Crispy Sage Flaky salt
Parsley Chives

Sauce PROV: Mozz   Red + green sweet peppers
hot pickled   peppers
Cherry peppers

The Rachael

Broc Rabe   Ricotta + thyme
Mozz + chile anch garlic Rabe parbol
3 min cold water

Marg   Sauce + mozz + parm + Basil
pepperoni   ± pepperoni
55y   + parsley (chroile)

Cook 10

grilled ASP. + SPRING onions
Steaks - Tenderloin + tarragon garlie
Cast IRON + grilled + more Butter
lemon   Blue + tarragon

cider Brine + glaze
¼C DB Sugar
2T Honey
STOCK   1/2 c cider
1/3 c Worcestershire
¼C BOURBON
325
90-24 HRS smoked TURKEY

SQUASH
400, invert OO SP to tender
Shred

Ricotta
garlic
-1 c Grana or Parm
nutmeg
drained spinach
eggs beaten lightly
combine
Butter Lasagna dish
top mozz

THXGVG
Brussels Sprouts
Pancetta or bacon onion garlic
SP Caraway grainy Dij. Apple cid
Honey Sage nutmeg Blanched vin
Brussels Sprouts

GREEN Beans
Shallots low in Butter to soft
chicken Stock
Blanched greenbeans

SPAG
SQUASH — 3c Ric. garlic 3-4
2 400 to ½ Parm eggs
tender nutmeg moz
30 min.

PEAS w/ Butter

Butter apple 2 lg onion 5-6 celery
1½   219   219
parsley (±) 1½ c chestnuts   herbs Stuffing
sage   3-4 c Stock   1½ Bag
thyme   Bay Butter

Baked Blue Plumpkin
gravy   Butter SP curry +
Show stock   nutmeg   2-2½ hrs
STUFFED APPLES   Whiskey Brine + cider turkey   450 20 min
Herb citrus garlic   400 to 165
REST 30
mashed pot + parsnip BOURSIN

Chix Livers + f
12/27   32
English beef R
Kosher salt
Garlic Ros
Roast w/ 1c stock
finish 425 25
WB ove
fresh horseradish
Garlic chives s
Panko w/
OR
no BC
tosp cin cha ½
1 onion, 2T butt
6oz cin chos ½
nutmeg ¼ c
Shall gar Sher
Pot p

w pecorino
Aglio e Olio

S+P M H heat
more OO if
first 3-4 pc
sides. Remove.
¼C.
¼ lb dice)
sm 1 med carrot
pped fine dice
on chop
cook to tender
partially covered

24   Stuffed Artichokes   Cod Agrodolce
Scampi   Winter Salad
Crab cake (Brunch?)
Romaine   pommegranate & fennel

25   Caviar + Chips   Ro Tenderloin
Caesar w/   horseradish sauce
Blue   green beans
n Bacon   Beets
carrot
Broccolini

Sage
Caviar + Chips   Truffle eggs   Panetone Sundays
BEET ARANCINI   GOUGERES   mousse
moms livers   lemon wedges
(c/ Reardons   Porchetta   Beet arancini

ai   mo
orecchiette with   Mama Caulif
or
Brocco
Salted   florets Remove
Boil   1t o   spider or
slotted spoon
Chop the stem bite size
cook pasta & stems 9-10
Sa
1/3 c OO
6 garlic
16 or 1sm chili
8 to flat filet anch.   Si
add florets

rachael ray

MEMORIES AND MEALS FROM
A SWEET AND SAVORY LIFE

FOOD PHOTOGRAPHY BY CHRISTOPHER TESTANI

BALLANTINE BOOKS / NEW YORK

Published in the United States by Ballantine Books,
an imprint of Random House, a division of
Penguin Random House LLC, New York.

BALLANTINE and the HOUSE colophon are registered
trademarks of Penguin Random House LLC.

Photograph credits and permissions appear on page 317.

Hardback ISBN 978-1-984-81799-0
Ebook ISBN 978-1-984-81800-3

Printed in China on acid-free paper

randomhousebooks.com

9 8 7 6 5 4 3 2 1

First Edition

Book design by Debbie Glasserman
Food photography by Christopher Testani

If it's about who brought me to this day fifty plus years in the making, there are too many people and animals to list. Instead, I'm dedicating this book to my four favorite four-letter words:

BOOK. The more we read, the more pages we turn in books, the more pages we can turn in our lives and the closer we will become to one another.

FOOD. Food brings us together and connects us. Food nurtures and provides the most basic building block of feeling secure in this world.

LOVE. Love always wins and it is the only force stronger than those creepy teammates, fear and hate.

HOPE. Hope gets me out of bed and excited to try again each and every day.

Contents

Introduction

My husband, John Cusimano, turned fifty in 2017, a year before I did, and what a party we had—more than two hundred people at a club in Manhattan. He loved it. I gotta say, I hated it. It overwhelmed me. I felt crowd-drunk and claustrophobic, and I didn't get to spend quality time with any of our closest friends. But it did get me thinking about my fifty years on this planet. And about what I'd learned from them.

For me, aging has never been a big emotional thing. I guess that's because I've always gravitated to people much older than myself. As a little girl, I couldn't wait to leave school and run home to hang out with my grandpa and his friends, *my* best friends, a group of Sicilian men in their seventies who played cards and told stories all day. And I've always felt comfortable with my actual age, never fretting or freaking out or dreading birthdays. In fact, for most of my life when asked how old I was, I lied and aged myself *up* a year. When I got to thirty and forty I was already used to the idea. Old news.

So I didn't dread my fiftieth, but I knew I wanted to take stock of what's important to me, and to celebrate the moments that influenced me most along the way. Writing this book is the party I planned for myself. In these pages I share who I am, what my favorite memories are, and the food I love to cook when I'm not in front of a camera.

It was *hard.* I've never sat down and written about myself before, beyond some headnotes and acknowledgments. I don't like drawing attention to myself—yes, I realize how ironic that is, considering what I do for a living. But I'm a pretty private person, and this was the most personal project I'd ever taken on. I developed a love-hate relationship with it. In its best moments, the book felt like a dear friend and confidant, and helped me remember all the adventures I've packed into the last few decades. In its worst, it made me cry, or wince with embarrassment. But overall my ride in this life has been off-the-charts beyond my wildest expectations for myself, and I wanted to share some of it in a way I hadn't before.

This is not a memoir. It's a series of recollections, a scrapbook of my life so far. Most of the essays lead into recipes, the food I make for family and friends when I have days to prepare dishes, rather than just thirty minutes. Other episodes in the book have nothing to do with food, but they remain important ingredients that have helped give my life its particular flavor.

When I'm writing recipes, I use a freehand equivalent for most of the measurements—a handful of an herb or a turn of the pan of EVOO. I want anyone who gives me the compliment of trying to cook my recipes to at the same time have the freedom to make them their own. My wish, especially for nervous cooks, is that they'll learn that while in cooking you need balance and to follow basic rules, it's also very personal. No matter the recipe, each of us changes a dish by our own preparation of it.

It's the same with stories—once you put them out there, readers get to interpret them and be affected by them as they will. Ultimately, it's my hope that this book leaves the reader with that quiet smile we all get after we eat our favorite comfort food. Basically, I'm going for the afterglow of a big bowl of spaghetti. I'm a waitress at heart and a cook in my soul, so as long as I'm making you something good to eat, or read, I'm happy.

I draw recipes for friends as thank-you cards. Here's my "foodle" for Greens and Beans Minestra (recipe on page 8).

family

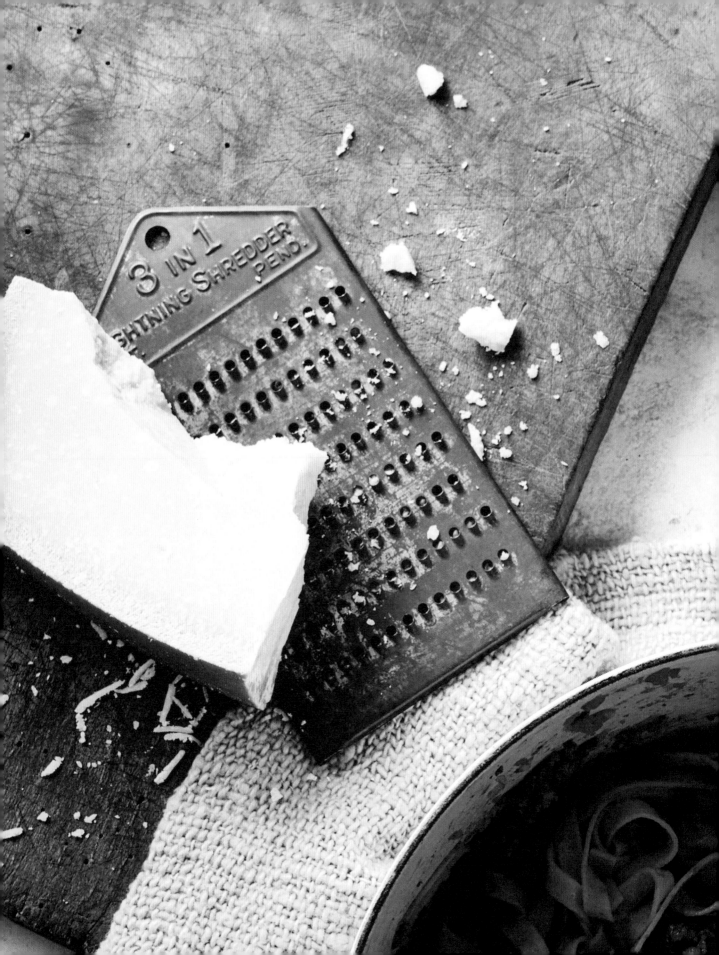

1 The Princess Who Lived in a Fort

Once upon a time, by a lakeside in the woods, there lived a beautiful little girl with dark wavy curls, rosy round cheeks, and a heart so big, a soul so bright, that her energy was boundless morning, noon, and night. My favorite fairy tale is actually the reality of my mother's childhood. I've spent my life in pursuit of it, because the pictures in my head of how things were are the most beautiful scenes imaginable to me.

My mother, Elsa Providenzia Scuderi, was born on July 18, 1934, the first of ten kids. She grew up in a house on the edge of Lake Champlain in Ticonderoga, New York. The main feature of the house was a tower of stone that helped to keep the house warm and cozy in the harsh, cold winter and cool during the long, hot days of summer. The tower stood at the heart of this home, and was actually a hand-stacked, artisan-crafted chimney that ran through the center of the house from bottom to top. It was built by her dad, my grandpa Emmanuel, a master stonemason. The house is gone now, but the stones of that tower still stand today. To look at it back then, I suppose to some people it was just the too-small house of a blue-collar worker with too many kids. To my mother, it was a fortress and she was a princess.

Growing up by a lake is wonderful in and of itself. (Mom would raise me on the same lake years later.) During their childhood summers, Elsa and her sisters would gather the tall grasses that grew by the lake and make skirts, while the boys swam and chased each other. The uncles would play tricks on the children, like diving deep and floating a hat on the water to make the kids think they'd drowned, then rising up like a lake monster to scare them! Grandpa would play his concertina and all would sing and dance around big bonfires, Zia (Aunt) Patrina waving her *moppina* (Italian American slang for a dishcloth) over her head, leading them on.

In the spring and winter, Daddy Emmanuel would wake his kids in the middle of the night and take them outside to sit in the notches he carved for each of them in the old tree that had fallen down long ago. He would tell them stories of sea turtles and of his life as a boy in Sicily. They would listen and giggle and yawn and try to keep their eyes open, waiting and watching the dark night skies for the northern lights. Then, when the light shows began, Emmanuel would sing to his kids, serenading them with Italian arias and old standards like "O Sole Mio."

My grandpa was a wonderful gardener, and tended huge vegetable gardens, fruit trees, rabbits (Elsa learned at a tender age not to name them), and chickens, necessary skills with so many mouths to feed and a limited budget. At their house there was always plenty of food, and not just for the ten kids but for the whole community. On sunny Sundays, Emmanuel would enlist help to move the kitchen table outside to accommodate guests. He'd make a huge, industrial-size braising pot full of Sunday Sauce—meats and home-made sausages and tomatoes canned with basil. He'd cook pounds of spaghetti and toss it in the red sauce and serve it with lots of grated cheese. He'd arrange the meats separately on large wooden platters and boards. Next, he'd set out a huge wooden bowl of mixed greens from the garden dressed with lemon or vinegar and olive oil, salt, and pepper. The last stop on the buffet he would man himself. Emmanuel would grab the machete that hung from a strap on his belt and worked as an extension of his arm, and he would swipe at ripe hand-melons from his gardens, whacking them open. One by one, he'd scoop out the seeds with the side of his hand and fill the melons with vanilla ice cream from a five-gallon tub. The quality of his family's life was all about the quality of their food and their time together.

These scenes, these painted pictures in my mind's eye, remind me of an old nightclub song. I think it's Russian, and the lyrics put to it in English have always spoken to me. I sing along every time I hear it.

Those were the days my friend
We thought they'd never end
We'd sing and dance forever and a day
We'd live the life we choose
We'd fight and never lose
Those were the days, oh yes those were the days

Back then, food was also a commodity. When the kids were good, they'd get treats like their own bucket of fruit that they didn't have to share with their brothers or sisters. Mom is a little embarrassed but mostly proud that, as the oldest, for a while she could outrun the others after school. She'd get home first and sneak into the canning cellar and hoard a jar of caponata (eggplant and vegetables) or dandelion greens all to herself.

My favorite of Elsa's childhood memories is of one special Christmas morning. Every year each of the kids got one toy of their own and some toys to share with their brothers or sisters. One year, my mother tiptoed down the stairs with her sisters and their mouths opened wide in awe. There by the tree was a small table and chairs, the table set with china for tea and in each chair a dolly with a tag marked for each girl. Elsa's dolly had an extra-special surprise. It had a gold necklace with a little heart attached to it.

My mom still cries when she remembers that morning and how special and loved she felt. My idea of her facial expression at that moment and how that memory has stayed with her all this time is a constant motivation for me. I want to give all I can in every way in anything I do for others—a passing comment, a sketch or note or a piece of furniture or kitchenware that I doodle, a meal I cook or write about or anything I buy for someone else. I daydream about catching that look in someone's eye, the joy of a pleasant surprise. I believe in the wonder and possibility of every day. I am a romantic because I was born to my mother, and she is one because she was born to her father.

Caponata / SERVES 8 AS A SNACK

1 large, firm eggplant

Salt

About ¼ cup EVOO

3 ribs celery with leafy tops, chopped into ½- to ¾-inch pieces

1 large or 2 medium onions, chopped into ½- to ¾-inch pieces

2 cubanelle peppers (light green mild frying peppers), seeds removed and chopped into ½- to ¾-inch pieces

1 large or 2 medium red frying peppers or field peppers (sweet bell-like peppers but more rectangular in shape), seeds removed and chopped into ½- to ¾-inch pieces

1 bulb garlic (5 or 6 cloves), cracked from skin and chopped or thinly sliced

1 cup black and green olives combined, pitted and coarsely chopped

¼ cup Italian capers in brine, drained

1 teaspoon crushed red pepper flakes (⅓ palmful)

1 (28-ounce) can San Marzano tomatoes or 2 (14-ounce) cans Sicilian canned cherry tomatoes

A few leaves of fresh basil, torn

1 handful of fresh flat-leaf parsley, chopped

⅓ cup pistachio or pine nuts, toasted and chopped for garnish (optional)

Caponata is a traditional Italian cold appetizer. In my family, we eat it hot, room temperature, or cold, and sometimes as a meal on creamy polenta or just with hunks of bread. Many recipes add sugar and vinegar, for a sweet-and-sour approach to the eggplant-based dish. We do not. We keep it simply about the balance of salty olives and capers and the crunch of tender-crisp celery, peppers, and onions. (When my mom was a kid, this was her favorite snack.) For the olives in this recipe we use what's on hand—sometimes we pit buttery Cerignola green olives and mix them with briny, black, oil-cured olives. Sometimes I have Kalamata olives on hand or giant Sicilian varieties in brine. Around the holidays we add a small handful of currants or golden raisins for sweetness and heartiness.

/ / /

TRIM THE TOP AND BOTTOM OF THE EGGPLANT and trim the skin from two sides—a half-peeled eggplant. Stand the eggplant upright and cut into ½-inch planks lengthwise. Stack the planks two to three high and cut into long sticks also about ½ inch wide, then cube. Arrange the eggplant on a kitchen towel and season with kosher salt. Let the eggplant set and drain for 30 minutes, tossing often.

HEAT A LARGE DUTCH OVEN OR HEAVY POT over medium-high heat with EVOO, 4 turns of the pan. Add the celery, onions, peppers, garlic, olives, and capers and partially cover. Cook for 12 to 15 minutes, stirring occasionally, to tender-crisp. Add the eggplant and red pepper flakes and cover. Cook for 5 minutes, stirring occasionally. Add the tomatoes and break up with a spoon. Add the basil and parsley. Reduce the heat to medium-low. Cook uncovered for 15 minutes more, stirring occasionally, then season with salt to taste. Garnish with nuts, if using.

Scuderi-Style Rigatoni / SERVES 6-8

MAKE THE SAUCE: Heat a medium Dutch oven or 6-quart pot over medium-low heat with EVOO, 2 turns of the pan. Add the butter and melt into the olive oil. Add the onion and garlic and season with salt. Cook for about 15 minutes, until the onion is very soft and sweet but not brown. Add the stock, raise the heat a bit, and cook until the stock is reduced by half. Add the tomatoes and break them up with a wooden spoon. Wilt the torn basil into the sauce. Simmer at a low bubble for 30 minutes to thicken the sauce.

MAKE THE PASTA: Preheat the oven to 425° F and bring a large pot of water to a boil over high heat. Salt the water and cook the pasta 6 to 7 minutes, 2 to 3 minutes less than the package directions for al dente. Reserve ¾ cup of the boiling starchy water just before draining. Place the pasta back in the hot pot. Add the butter, ricotta, enough water to bring the sauce together, and half the sauce. Toss to coat the pasta evenly and transfer to a large casserole. Cover the rigatoni with the remaining sauce and the Parmigiano-Reggiano. Bake for about 15 minutes to brown the cheese.

MAKE THE BREADCRUMBS: Heat the EVOO over medium heat. Melt the butter into the olive oil and swirl with the garlic a minute or so. Add the breadcrumbs and stir to toast for 8 to 10 minutes, until a deep golden brown. Cool the breadcrumbs in a bowl and combine them with parsley, lemon zest, and grated cheese. Pile the basil leaves all together, then roll them and shred them. Combine the basil with the breadcrumbs and parsley.

TOP THE RIGATONI with the breadcrumb mixture and serve.

TOMATO-BASIL SAUCE

2 tablespoon EVOO

2 tablespoons butter

1 small onion, finely chopped

4 cloves garlic, crushed or chopped

Salt

1 cup chicken stock or vegetable stock

2 (28-ounce) cans San Marzano tomatoes

10–12 leaves of fresh basil, torn

PASTA

Salt

1 pound (500 grams) rigatoni or imported Italian pasta

2 tablespoons butter

1½ cups fresh ricotta

1½ cups freshly grated Parmigiano-Reggiano

BREADCRUMBS

2 tablespoons EVOO

2 tablespoons butter

1 clove garlic, crushed

1½ cups large homemade breadcrumbs from stale white peasant-style Italian bread (pulse chunks of bread in a food processor)

1 fat handful of fresh flat-leaf parsley tops, finely chopped (about 1 cup)

Zest of 1 lemon

1 cup freshly grated Parmigiano-Reggiano

1 fat handful of fresh basil leaves

Greens and Beans Minestra / SERVES 4–6

1 cup dry white beans (cannellini)

1 onion, halved and peeled

2 fresh bay leaves

Salt

About ¼ cup EVOO

2 large shallots, thinly sliced

2 lemons, 1 thinly sliced and
seeded, 1 halved

4 cloves garlic, crushed and
chopped or sliced

Freshly ground black pepper

8 to 10 cups fresh flat-leaf kale, stemmed
and sliced into 1-inch ribbons, or 1 large
head escarole, coarsely chopped

A little freshly grated nutmeg to taste

1 quart chicken or vegetable stock

Minestra is a simple soup of greens and beans—escarole and white cannellinis for our family. Minestrone is a bigger soup, with more vegetables and mixed varieties of beans and pasta, too.

Greens and beans is more of a meal but we often use it as a side with a lighter entrée like a crispy-skin fillet of branzino.

///

PLACE THE BEANS IN A BOWL and soak overnight. (For a quick-soak method, cover the beans with boiling water and let stand for 1 hour.) Rinse the beans and place in a pot. Cover with 7 to 8 cups water. Add the onion and bay leaves, bring to a boil, season with salt, and cook for 30 to 40 minutes until tender, skimming as necessary. Remove the onion and bay leaves and drain the excess water if there's more than ½ cup.

IN A LARGE SAUTÉ PAN, heat the EVOO over medium to medium-high heat. Add the shallots, sliced lemon, and garlic and cook for 3 to 4 minutes, flipping or stirring occasionally. Season with salt and pepper. Add the greens in bunches to wilt in, season with salt, pepper, and nutmeg, and add the stock and the beans. Simmer until ready to serve. Douse with lemon juice and adjust the salt and pepper to taste.

Beef Shank Minestra / SERVES 6

BEEF STOCK
MAKES 3–4 QUARTS STOCK

5 pounds beef bones with marrow, cut into 1½- to 2-inch pieces, from butcher counter

4 large carrots, coarsely chopped

1 large parsnip, quartered

1 parsley root, if available, quartered

4 ribs celery with leafy tops, coarsely chopped

2 onions, quartered through root

1 large bulb garlic, halved across to expose cloves

Salt

EVOO for liberal drizzling

3 large dried bay leaves

1 bundle of fresh flat-leaf parsley or parsley stems and fresh thyme, tied with kitchen string

10 black peppercorns

MINESTRA

Beans
1 rounded cup dry white beans (cannellini)

2 large dry bay leaves

1 onion, halved through root

2 large cloves garlic, crushed

Salt and freshly ground black pepper

This dish is delicious prepared with a few quarts of store-bought stock. But whenever you have the time to make homemade beef stock, for sure it's always worth it and you can freeze the surplus (or slurp-plus).

/ / /

PREHEAT THE OVEN TO 400°F. Position the oven rack one rung above the center of the oven.

IN A LARGE ROASTING PAN, place the bones, carrots, parsnip, parsley root if using, celery, onions, and garlic. Season with salt and drizzle to coat evenly with EVOO. Roast for 50 to 60 minutes, turning the ingredients once. Transfer the bones and vegetables to a stock pot, and add the bay leaves, herb bundle, and peppercorns to the roasting pan. Place the pan over two burners over medium-high heat. Loosen the pan drippings with a couple of cups of water. Loosen the bits and pour the liquid over the bones along with the bay leaves, herb bundle, and peppercorns. Then continue to fill the pot to cover the bones and vegetables by 3 to 4 inches. Bring the stock to a boil and reduce the heat to a simmer. Simmer for 4 hours, skimming any solids that float to the top. Strain the stock through a fine mesh strainer or cheesecloth.

TO MAKE THE BEANS: Soak the beans in a large bowl overnight, covered by 3 inches of water. Drain and rinse them. (To quick-soak, cover the beans with boiling water and let stand for 1 hour, then rinse and drain them.)

PLACE THE BEANS IN A LARGE POT and cover with 2 to 3 inches of water. Add the bay leaves, onion, and garlic. Bring the beans to a boil and cook at a medium rolling boil for 40 to 45 minutes, until just tender. Top off with more water as they cook, if necessary. Remove the onion and bay leaves.

TO MAKE THE SOUP: Bring the shanks to room temperature and season with salt and pepper. Heat a large Dutch oven over medium-high heat with EVOO, 3 turns of the pan. Add the beef shanks and brown on each side for about 5 minutes, until they are a reddish brown color and nicely crusted; remove the shanks to a plate. Add onions, celery, fennel, garlic, and sage and reduce the heat to medium. Partially cover and cook the vegetables for 10 to 12 minutes, stirring occasionally, until the onions are translucent. Wilt in the kale and escarole a few handfuls at a time and season with a little nutmeg. When the greens have wilted, add rind, stock, and beef and cook, over medium-low heat, at a low rolling boil for 45 minutes. Add the beans and 1 to 2 cups of their starchy liquid. Simmer for 15 minutes to heat through. Remove the beef shank steaks. Remove the meat from the bone, pull or chop the beef, and add to soup. Remove the sage bundle and rind. Add the lemon juice. Serve with a drizzle of fruity finishing EVOO and minced white onion. Add the buttery breadcrumbs, if using.

TO MAKE THE BREADCRUMBS, if using: Preheat the oven to 350°F. Scatter the breadcrumbs on a small rimmed baking sheet. Toast them for 15 to 18 minutes, until they are deeply golden in color. Place the breadcrumbs in a bowl.

IN A MEDIUM SKILLET over medium to medium-high heat, melt the butter and let it foam. Add the sage and cook for 2 minutes, until the sage is crisp and the butter browns. The butter should be nutty and fragrant. Using a fork, remove the crispy sage leaves to a paper towel–lined plate. Pour the butter over the breadcrumbs and combine. When cool, crumble the sage leaves and add them, along with the cheese, to the breadcrumbs.

Soup

2 beef shank steaks about 1¼ to 1½ inches thick

Salt and freshly ground black pepper

3 tablespoons EVOO

1 large onion or 2 medium onions, peeled and chopped

2 ribs celery with leafy tops, chopped

½ bulb fennel, chopped

4 cloves garlic, thinly sliced or chopped

1 bundle of fresh sage, tied with kitchen string

1 bundle of lacinato kale, stemmed, washed and dried, and coarsely chopped

1 large head escarole, washed and dried and coarsely chopped

Freshly grated nutmeg, to taste, no more than ⅛ teaspoon

Rind of Parmigiano-Reggiano and grated cheese to serve

2 quarts beef stock

Juice of 1 lemon

Fruity green EVOO, for finishing

White onions, rinsed and finely chopped

BROWN BUTTER AND
SAGE BREADCRUMBS
(*optional garnish for soup*)

2 cups large, fresh breadcrumbs

¼ cup (½ stick) butter

12 to 16 leaves sage

½ cup grated Parmigiano-Reggiano

Sunday Sauce / SERVES 8

3 pounds English-cut (3 inches) meaty, trimmed beef short ribs

Salt and freshly ground black pepper

About ¼ cup olive oil

2 medium onions, chopped

1 large fresh bay leaf

1 large carrot, peeled and halved across

1 large rib celery with leafy tops, halved across

4 cloves garlic, crushed

2 tablespoons sun-dried tomato paste or regular tomato paste

1½ teaspoons dried oregano (½ palmful)

1 cup red or white wine

1 cup beef stock or chicken stock

2 (28-ounce) cans San Marzano tomatoes

1 pound Italian sweet sausage with fennel or anise

1 pound hot sausage

1½ to 2 pounds spaghetti

3 tablespoons butter cut into pats or 3 tablespoons EVOO

1 to 1½ cups freshly grated Parmigiano-Reggiano (cow's milk, nutty) or Romano (sheep's milk, tangy), plus more to pass at the table

Sunday Sauce can include any braising meats such as beef short ribs, chunks of beef chuck, veal or beef shanks, and pork shoulder. Emmanuel always included his sausages, but the sauce makes good use of a range of leftover meats. When cooking the sausages in sauces, we prick and crisp the casings, then simmer at a low bubble until cooked through. When we serve sausages separately, the method is the reverse. We pierce the casings and simmer them in ⅛ inch of water to cook through, then brown their casings to serve. This is our procedure for grilling sausages as well, par-cooking them in a little water, then crisping the casings to serve. This sauce slow cooks all afternoon, and it always seems to stretch to feed as many as need be.

Italian spaghetti is often packaged in 1,000-gram packages (a little more than 2 pounds), enough for ten people. I have found 750 grams or about 1½ pounds to be the perfect portioning for eight people. I reserve the ½-pound and use it to break into pieces for rice pilaf or for soups.

/ / /

PREHEAT THE OVEN to 325°F.

BRING THE MEAT TO ROOM TEMPERATURE and season with salt and pepper. In a large Dutch oven over medium-high to high heat, heat the olive oil, 2 turns of the pan. Brown the meat for 10 to 12 minutes, until the meat is browned evenly all over. Remove the meat and drain off some of the fat if necessary. Reduce the heat to medium. Add another tablespoon of olive oil and add the onions and bay leaf. Season with salt and pepper. Partially cover and cook for 4 to 5 minutes, until softened. Add the carrot, celery, garlic, and tomato paste and stir. Add the oregano and wine and reduce for a minute. Add the stock and tomatoes, breaking up the tomatoes with a wooden spoon. Bring the sauce to a bubble and cover the Dutch oven with a tight-fitting lid. Place the pot in the oven and cook for 4 hours, or simmer on the stovetop on the lowest heat, stirring occasionally.

AFTER ABOUT 2½ HOURS, in a large nonstick skillet over medium-high to high heat, heat 1 tablespoon olive oil, then brown the sausages. Remove the sauce from the oven. Remove the carrot halves and celery from the sauce and discard; add the sausages. Roast for 1 hour more. Transfer the sauce to stove and simmer uncovered for 20 to 30 minutes on the lowest heat.

BRING A LARGE POT of water to boil for the spaghetti.

REMOVE THE MEAT AND SAUSAGES from the sauce and arrange on a platter. Trim away the cartilage and slide the bones from the beef. Halve the sausages on a bias. Cover the platter with foil. Skim the fat from the sauce.

SALT THE PASTA WATER LIBERALLY. Cook the pasta for about 8 minutes, 1 minute shy of the package directions for al dente. Reserve 1 cup of starchy water before draining the pasta.

RETURN THE PASTA to the pot and add the butter or EVOO, half the sauce, half the starchy water, and the cheese. Adjust the seasoning of the pasta and transfer to a large platter.

TOP THE MEATS and pasta with remaining sauce and serve with extra cheese to pass.

Big Pan Roast Shrimp with Garlic / SERVES 6-8

The kids in my mom's family would come running and mop and sop the juices up from this dish with the big chunks of crusty bread. They're essential for this dish.

/ / /

HEAT A LARGE CAST-IRON SKILLET or a roasting pan over medium heat. Preheat the oven to 500°F. Position the oven rack at the center of the oven.

ADD THE EVOO TO THE PAN, 6 to 7 turns. Stir in the shallots and garlic, thyme, 2 tablespoons lemon zest, and the red pepper flakes. Add the shrimp to the pan and toss to coat evenly. Add the 4 lemon halves to the pan, cut-side down, and roast the shrimp in the oven for 3 to 5 minutes, until not quite opaque. Remove from oven and remove the lemons to cool. Add the vermouth and the pieces of butter to the pan, toss with tongs, and return to oven for 3 to 5 minutes more; the shrimp should be opaque now, the tails should be red and crispy, and the whole pan should be bubbling and crackling. (Note: Italians like our seafood almost overcooked. If you don't, adjust cook times accordingly.) Remove the pan from oven, top with parsley, and douse with the juice of the lemons. Toss again with tongs and place on a trivet on the table to serve.

About ½ cup EVOO

2 large shallots, chopped

1 large bulb garlic (7 or 8 cloves), sliced or chopped

2 tablespoons chopped fresh thyme

2 lemons, zested and cut in half

2 teaspoons crushed red pepper flakes, or 1 tablespoon Calabrian chili paste

2 to 2½ pounds jumbo shrimp (the biggest you can find), peeled and deveined, tails on

1 cup dry vermouth

5 tablespoons butter, cut into small pieces

½ cup fresh flat-leaf parsley, finely chopped

Crusty bread, to pass

2 Sardines Don't Make You Friends

At the end of my first day of kindergarten, in Mashpee, Massachusetts, I went home with a hot, red face, fighting back tears and wondering how I could ever go back to school again.

My Grandpa Emmanuel lived with us when I was little, and he was my best friend. Our bond started when I was still in the cradle, and he'd watch me when my mom was at work. I didn't like formula. I would throw my bottles back at him at feeding time. Grandpa was in his seventies, a proud and once very strong Sicilian, but at this age, and with his diabetes, he sometimes used a walker to get around. Chasing after bottles that had rolled under furniture was not his idea of fun. His solution was to fill my bottles with a mix of a little of his homemade wine and water. (Visitors thought I was a good, quiet baby but I think I was just a little drunk.) He'd hold the bottle up over my face and say, "Vino, vino!" and that's how Grandpa taught me my first word. My mom took a Polaroid of me in a high chair (the kind that hooked onto a table and was later made illegal for killing kids by dropping them on their heads), trying to ask for my bottle. I waved my arms in

I'm a corny girl. My mom would let me gnaw on an ear to keep me busy, and I loved it so much, I was known to fall asleep with it gripped tightly in my little hand.

the air, and loudly called, *"Vino!"* Scribbled on the back in my mother's handwriting was "Rachael's first word—Vino!"

I didn't know it then, but Grandpa Emmanuel was the best teacher I would ever have. He taught me how to read, just as he'd taught himself to read and write in English when he immigrated to the United States from Sicily as a boy. Most important, he taught me how to laugh with my whole body. The first image that comes to mind when I think of him now is of him sitting in his blueberry chair—what I called the upholstered wing chair with blue roses in our TV room—laughing. Small moments in his everyday life could bring him to fits of laughter. My aunt Geraldine Domenica painted his portrait in that chair and she made his eyes dance. They had a way of twinkling and the joy would just wash through him.

Grandpa would turn the blueberry chair so he could watch me instead of the TV each week during the TV show *This Is Tom Jones*. I would wear a dress, even though I did *not* like dresses, because I thought Tom could see me through the TV and I had a mad crush on him—even as a toddler. I'd mimic Tom and dance and try to sing along. "Delilah" was my favorite. It was odd for a small child to learn all the words to one of the most misogynistic songs ever (the narrator sings of stabbing Delilah for cheating on him, but somehow it's all her fault). But it was my favorite, and Grandpa loved to watch me perform it for him while he sat in his favorite chair.

From that chair he also taught me to tie my shoelaces. I would crawl

My grandpa, Emmanuel Scuderi, in the "blueberry chair."

under the chair without him seeing me, but my giggling gave me away. "What is that at my feet?" he'd say. "Is that a rabbit?" I would untie his laces, then I'd try and try and eventually I got it! I tied *his* shoelaces together! For a man in his seventies with a walker and diabetes, pratfalls could kill, literally, but he would stand and fall just to make his "little rabbit" giggle.

Grandpa taught me about the true meaning of food, too. He taught me that meals are as much about stories and life lessons as they are about ingredients and flavor and preparation. He was a wonderful cook, the main cook in his home for his ten children.

I liked to hang with Grandpa and watch him play Tre Sette or Scopa with his friends, the Runzo boys. I loved the feel of his flannel shirts, and the smell of his pipe smoke. It mixed with the aromas of something good cooking in the kitchen, always with lots of garlic and onions. I didn't have other friends. I didn't want them or need them. Grandpa was my best friend. I ate what he ate, did what he did, and we were together around the clock.

Then I started school.

For the first morning of kindergarten, my mom and Grandpa had put out my best dress and shined shoes (shoes are very important in Italian culture, as is caring for them). I packed up my favorite pencils, pad, and notebooks, and my favorite book, *The Casual Observer*. Grandpa packed me my favorite lunch: two slices of good bread, with sardines, onions, lemon, and olive oil, and some fruit for dessert.

Off I went to greet my teacher and classmates. When I arrived at my

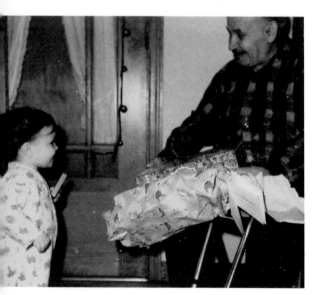

classroom I noticed all the other kids were in dungarees (what we now call jeans) and sneakers. So, I dressed funny. Also, none of the other kids knew how to read yet, so my teacher took away my security blanket: *my book*! (She did give it back at the end of the day.) At lunch, the other kids ate the school lunch from the cafeteria, which was something they called "pizza," but it looked more like ketchup on cardboard with weird old white cheese; a few kids had cool lunch boxes with peanut butter and jelly or ham, cheese, and mayo sandwiches on white bread. My lunch was salted fish with onions. So I became the smelly kid who dressed funny. Sardines do not make friends. At least, in American kindergartens they don't.

After school, I ran off the school bus and burst into the house in a blur. The tears! The gasps! The drama! Grandpa stretched me out on my bed and put a cool cloth on my forehead. I could barely catch my breath to list my complaints, the reasons I should never, ever go back to school. Grandpa looked at first to be empathetic to me and to my plight. Then he did something so strange. He started to laugh! Why was he laughing? Laughing at me? He laughed so hard he made the whole bed shake. That made me cry even harder. Then Grandpa did something hor-

rible. He started tickling me! What? The nerve! I continued my wailing and choking as I thought to myself I might just die this way. Then, almost as suddenly as flipping a light switch, I realized that I had stopped crying and I had begun laughing, too.

Grandpa wiped my face, took off my shoes and socks, and asked me to do the weirdest thing: to count off all my fingers and all of my toes with him. Well, I still had ten of each. Then he put his hand on my forehead and asked me, "What's inside here?"

"My brain," I answered.

"So, if you have ten fingers and ten toes and a brain in your head, what do you have to be crying about?"

Grandpa believed that life would provide plenty of tears that are necessary. The rest of our tears, the ones we work ourselves up into, are a choice that we make. Each day will have ups and downs, but when we feel frustrated or overtired or beat up by life, we can choose to laugh (at ourselves, at life) or to cry. Laughing feels much better.

I went back to school the next day in jeans (yay!) but still carrying my sack lunch and my favorite pencils—and a newfound resilience.

My grandpa passed away about a year later, but his lessons are always with me.

/ / /

Here are a few recipes Grandpa cooked, and a few he'd appreciate, thanks to the presence of salty little fish.

Spaghetti Aglio e Olio (Garlic and Oil) / SERVES 4–6
WITH ANCHOVIES, BROCCOLI RABE, PRESERVED LEMON, AND GARLICKY BREADCRUMBS

CRUMBS/CROUTONS

¼ cup (½ stick) butter

1 large clove garlic, crushed

About 2 cups coarse homemade breadcrumbs from Italian or white bread

Salt (optional)

1 cup loosely packed freshly grated Pecorino (optional)

½ cup fresh flat-leaf parsley, chopped

PASTA

Salt

1 large bunch of broccoli rabe, trimmed of tough ends

½ cup EVOO

8 anchovy fillets, drained

6 large cloves garlic, very thinly sliced

About 1½ teaspoons crushed red pepper flakes (½ palmful), or a generous spoonful of Calabrian chili paste

½ cup dry vermouth

½ cup fresh flat-leaf parsley, finely chopped

1 pound spaghetti

About ¼ cup preserved lemon, finely chopped, plus a splash of brine

To cheese or not to cheese, that is the question. Most Italians use breadcrumbs rather than grated cheese on pasta with fish. In my family, we like both. The more salt and texture, the better! We use dry vermouth—herb-fortified white wine—in many recipes with seafood because "it takes the smell out of the drapes," but of course white wine or a little chicken stock works well, too.

/ / /

PREHEAT THE OVEN to 350°F.

MAKE THE CRUMBS: In a skillet over medium heat, melt the butter and, when it foams, add the garlic and swirl for 1 to 2 minutes. Add the breadcrumbs, toss with the butter, transfer to a rimmed baking sheet, and season with salt or sprinkle with Pecorino, if using, then bake for about 12 minutes, until deep golden. Cool and toss with parsley.

MAKE THE PASTA: Bring a large pot of water to boil. Season with salt.

MEANWHILE, IN A MEDIUM TO LARGE POT, heat a few inches of water to a boil, salt the water to season it, and parboil the broccoli rabe for 4 to 5 minutes. Cold shock the broccoli rabe in an ice bath, then drain it and dry it. Chop it into 1½-inch pieces.

IN A LARGE SKILLET over medium to medium-high heat, heat the EVOO, 6 slow turns of the pan, and butter. Add the anchovies and stir with a wooden spoon to break the fillets up until they literally melt into the oil. Then reduce the heat to medium and add the garlic and red pepper flakes or paste. Swirl or stir for 1 to 2 minutes, then add the dry vermouth and parsley. Reduce the heat to low and add the broccoli rabe.

COOK THE PASTA to 1 minute less than the package directions for al dente. Reserve about ½ cup of the starchy cooking water and drain the pasta. Transfer the pasta to the anchovy and broccoli rabe pan. Add the chopped preserved lemon and a small splash of brine. Combine the pasta with the sauce and broccoli rabe for 1 minute using tongs, adding the starchy water as you toss. Transfer to shallow bowls and top with breadcrumbs.

Bucatini con le Sarde / SERVES 6

MAKE THE BREADCRUMBS: In a medium skillet over medium heat, melt the butter. Add the breadcrumbs and cook until golden and toasted. Cool the breadcrumbs. Drizzle with the EVOO, add the parsley, and season with salt to taste.

MAKE THE PASTA: Bring a large pot of water to a boil.

IN A LARGE, DEEP SKILLET, heat the ¼ cup EVOO, 4 turns of the pan, over medium to medium-high heat. Add the celery, onion, fennel, garlic, red pepper flakes, fennel seeds, currants, and capers. Stir and arrange in an even layer. Cook for 7 to 8 minutes, turning over occasionally. Transfer the vegetables to a plate, then add the remaining tablespoon EVOO to the pan. Add the fish and cook until lightly browned. Add the Pernod and the wine and scrape up any brown bits that may have accumulated. Add the vegetables back to the pan and stir to combine. The fish will break into bite-size pieces. Reduce the heat to medium-low to medium and season the sauce with salt and pepper to taste.

SALT THE PASTA WATER and cook the pasta about a minute less than the package directions for al dente. Remove about 1 cup of starchy water and add to the sauce just before draining the pasta or transferring the pasta with a spider or tongs. Combine the pasta, sauce, parsley, fennel fronds, and nuts. Serve the bucatini in shallow bowls topped with breadcrumbs.

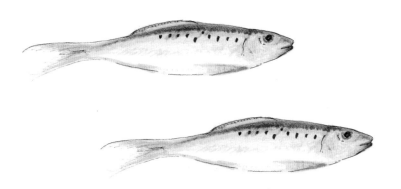

BREADCRUMBS

2 tablespoons butter

1 cup homemade large breadcrumbs from white peasant-style bread

2 tablespoons EVOO

½ cup fresh flat-leaf parsley, chopped

Salt

PASTA

About ¼ cup plus 1 tablespoon EVOO

2 or 3 small ribs celery plus leafy tops from heart, finely chopped

1 small onion, yellow or red, finely chopped

1 bulb fennel, trimmed, quartered, cored, and finely chopped

4 large cloves garlic, thinly sliced

½ to 1 scant teaspoon crushed red pepper flakes

1 scant teaspoon fennel seeds (⅓ palmful)

¼ cup dried currants

¼ cup Italian capers in brine, drained

2 pounds fresh sardines, trimmed and deboned, or 3 jars or cans of sardines, spines removed

About 3 tablespoons Pernod

½ cup white wine

Salt and freshly ground black pepper

1 pound bucatini

½ cup fresh flat-leaf parsley plus small handful of fennel fronds, finely chopped

⅓ cup pine nuts or sliced or slivered almonds, toasted

Spaghetti Puttanesca / SERVES 4

PLACE A LARGE POT OF WATER over high heat and bring to a boil for the pasta.

IN A LARGE SKILLET over medium to medium-high heat, heat the EVOO, 4 turns of the pan. Add the anchovies and cover the pan with a tight-fitting lid or splatter guard. Shake the pan for 1 minute to begin to break down the anchovies. Stir with a wooden spoon until the anchovies melt away into the oil. Reduce the heat to medium-low and add the garlic, capers, olives, and chili paste. Stir for 2 minutes more, then add the dry vermouth and reduce by half. Add the canned tomatoes, break them up with a spoon, and stir in the basil. Reduce the heat to a simmer to thicken the sauce while the pasta cooks.

SALT THE PASTA COOKING WATER and cook the pasta about a minute less than the package directions for al dente. Reserve ½ mug of the cooking water and use a spider or tongs to transfer the pasta to the sauce or drain the pasta in a colander. Toss spaghetti with the sauce and parsley for 1 to 2 minutes, using the cooking water as needed to keep the pasta from getting dry or the sauce from getting too thick.

About ¼ cup EVOO

10 to 12 good-quality Italian anchovy fillets in oil, such as anchovies from l'Escala, drained

6 large cloves garlic, thinly sliced

¼ cup Italian capers in brine, drained

1 cup oil-cured black olives, pitted and coarsely chopped

1 scant tablespoon Calabrian chili paste, or 1½ teaspoons crushed red pepper flakes

1 cup dry vermouth

1 (28-ounce) can whole San Marzano tomatoes (in the summer I use halved cherry tomatoes instead, a couple of pints)

A few leaves of fresh basil, torn

1 cup fresh flat-leaf parsley, loosely packed, then finely chopped

Salt

1 pound spaghetti or linguini

Linguini con le Vongole / SERVES 4

4 pounds (36 to 48) Manila or littleneck clams, scrubbed

¼ cup EVOO

4 to 6 anchovy fillets

4 large cloves garlic, chopped

1 teaspoon fennel seeds, crushed

1 teaspoon crushed red pepper flakes

1 cup dry vermouth

Salt

1 pound linguini or other long pasta

2 tablespoons fresh thyme, chopped

Juice of ½ lemon

1 cup fresh flat-leaf parsley, loosely packed, then finely chopped

SOAK THE CLAMS in cold water.

HEAT A LARGE POT of water to a boil for the pasta.

IN A LARGE SKILLET over medium-high heat, heat the EVOO. Add the anchovies and break them up with a wooden spoon. Add the garlic, fennel, and red pepper flakes to the pan and swirl or stir for 1 minute. Add the vermouth and swirl.

SEASON THE PASTA WATER liberally with salt. Add the linguini and cook for 5 to 6 minutes, a few minutes shy of al dente, as it will finish cooking in the sauce.

REMOVE THE CLAMS from the cold water and drain. Add the clams to the sauce and cover with a tight-fitting lid; the clams will open after 2 to 5 minutes. Once the clams are open, add the thyme, lemon juice, and parsley. Transfer the pasta to the clams and sauce with tongs or a spider and simmer together for 3 to 4 minutes, adding starchy cooking water if the pasta gets dry. Serve hot in shallow bowls.

Grandpa Emmanuel's Sardine Sandwiches

Very thinly sliced red or white onion

Very thinly sliced fennel

Baby kale or arugula

Lemon juice

Salt and freshly ground black pepper, or crushed red pepper flakes

Sliced white peasant-style bread, lightly toasted or charred

1 large clove garlic, peeled and halved

EVOO for drizzling

Dijon mustard combined with aquafaba (chickpea mayo substitute), mayo, or Greek yogurt

Good-quality jarred or canned sardines, spines removed

SOAK THE ONIONS AND FENNEL in cold water for a few minutes, then drain and dry. Combine them with the greens, lemon juice, and salt and black pepper.

RUB THE TOASTED BREAD with the garlic and dress with the EVOO. Mash the sardines into the bread a bit in an even layer and top with the onion-fennel mixture. Spread the top slice of bread with Dijon dressing and set into place. Halve the sandwiches to serve.

notebooks

When I was a little girl I loved to draw. One day, my mom asked why I only drew girls. *What's she talking about?* I thought. I told her I draw all kinds of people and animals and of course there are boys and girls, men and women—DUH! Mom pointed out that everything—even the fish—had a purse.

"What?" I replied, offended. "Those are NOT purses! Those are bags to carry their notebooks and pencils in!" To me, no one, not even a Martian or a fish, should go anywhere without pens and a notebook, because I never would.

I am a pen-and-paper person. For decades every doodle, thought, assignment, and recipe has started with pen or pencil to paper. I do my part and then some in keeping the stationery business in business! On any given day my most prized possession is the notebook I'm using. I'm typing on a computer now, but every recipe and all my notes for the stories that fill the book you're reading started in a notebook. Literally more than twenty books and every 30-Minute Meal on TV or in every issue of *Rachael Ray Every Day,* along with everything I cook at home, every pot or pan or piece of furniture I design—all of it gets handwritten first on paper in my notebooks or on my Danish blue-paper pads.

I don't know what my obsession is with paper, but it's as much a part of me as any cell in my body. I've always been obsessed with lists and I make them around the clock. I sleep within arm's reach of a notepad; I have them in every corner of the house, apartment, and office. I keep a roll of paper attached to the fridge to pull from. I have "dress notebooks"—tiny enough to fit into fancy evening handbags. I've lost wallets and passports and credit cards and even computers, but they can all be replaced. My notebooks cannot.

Part of the reason I love them so much is because they're *mine*. My work is in them—my ideas, my inspiration. I make everything I put my name on myself, and it all starts there. The biggest insult I ever received was when *The*

New York Times wrote that I didn't write my own books. What?! I wrote them all myself and have proof: They're all in my notebooks, thank you very much! I called the public editor crying hysterically and asked for a retraction. I don't think I ever got it, but he did say he thought the *Times* might have gotten that one wrong. (I still lick this wound, but I'm the biggest fan of the *Times*. I read it every day, and Wednesday is my favorite because it's Food Section day!)

My preferred notebooks are Decomposition Books, with 100 percent post-consumer recycled pages. I go through one every two to three months, and I label them simply by the quarter and the year—I finished this book in Q1 2019. I record each meal John and I make at home, even if it's something we've made hundreds of times, because recipes evolve. I code ideas for TV as DTS (for a daytime show), TVFN (for Food Network), and ED (for the magazine, *Every Day*).

Lists go outside the notebook, which is why I am also obsessed with blue pads from Denmark made by Normann Copenhagen. My grocery lists are always written on my blue sheets. It starts with a menu plan for the week or weekend. Next come sublists of what I need for each menu. Next I note how many items repeat, to get the total weight or number of units correct. I have my produce list, my Italian import store list, my seafood list, my meats list, my dry pantry list, and my beverage list, which John takes off my hands and orders for us.

I know I sound crazy and like I need a hobby—get a life, Rachael! The truth is, cooking food for those I love is my absolute happiest state of being. I love my lists because they allow me to organize and daydream about the next meal to be shared, the next chance I get to light up someone's eyes with a dish I've made. And, thanks to my lists, I can always make it again, and even better.

3 Nixon Was My Favorite President

When I was five, my family lived on Cape Cod, Massachusetts, in a little community called New Seabury. The house was a Yankee Barn—a big old place with all the modern amenities but also with exposed beam work as its bones, and lofts and ladders and rafters.

At the time, we owned three restaurants, all called The Carvery, steakhouses with classic French and Mediterranean influences. My mother developed every recipe and drew the original menu designs by hand. (My aunt, her sister, Geraldine, drew the logo of a butcher that looked more than a little like my grandpa.) Mom decorated the restaurants, as she did our barn, with classic Thomasville and Hunt Country furniture and eclectic accents like large, intricately carved candlesticks, cut-metal lanterns, and striking statues that were surprisingly moving and alive—old men fishing on a stone bridge or a family intertwined, the children literally climbing their parents.

I loved playing in both the restaurant and in our house, as they felt similar to me, one an extension of the other. The one thing I would have changed if I could? I desperately wanted us to upgrade to a color TV.

Like everyone, regardless of age, I appreciated Bugs Bunny, especially the mock operas, and the mad scientist and Gossamer the Monster. Pink Panther was cool, too. But I was not a kid who got into Saturday morning cartoons. For me, *Columbo, McCloud,* and *McMillan and Wife* were where it was at. I loved to watch murders get solved, and *60 Minutes,* especially the news and commentary from Harry Reasoner. (I know. Weird kid.)

Now, I realize that mysteries and news programming are not nearly as important to see in color as cartoons are, but I felt very put out by being "forced" to watch my quality television shows in black-and-white. I made this clear to my mom, but she wasn't budging.

Watching as much news as I did for a kid my age, it's no surprise that Nixon was a major figure in my life during that time. At the height of the Watergate scandal and up until his resignation speech in August 1974, just a few days before my sixth birthday, he was on TV constantly, professing his innocence over and over.

My mom's personal style was as great as her knack for decorating and for preparing food. Her look was bold, simple, and elegant. Back in the day, she wore a size 0 or 2 and had a teeny waist. She wore long skirts, wide belts, and simple white or ivory blouses, and skinny tall heels or booties. She could work a twelve-hour day in them. She had short, dark brown hair cut in a Vidal Sassoon bob, and it moved with her every quick step and turn. She

Really, Mom?! Thanks for the whale-tail hairdo (right). And on picture day, no less!

stood four foot eleven inches tall but carried herself as if she were a tall man with a long stride, and had a Sicilian passion and temper at her core. (Today, at eighty-four, she still looks beautiful and could still kick my ass.)

Mom voted for George McGovern. So one day, when Nixon was on TV yet again, in an extreme close-up, and he said, "I am not a crook!" she snapped. At twenty paces, just beyond the sofa and trestle drop-leaf table, she took off her size 5½ spike-heeled shoe and hurled it with fury at the target: our black-and-white Sylvania television. The shoe must have hit that old screen at just the right angle or with just the right velocity, because it caused the screen to crack and the TV to literally explode, smoke and sparks coming out of the hole. Her shoe then fell to the ground as if to drop the mic.

Three days later we finally got a color TV! And that's why, for a long time, Nixon was my favorite president.

The seventies were ground zero for the oil crisis and gas shortages. Eventually people could no longer afford the gas to go to Cape Cod and sadly, our Carvery restaurants went bankrupt. We moved to New York State and Mom started her life in restaurants all over again, from the bottom up. She became a success all over again, but I know we both miss her restaurant, done her way, with her food.

/ / /

Here are some recipes that remind us of the Carvery days. Together they make for a very special meal, fancy enough for the holidays but easy enough to prepare in part or whole more than once a year.

.

Crab-Stuffed Mushrooms with Mornay Sauce

MAKES 24 LARGE STUFFED MUSHROOMS

MUSHROOMS

24 large white stuffing mushrooms

Cooking spray or olive oil for brushing

Salt and freshly ground black pepper

CRAB STUFFING

THIS WILL FILL 24 LARGE MUSHROOMS, 6 FLOUNDER FILLETS, OR 18 TO 20 JUMBO SHRIMP.

6 tablespoons butter

Stems of 24 mushrooms or, if using with fish or shrimp, 6 mushroom caps, finely chopped

2 tablespoons fresh thyme, chopped

1 large shallot or 2 medium shallots, finely chopped

2 small ribs celery with leafy tops, finely chopped

2 large cloves garlic, finely chopped

1 bay leaf

Salt and freshly ground black pepper

½ cup sherry, dry vermouth, or white wine

1 handful fresh flat-leaf parsley, chopped

3 slices of white toasting bread

1 pound king crab meat

Juice of 1 small lemon

1 tablespoon Old Bay seasoning (scant palmful)

A few dashes each of Tabasco and Worcestershire sauce

My mom's crab stuffing is a favorite of mine and can be used in several ways. Here, it fills large white stuffing mushrooms, a classic starter for a dinner. I've requested it for my birthday many times over the years. Mom would place flounder on parchment paper–lined baking sheets and cover half of the fillet with a mound of crab, pull the fillet up over the stuffing, and top with Mornay sauce to bake to golden and the fish just cooked through. She used the same trick to stuff 6- to 8-count jumbo shrimp. She'd butterfly the shrimp, set them butterflied-side down, fill and stand the tails up, nesting them in the stuffing, then baste them with butter and bake them to perfection. Then she served them immediately with lemon wedges. To turn this stuffing into crab cakes, add an egg and chill, form patties, and coat in superfine flour (like Wondra), eggs, and breadcrumbs seasoned with Old Bay and parsley.

/ / /

MAKE THE MUSHROOMS: Par-bake the mushrooms. Before you roast the Classic Prime Rib au Jus (page 37), if serving as a meal, preheat the oven to 450°F and position the oven rack one rung below the top. Arrange the mushroom caps on a parchment paper–lined rimmed baking sheet, cap-sides up, and spray with cooking spray or brush with olive oil, then season with salt and pepper. Roast the mushrooms for about 12 minutes, until they have released a considerable amount of moisture, then remove from the oven and cool.

MAKE THE CRAB STUFFING: In a large skillet over medium to medium-high heat, melt 3 tablespoons butter, add the finely chopped mushrooms, and brown them, about 7 minutes. Then add the thyme, shallots, celery, garlic, and bay leaf. Season with salt and pepper. Sauté the vegetables for 4 to 5 minutes to soften them, then add the sherry, dry vermouth, or white wine and let it absorb, about 3 minutes. Remove the pan from the heat and cool the mixture in a large bowl. Add the parsley and combine.

MELT THE REMAINING 3 TABLESPOONS BUTTER. Toast the white bread in a toaster to medium golden and brush liberally with the melted butter. Finely chop the bread into coarse, small-dice toast crumbs. Add the toast crumbs to the bowl.

PICK AND CHOP THE CRABMEAT and douse with the lemon juice. Add the crabmeat to the bowl and add Old Bay seasoning and a few dashes of Tabasco and Worcestershire sauce. Mix the stuffing to combine, then place the bowl in the fridge to chill.

MAKE THE MORNAY SAUCE: In a medium saucepan over medium heat, warm the milk. In another medium saucepan, melt the butter over medium heat and whisk in the flour. Combine and let the roux bubble. Whisk in the warm milk, bring to a simmer, then cook for about 2 minutes to thicken sauce a bit, and season with salt, white pepper, and nutmeg. Stir in the Gruyère, cover the sauce, and remove the pot from the heat.

TO BAKE OFF THE MUSHROOMS, transfer the mushroom caps to another parchment-lined baking sheet, cap-side down, and fill each mushroom with a small round scoop of stuffing or mound by hand. Top each mushroom with sauce and a sprinkle of grated Parmigiano-Reggiano. Bake at 450 degrees temperature to golden and bubbly and hot through, about 10 minutes, and garnish with chives or parsley.

MORNAY SAUCE

1½ cups milk

2 tablespoons butter

2 tablespoons flour

Salt and white pepper to taste

A little freshly grated nutmeg (1/16 teaspoon)

½ cup finely grated Gruyère cheese

1 cup finely grated Parmigiano-Reggiano

Finely chopped fresh chives or fresh flat-leaf parsley, to serve

Proper Popovers / MAKES 12 POPOVERS

3 cups AP flour

1 tablespoon kosher salt

3 cups whole milk

6 large eggs

5 tablespoons butter:
3 tablespoons melted and
2 tablespoons softened

PREHEAT THE OVEN to 450°F.

COMBINE THE FLOUR and salt in a medium bowl.

IN A SMALL POT over low heat, barely warm the milk, to take the chill off.

IF THE EGGS ARE CHILLED, place them in a warm water bath for 10 minutes. (I keep eggs at room temperature.)

IN A LARGE BOWL, whisk together the milk and eggs to combine and until the whites are incorporated and frothy. Add the flour mixture to the eggs and milk and incorporate until no lumps remain. Add the melted butter and whisk to combine.

BRUSH THE CUPS of two 6-ounce nonstick popover/custard pans with the softened butter and fill just over halfway, about two-thirds full or ¼ cup batter in each tin. (A liquid measuring cup is very useful here.) Carefully place the tins in the oven and bake for 20 minutes. Reduce the oven temperature to 350°F and bake for 20 minutes more. Turn the popovers out on a wire rack and cut a small slit in each to allow the steam to escape. Serve immediately.

Classic Prime Rib au Jus / SERVES 8

Like my Grandpa Emmanuel, my mom loves to roast meats and whole fish at very high temps, then let the oven slowly cool for carry-over roasting. You will need a probe thermometer that can be inserted in the meat and read from outside the oven. And before roasting, let your meat stand for 2 to 4 hours, until it comes to room temperature.

/ / /

POSITION THE OVEN RACK one rung up from the bottom of the oven and preheat the oven to 500°F.

PLACE THE ROAST, bones down, in a large cast-iron skillet or in a roasting pan. The ribs make a natural rack for beef.

COMBINE THE SALT, pepper, rosemary, thyme, oregano, granulated onion, and granulated garlic. Place a meat thermometer in the center of the roast. Slather the roast with EVOO and rub all of the beef—the top and sides—with the mixture. Place in the oven and roast 5 minutes per pound. Turn the oven off and DO NOT OPEN THE DOOR. Roast the beef this way for 2 hours or until it reaches an internal temperature of 135°F. (If your oven doesn't retain heat well, roast the meat at 325°F to an internal temperature of 125°F, then flash-broil it to crisp the fat.) Let the beef stand for about 15 minutes, or cover it with foil and dishtowels to keep it warm. Carve 2 portions per rib. Serve with Au Jus and parsley and pass Horseradish Sour Cream (recipe follows) at the table.

MAKE THE AU JUS: Place the drippings in a small sauce pot and heat over medium-high heat. Whisk in the flour and then the stock. Season the gravy with granulated garlic, soy sauce, Worcestershire, and pepper to taste. Remove from the heat, cover, and reheat over medium heat to serve.

MAKE THE HORSERADISH SOUR CREAM: Combine all of the ingredients in a bowl and chill to serve.

1 (6-pound, 4-bone) prime rib (each rib is 2 portions), boned and tied (your butcher should be able to do this for you)

2 tablespoons kosher salt

1½ tablespoons coarsely ground black pepper

1 tablespoon each fresh rosemary and thyme, chopped

1 tablespoon each (1 palmful) dried oregano or marjoram, granulated onion, and granulated garlic

EVOO for liberal drizzling

Chopped fresh flat-leaf parsley and Au Jus (recipe follows), to serve

AU JUS
MAKES ABOUT 2 CUPS GRAVY

3 to 4 tablespoons beef drippings

2 tablespoons flour

2 cups beef stock or consommé

1 teaspoon granulated garlic

1 teaspoon soy sauce

2 teaspoons Worcestershire sauce

Freshly ground black pepper to taste

HORSERADISH SOUR CREAM
MAKES ABOUT 2 CUPS

1½ cups sour cream

About ¼ cup prepared or freshly grated horseradish

About ⅓ cup minced fresh chives

3 tablespoons unsweetened applesauce

2 tablespoons fine breadcrumbs

1 tablespoon coarsely ground black pepper

Salt to taste

Pucky Huddle Fries / MAKES ONE SERVING; MULTIPLY FOR MORE

1 large russet potato per person, skins scrubbed and dried

Oil for frying

Fine salt

"Pucky Huddle" derives from old Irish and old English. "Pucky" refers to land that is rough terrain, like much of the Northeast. A "huddle" is a gathering or a crowd. My mom used the term to describe her oven-roasted then flash-fried potatoes. They're so good they would cause people to gather around in a pucky huddle. The recipe is really just a method and can be adapted to any yield. Serve Pucky Huddle Fries with ketchup or Dijon mustard mixed with a little crème fraîche and black pepper or Horseradish Sour Cream (page 37).

CUT THE POTATOES, skin on, into ½-inch squared planks, then slice into fries

SOAK THE CUT POTATOES in cold water for 3 hours, then drain well. Preheat the oven to 350°F. Line a rimmed baking sheet with parchment paper and arrange the potatoes in a single layer. Roast them for 45 minutes. Meanwhile, heat a deep pot of oil or tabletop fryer to 400°F.

FRY THE PAR-BAKED POTATOES for 4 minutes or until deeply golden. Drain on a wire rack and season with fine salt.

Green Beans and Shallots / SERVES 8

Salt

2 pounds trimmed beans, topped and tailed

¼ cup (½ stick) butter

3 large shallots, peeled and thinly sliced

1 cup chicken stock or broth

These beans can be made well ahead and warmed to serve.

IN A LARGE POT, heat 3 to 4 inches of water to a boil and prepare a large bowl of ice water for a cold shock.

ADD SALT to the boiling water and add beans. Cook for 4 minutes, then drain in a strainer. Rinse under cold water, set the strainer in the cold ice bath to shock the beans, then drain again.

IN A LARGE SKILLET over medium-low to medium heat, melt the butter. Add the shallots and season with salt. Cook for 12 to 15 minutes, until the beans are very tender. Reduce the heat if the beans begin to brown. The shallots should become sweet and translucent. Add the stock and turn off the heat. Place the beans in the pan and toss to combine with the shallots and broth. Cover the pan and reheat over medium heat to serve.

4 No Baloney Bolognese

My mom, Elsa Providenzia Scuderi, is "no baloney." She's tough and smart and, to me, oh so cool. She's my favorite cook and my favorite person. She's the hardest worker I have ever known and, although one of the toughest humans, she's also the most empathetic and compassionate. She wants to save every living thing and champions every underdog, child, and animal great or small. If the meek inherit the earth, Mom will be their not-so-meek leader.

Among the long list of things to love and admire about Elsa, her gratitude may be her best attribute. Elsa, at under five feet tall and barely a hundred pounds, could outwork any ten men, and often pulled a hundred-hour workweek. She didn't complain or give in to the aches and pains or exhaustion. She was always positive-minded and grateful. My mother has always believed and taught each of us kids and all of her employees to have gratitude for work itself, that work is a privilege, not a right.

Elsa was a forerunner in her day, self-taught in many areas including home and industrial kitchens. She educated herself and carved out a sixty-year career as a mother of three in a world that told her the choice after high school for "someone like her" was motherhood or secretarial school.

Over the years, my mom passed many of her favorite cookbooks on to me. One of my favorites from her collection, a book we both consider an essential, is *The Classic Italian Cookbook* by Marcella Hazan. It was first published when I was five. What I love about this book can't be explained in its recipes, but in the story of Marcella herself.

Marcella earned a doctorate in natural sciences and biology in Italy in the mid-fifties, when I imagine very few of her fellow graduates were female. She never cooked an entrée until she married a Jewish man and moved to Manhattan, where she navigated home cooking and adapted classic Italian food. She opened her apartment to others and started a small cooking school. Marcella was a forerunner, too, a self-made woman in many ways. She was a badass with a great personality: tough, smart, and, to me, oh so cool. Of course Marcella reminded me of my mom, who also loved her and cherished her books. We were both more than fans of Marcella; we considered her and her food part of our family. Mom and I are forever devoted and often make our versions of many of her basic and beautiful meals.

Marcella never measured. She said that exact measurements to a cook are like placing a bird in a cage. For this reason, I write my recipes with a freehand equivalent for most of the measurements—a handful of this or a turn of the pan. I want anyone who makes them to be able to make them their own at the same time.

Marcella Hazan's recipe for classic Bolognese is perfect. It is delicious and rich, as those of us who've made it know. That said, I've added a few things over the years to make it our family recipe. When I use onions, as in this sauce, I often add a fresh bay leaf for sweetness and a floral note. Also, classic Italian recipes from Bologna to Naples allow onions to stand on their own. If I cook with onions I *must* add some garlic. It's literally in my blood. I digest so much of it that garlic comes out of my every pore like perfume. (If my husband, John, didn't care for garlic, it would have been a deal breaker. I tend to smell more like spicy salami than a delicate flower.) Also, I love grassy parsley stems in most any homemade stock or sauce and I often add a chunk of rind from Parmigiano-Reggiano as well (I save them from every piece I buy). It adds a buttery, nutty, and salty finish that's addictive. Marcella simmered Bolognese for a minimum of 3 to 4 hours, adding water when needed. I keep a warm pot of chicken broth or stock with Parmigiano-

Reggiano rind on the stove alongside the Dutch oven that I make Bolognese sauce in and I draw from it as needed, as if I were making risotto.

I never met Marcella in person. Once, years ago, my friend Kim Severson, at the time a columnist for the food section of *The New York Times*, now a bureau chief there, interviewed Marcella. Kim called me from the interview and left me a message that said, "I'm with Marcella and she's drinking whiskey and smoking Marlboro Reds." Kim then passed the phone to Marcella, who said in Italian that Rachael Ray teaches American mamas how to feed their babies, and American families how to appreciate Italian food. To this day I have kept the message in my voicemail. When I feel discouraged, when it's the wee hours and I still have eight more shows to write before I can let myself go to bed, I play that message and it makes all the difference.

Bolognese Sauce / SERVES 4 TO 6

About 2 tablespoons EVOO

About 2 tablespoons butter
for sauce, plus a few pats to toss with
the pasta

1 onion, finely chopped

1 rib celery with leafy tops, finely
chopped

1 carrot, finely chopped or grated

2 fat cloves garlic, chopped

1 pound ground beef chuck, or ¾ pound
beef plus ¼ pound ground veal or pork

Salt and finely ground black pepper

1 bay leaf

1 bundle fresh parsley stems,
tied with kitchen string

1 cup whole milk

Freshly grated nutmeg,
about ⅛ teaspoon

1 cup white wine

1 (15-ounce) can diced or crushed Italian
tomatoes (about 2 cups)

3 cups chicken stock or water

1 chunk of rind of Parmigiano-Reggiano,
plus grated cheese to serve

1 pound (500 grams) pasta such as
egg pasta or semolina tagliatelle or
other long pasta of choice

You need time for this meat sauce to simmer, but you can mostly ignore it. Just keep it at a low bubble and add liquid anytime it looks dry.

/ / /

IN A LARGE DUTCH OVEN over medium to medium-high heat, heat the EVOO, 2 turns of the pot. Add the butter to oil. When it foams, add the onion and cook for 5 minutes, until it softens. Add the celery, carrot, and garlic. Stir for 1 to 2 minutes, to coat the vegetables in the fat. Add the beef and season with salt and pepper. Break up the meat until it loses its pink color. Then add the bay leaf, parsley, and milk. Season with a little nutmeg and reduce the heat to a simmer. Let the milk absorb into the meat completely, about 20 minutes, then add the wine and let it absorb completely, about 20 minutes more. Stir the tomatoes into the sauce and reduce the heat to low. Simmer for 3 to 4 hours.

MEANWHILE, IN A MEDIUM POT over medium-high heat, heat the stock with the chunk of rind to a simmer, then reduce the heat to low. When the sauce looks like it may be drying out, add a few ladles of the warm liquid to moisten it, keeping the Bolognese at a low bubble. To serve, remove the bay leaf and parsley stems.

BRING 6 QUARTS of salted water to a boil over medium-high heat. Add the pasta and cook for a minute to a minute and a half less than the package directions. Reserve ½ mug of starchy cooking water if you have used all of your stock or Parmigiano-Reggiano-infused warm water. Drain the pasta or remove it from the water with a spider. Toss the pasta with a few pats of butter and combine with the sauce and a little stock or reserved water if necessary. Pass grated Parmigiano-Reggiano at the table.

5 Memories of Mamma Leone's

In the dining room of our house upstate hangs a framed menu from Mamma Leone's restaurant in New York City, dating way back some forty years ago, to a time when Mamma was alive and hosting her guests and I was just a little girl. My friend Kim gave me the menu as a gift—she knew what Mamma's meant to me. Every time I look at it, I think of my childhood Christmases and of some of the happiest days of my life.

When I was young we weren't rich but we weren't hand-to-mouth, either. Mom's budget was more like check to check, but every year she would save up, not for a rainy day or her retirement, but to take us to New York City during Christmas. It was part of our education: New York City was our exposure to the arts and our understanding of diversity in people, cultures, customs, and food.

Stepping onto the plaza of Rockefeller Center, the lights of the tree and the rows of trumpeting angels seemed the stuff of dreams and glitter-filled snow globes. Magic. Each year Mom always made sure that my brother and sister and I had on well-made dress coats and good shoes. We would walk

Fifth Avenue together, go to church at St. Patrick's, and we'd always get a little lost, on purpose, taking in a new neighborhood with each visit. Next we'd go to the theater, to see *The Nutcracker* at the Metropolitan Opera or a Broadway show. We saw *Fiddler on the Roof* twice, once with Topol and once with Zero Mostel. What a lucky, lucky girl I was.

Each trip also included a visit to FAO Schwarz. It used to be five stories high and it was the most wonderful place imaginable. You could play with every toy in the store. You could drive the toy cars or build bridges or castles with blocks or Erector sets, then curl up for a catnap in piles of Steiff stuffed animals. There was a salon on the top floor for kids only. We even got our hair done. We were allowed hours at FAO and the best part was that after all that playing around, we actually got to pick a toy, any one gift, to take home with us.

As if out of a storybook, we'd ride all dressed up and rosy cheeked in horse-drawn hansom cabs, touring the forest of lights surrounding Tavern on the Green. When we finally made our way to Mamma Leone's on Forty-Eighth Street, we were welcomed with open arms by Pasquale, our waiter. He wore a badge on his jacket and the numbers changed every year but I think the last time I saw him it said twenty years of service.

Going to this restaurant in its heyday was like visiting Italy for the night. The bar looked like the Blue Grotto of Capri. The dining room looked like a piazza in an Italian village, with balconies hanging out over an open square with fountains. There was always music in the air, courtesy of strolling troubadours and accordion players. I remember sitting on

Pasquale's right shoulder, my hands in his, and we'd dance and twirl till the room was spinning, the smile on my face so big my cheeks hurt. I'd put olives on my fingers and bite them off and Mom would even let us sip Chauvenet Red Cap sparkling red wine from aperitif glasses. We would twirl our forks into big bowls of pasta or dig into lasagna with giant silver spoons. We'd have soup and fish and meats and vegetables. My sister, Maria, loved the desserts like the spumoni and the cream-filled rum cakes, all of the cookies and the crispy fried dough bits with powdered sugar on top. It was all simply magic to us.

I love my mother so much for the thousands of hours she worked for us, for the roof over our heads, the food we ate, the dentists' and doctors' appointments she paid for and the education she made sure we had. But I'm most grateful for the exposure she gave us to the world. She showed me that it's much bigger than where you come from, or how you're raised, and that there's nothing out there to be afraid of. The world is where we meet the people, places, and things that make us reimagine who we are and what we could become. Those trips made me love New York City and the wide world that waited beyond it.

/ / /

Here are a few heavy, saucy, Italian American meals like the ones Mamma's was famous for.

Mamma Leone's-Style Spaghetti and Meatballs

WITH MOZZARELLA / SERVES 4 TO 6 IF MAKING 1 POUND OF PASTA, 6 TO 8 IF MAKING 1½–2 POUNDS OF PASTA

POMODORO SAUCE

About ½ cup EVOO, plus more for serving

1 onion, finely chopped

3 large cloves garlic, finely chopped

Salt and freshly ground black pepper

2 (28-ounce) cans San Marzano tomatoes

2 cups passata or tomato puree or tomato sauce

1 chunk of rind of Parmigiano-Reggiano

1 fat handful of basil leaves, torn

1 to 2 pounds spaghetti

MEATBALLS

2 tablespoons olive oil, plus EVOO for drizzling

1 small onion, finely chopped

2 large cloves garlic, finely chopped or grated

1 cup whole milk

4 slices of 1-inch-thick stale Italian bread

1½ pounds ground beef

1½ pounds ground pork

Salt and freshly ground black pepper

About ¼ teaspoon ground allspice

About ¼ teaspoon grated nutmeg

1½ teaspoons fennel seeds

1 teaspoon crushed red pepper flakes

About ½ cup grated Pecorino

About ½ cup grated Parmigiano-Reggiano

2 large eggs, lightly beaten

1 ball fresh mozzarella, halved and thinly sliced and chopped or coarsely shredded

Basil to serve

HEAT A LARGE DUTCH OVEN over medium heat. Add the EVOO, 6 slow turns of the pan. Add the onion, garlic, salt, and pepper and cook slowly for 15 minutes, until very soft, stirring frequently and reducing the heat if the onion begins to brown. Add the tomatoes and break them up with a wooden spoon. Add the passata, cheese rind, and basil and simmer at a low bubble for a minimum of 30 minutes.

BRING A LARGE POT of water to a rolling boil over high heat. Add salt to liberally season the water and cook the pasta 1 to 2 minutes less than al dente. Reserve 1 cup of the starchy water and drain the pasta.

TOSS THE PASTA with half of the sauce and add the starchy water and more grated cheese if you like. Add EVOO to gloss the sauce and the pasta once it emulsifies.

TO MAKE THE MEATBALLS: In a small skillet over medium-low heat, heat the olive oil. Add the onion and garlic and sauté them for about 15 minutes, until very soft. Add a splash of water if the onion begins to brown. Cool the mixture.

POUR THE MILK into a bowl. Add the bread and soak it in the milk for 10 minutes. Squeeze out any excess liquid and crumble the bread into moist crumbs.

PREHEAT THE OVEN to 350°F.

PLACE BEEF AND PORK in a large bowl and season with salt and black pepper. Then add the breadcrumbs and season with the allspice and nutmeg. Add the onion-garlic mixture, fennel seeds, red pepper flakes, grated cheeses, and eggs to the bowl and mix. Roll the meat into large meatballs about 2½ inches in diameter and arrange in a baking dish (you may need to use two baking dishes). Drizzle with EVOO.

BAKE THE MEATBALLS for about 15 minutes, then cover with about half of the Pomodoro Sauce and mozzarella and bake for about 15 minutes more. Top with torn basil and serve. Pass the meatballs at the table to place on top of the pasta.

NOTE: *Meatballs freeze well, but do not add the mozzarella if freezing.*

Mamma Leone's–Style Meat, Spinach, and Sausage Lasagna

SERVES 20

TOMATO-BASIL PUREE

4 cups passata

About 2 tablespoons EVOO

Salt

A few leaves of fresh basil, torn

MARINARA

About ¼ cup olive oil

1 onion, finely chopped

1 carrot, grated or finely chopped

1 rib celery with leafy tops, finely chopped

3 cloves garlic, thinly sliced or grated

1 rounded teaspoon sugar

Salt and white pepper

About 1½ teaspoons dry oregano (½ palmful)

About 1 teaspoon crushed red pepper flakes (⅓ palmful)

About 2 tablespoons fresh thyme, chopped

¼ cup tomato paste

1½ cups white wine

1 (28-ounce) can San Marzano tomatoes, hand crushed or broken up with spoon

4 cups passata or tomato puree

A few leaves of fresh basil, torn

MEAT SAUCE

2 tablespoons olive oil

1½ pounds ground beef, 80%–85% lean

1 teaspoon fennel seeds (⅓ palmful)

1 teaspoon crushed red pepper flakes (⅓ palmful)

Salt

Why choose between meat and veggie lasagna? Have both in one dish! This is an Italian American classic-with-a-twist, great for serving many people who are *very hungry*.

/ / /

IN A MIXING BOWL, combine the passata with the EVOO, salt, and basil.

MAKE THE MARINARA: Heat a Dutch oven or medium sauce pot over medium to medium-high heat. Add the olive oil, 4 turns of the pan, onion, carrot, celery, garlic, sugar, salt and white pepper, oregano, red pepper flakes, and thyme. Cook for 10 minutes, until the vegetables soften. Add the tomato paste and stir for 1 minute. Add the wine and reduce by half. Add the tomatoes, passata, and basil and simmer uncovered for 20 to 30 minutes, until it's fragrant and flavors have melded.

MAKE THE MEAT SAUCE: In large skillet over medium-high heat, heat the olive oil. Add the beef to the pan and cook until browned. Add the fennel seeds, red pepper flakes, and salt. Combine the parsley and garlic and stir into the meat. Add about half of the marinara sauce to the beef.

MAKE THE SPINACH: In a large bowl, combine the spinach, ricotta, egg yolks, salt, pepper, and nutmeg.

MAKE THE WHITE SAUCE: In a small saucepan over medium heat, melt the butter, then whisk in the flour. Add the wine and reduce by half. Add the milk and season with salt and white pepper. Cook the sauce until it thickens, then stir in the grated cheese and remove the pan from the heat. Cool and combine with the spinach and ricotta.

MAKE THE SAUSAGES: In a medium nonstick skillet add sausages and ⅛ inch of water. Bring the water to a boil and simmer the sausages to cook through, about 6 to 8 minutes. In a separate pan, brown the casings with a touch of olive oil. Remove the sausages from the pan, cool, and slice them very thinly on the bias.

ASSEMBLE THE LASAGNA: Preheat the oven to 350°F. Position the oven rack in the center of the oven.

BUTTER A 12 X 16-INCH LASAGNA PAN. Alternate the ingredients: passata, a single layer of pasta, half of the meat sauce and half of the toasted breadcrumbs, pasta, all of the spinach-and-white-sauce mixture, pasta, sausage, marinara, pasta, remaining meat sauce and breadcrumbs, pasta, passata, mozzarella, and grated cheese. Bake covered for 60 minutes, then uncover and bake for 20 to 30 minutes more, until golden and bubbly. Cool for 20 minutes before cutting into pieces.

PASS EXTRA MARINARA at the table along with warm Italian bread.

½ cup fresh flat-leaf parsley, finely chopped (a generous handful)

3 cloves garlic, finely chopped

SPINACH

1 (16-ounce) package organic chopped frozen spinach, defrosted and wrung dry

2 cups fresh ricotta, drained

2 large egg yolks

Salt and pepper

About ¼ teaspoon grated nutmeg

WHITE SAUCE

3 tablespoons butter

3 tablespoons flour

½ cup white wine

2 cups milk

Salt and white pepper

1 cup grated Parmigiano-Reggiano or Grana Padano

SAUSAGES

1 pound (4 links) mild Italian sausage

Olive oil, for browning the sausage

TO ASSEMBLE

Softened butter

2 boxes no-boil lasagna sheets or half-cooked (5 minutes) curly lasagna noodles

2 cups homemade breadcrumbs tossed with ½ cup garlic butter, ¼ cup chopped fresh parsley, and toasted

2½ cups mozzarella, shredded or thinly sliced

Grated Parmigiano-Reggiano or Grana Padano (a couple of handfuls)

Mamma Leone's-Style Eggplant and Sausage / SERVES 4 TO 6

Another cheesy, heavy, indulgent dish. Mangia!

/ / /

SALT EGGPLANT AND DRAIN on kitchen towels or in a strainer for 20 minutes, then pat dry.

IN A LARGE POT over medium-high heat, bring water to a boil for the pasta.

IN A LARGE PAN over medium-high heat, heat the EVOO, 2 turns of the pan. Add the crumbled sausage and brown it. Add the eggplant, peppers, and onions and stir for 8 to 10 minutes, until the onions soften. Finely chop the parsley and garlic together and add to the pan. Stir in the wine and add the tomatoes, breaking the tomatoes up with a wooden spoon. Reduce the heat and simmer for 20 minutes.

SALT THE PASTA WATER and cook the pasta to 1 minute shy of the package directions for al dente. Reserve 1 cup of the starchy pasta water and drain the pasta. Toss the pasta with the sauce, starchy water, EVOO, and cheese.

SERVE IN SHALLOW BOWLS and pass additional cheese.

Salt

1 medium-large eggplant, firm and heavy, half the skin peeled off lengthwise and cubed into bite-size, ¾-inch pieces

2 tablespoons EVOO

1 pound Italian sweet sausage with fennel seeds, crumbled

2 Italian red frying peppers, or 1 large red field pepper (sweet bell-like pepper but more rectangular in shape), halved, or 2 small red bell peppers, cut lengthwise, seeded, and thinly sliced

1 large or 2 medium onions, halved, peeled, quartered through root end, and thinly sliced

½ cup fresh flat-leaf parsley tops (a fat handful)

4 large cloves garlic

½ cup white wine or water

1 (28-ounce) can San Marzano tomatoes

1 pound rigatoni with lines

Green fancy EVOO, to serve

About ½ cup grated Parmigiano-Reggiano to serve, plus more to pass at the table

6 Half-Baked

You won't find a lot of desserts in this book. One reason is that I don't really like sweets. The other is that I suck at baking.

My sister, Maria, has always been a gifted baker. She was eight years old when I came along, and by that time she was already making simple cookies and cakes all on her own. In high school Maria graduated to sculpted cakes, elaborately and painstakingly piped in a spectrum of colored buttercream frostings. She was well on her way to becoming a fantastic baker.

Never one to be outdone, when I was ten years old, I decided to try my own hand at baking. I had my heart set on making a birthday cake for my mom. I knew she loved "cottage cake"—a dense cake topped with lemon curd. I couldn't remember which of her cookbooks had the recipe, so I looked through all of them until I found it. I made a list of the ingredients that I would have to buy with my hard-earned allowance. But I knew it would be worth it to see the smile on my mother's face when I presented her with my amazing creation. Before I even pulled out the baking pan, I read through the recipe twice, making sure I was fully prepared. It was a real challenge

Wait, my sister, Maria, and I were *both* once brunettes?!

for me: all the bowls and precise measuring, the sifting of dry ingredients— multiple times—the painstaking process of making the curd. No easy feat for an adult, let alone a kid. After I got the batter into the pan and into the oven, I tiptoed around the kitchen trying not to peek at the cake, nervously watching the clock. It would all be worth it!

The result was not so much "dense" as it was a sugary rock with a thick, yellow, gelatinous glaze. It was a disaster. How could I give this mess to my mother? I cried and cried. I loved my mom so much and here I was with no gift for her. I was a failure. I didn't bake again for years.

The next time I dipped my toe into the baking pool was as a teenager. It was during the holidays, and again I was trying to surprise my mom. She was on vacation and due back a few days before Christmas. She loved gingerbread, so I baked literally hundreds of ginger people, each with a different frosting face. They looked great. Maybe baking wasn't so bad after all. I covered the tree with ginger folk and hung more all over the kitchen. Maria was also coming home with her husband and two dogs for the holidays. She beat Mom home by a few hours, and when she did, the door opened, and the rest was a blur. The dogs went straight for the cookie-covered Christmas tree, and down it went, ginger limbs flying, ginger heads rolling. I lost my mind and flew into a rage, purple-faced and eyes swollen from crying. Outraged, I took down the tree in record time. I was the Grinch who had stolen Christmas. My mother came home and was heartbroken. My sister took her dogs and her husband and left early. The holiday was ruined.

I have a competitive nature, so any time I feel like a complete failure at anything, it really sticks with me. I stayed away from baking for decades. Since I don't really like sweets, I didn't feel like I was missing anything. It wasn't until I turned forty that I owned a kitchen scale. Cooking fulfilled me and I practiced it freehand. It was making homemade fresh pasta that brought me to scales and measurements.

But it was eclairs that finally brought me back to baking. When we were kids, if my mom came home with eclairs, we knew to watch out. They were not intended to be a treat for us. Eclairs were a warning. They were a signal that Mom was very angry with one or all of us. My mom used eclairs as a pressure valve. If she was upset, she'd have one. Two eclairs meant she was very angry. Three or four eclairs in the box meant someone might not survive. They were her stress management tool. Eventually, I started to make them for her. I'm not a baker, but if you can make pâte à choux, the dough for gougères (which anyone can, including me), you can make eclairs. Eclairs are also easy to make, so I don't really need to measure when I make them anymore. I love knowing that if Mom is sad or mad, I have a way to make her happy again. Just give her eclairs.

I have a group of friends and guests who bake on our show and they've convinced me I can do it, too, and have taught me tricks and inspired me to bake more. I don't do it often because it doesn't make me as happy as cooking, but I know that I *can* bake thanks to Christina Tosi, Gail Simmons, Amirah Kassem, Buddy "the Cake Boss" Valastro, Grant Melton, and my sister, Maria. Each inspires me and baking with all of them really *is* fun! So I delve into it now and then, with cakes, meringues, and cookies. Maybe I'm cutting a baby sweet tooth after all these years!

/ / /

Here are a few of my favorite go-to dessert recipes.

Elsa's Stress-Less Eclairs / MAKES 16 TO 18 ECLAIRS

PASTRY CREAM

¾ cup sugar

1 pinch of salt

3¼ cups milk

¼ cup cornstarch

3 large egg yolks

1½ teaspoons vanilla extract

PÂTE À CHOUX

6 tablespoons butter

½ teaspoon salt

1 cup flour

4 large eggs

CHOCOLATE ICING

2 (1-ounce) squares semisweet chocolate

2 tablespoons butter

1 cup confectioners' sugar

1 teaspoon vanilla extract

Flaky salt (optional)

Stress less. Eat more eclairs.

/ / /

MAKE THE PASTRY CREAM: In a medium sauce pot over medium heat, combine the sugar, salt, and 3 cups of milk and bring to a bubble. While the milk is heating up, combine the remaining ¼ cup milk with the cornstarch in a small bowl and stir until completely dissolved. In a large bowl, break up the egg yolks and whisk them together.

USING A WHISK, stir while adding the cornstarch mixture into the simmering milk. Stir continuously for about 2 minutes, until thickened (it's okay if the mixture boils lightly).

WHEN THE MIXTURE has thickened, slowly add a couple of ladlefuls of the hot liquid into the bowl with the egg yolks while whisking constantly. Add the egg yolk mixture back to the pot, return it to medium heat, and simmer for about 5 minutes, until thickened. Remove the pot from the heat and stir in the vanilla.

TRANSFER THE PASTRY CREAM to a bowl and cover with plastic wrap, pushing the plastic wrap down so that it covers the surface of the cream. Refrigerate until chilled, at least 4 hours and up to overnight.

MAKE THE PASTRY: Preheat the oven to 400°F.

IN A MEDIUM SAUCE POT over medium-high heat, combine 1 cup water, the butter, and the salt. Heat until the butter has melted and the water is boiling. Add the flour and cook, stirring constantly with a wooden spoon. Stir for about 2 minutes, until the mixture begins to create a dough ball in the center of the pot and the dough is completely pulling away from the sides of the pot.

TRANSFER THE PÂTE À CHOUX to a mixing bowl or bowl of a stand mixer fitted with a paddle attachment. On low speed, add the eggs to the mixture one at a time, scraping the sides of the bowl well after each addition and beating until the bowl feels cool (the mixture should be very smooth and silky).

(recipe continues on page 60)

TRANSFER THE PÂTE À CHOUX to a plastic food storage bag and cut ½ inch off one corner to create a pastry bag. On a baking sheet, secure parchment paper at the corners with a dot of dough. Squeeze the mixture into about 5-inch lengths and bake for about 35 minutes, until golden brown and puffed. The pastry should look like it is sweating a bit.

THE PASTRIES CAN BE MADE a day or two ahead of time and kept in an airtight container at room temperature. If they feel soggy when you take them out, pop them into a 400°F oven for a couple of minutes until they crisp up again. Allow them to cool to room temp before filling.

GIVE THE PASTRY CREAM A STIR to break it up and smooth it out, then transfer it to a plastic food storage bag. Cut off about ½ inch from one corner to make a pastry bag. Use a chopstick or the tip of a pair of kitchen scissors to poke a hole in one end of each baked pastry. Squeeze the pastry cream into each opening to fill the pastries. If this process proves annoying, simply halve the pastry lengthwise and fill the lower half, then replace or set the top half.

MAKE THE ICING: In a small saucepan over medium-low heat, melt the chocolate and butter to combine. Stir in the confectioners' sugar and add 1 to 3 tablespoons of hot water to desired thickness. Add the vanilla and remove the pan from the heat to cool a bit. Slather the eclairs with chocolate glaze and sprinkle with flaky salt.

5-Minute Fudge

This is what I make every holiday season so I don't have to bake and decorate cookies (see pages 55–57). The fudge tastes like a "Chunky," which is my favorite candy bar. It really does only take 5 minutes to make. It's my mom's recipe. She calls it "disgusting," which means "delicious" in Elsa-speak.

/ / /

HEAT AN ENAMEL DUTCH OVEN over medium-low heat. Add the condensed milk, semisweet chocolate, butterscotch chips, walnuts, currants, and vanilla. Stir the fudge for 5 minutes to melt and combine the ingredients.

LINE AN 8- OR 9-INCH SQUARE PAN with parchment paper and butter the sides or, to make the fudge in the form of a wreath, butter a round cake pan, wrap the empty container of condensed milk with buttered plastic wrap, and place it in the center of the pan. Use a rubber spatula to spoon the fudge into the pan and leave it bumpy on top. At Christmas, Mom used to cut red and green candied cherries and decorate the fudge with them to look like holly.

COOL THE FUDGE in fridge for 30 minutes. Gift the fudge in bricks or as a wreath, or slice it ¼ inch thick in 3-inch-wide pieces and gift in parchment paper–lined rectangular boxes.

1 (14-ounce) can sweetened condensed milk

1 (12-ounce) bag semisweet chocolate chips

¾ bag (about 1½ cups) butterscotch chips

1 cup shelled walnuts, toasted

½ cup dried currants (a generous handful)

1 teaspoon vanilla extract

Butter, for greasing the pan

Baked Pears with Gorgonzola and Crispy Prosciutto / SERVES 6

When we entertain, John and I often offer a cheese course rather than a sweet—assorted cheeses with nuts, honey, and fresh, dried, or preserved fruits. This roasted preparation for pears is a more formal offering of fruit and cheese and it doubles as an elegant appetizer as well.

/ / /

PREHEAT THE OVEN to 400°F. Arrange the prosciutto on a parchment paper–lined baking sheet and bake for 10 to 12 minutes to crisp. Remove and cool.

TOAST THE NUTS in a small pan, stirring frequently. Remove the nuts from the pan. Then warm the honey in the same pan.

HALVE THE PEARS and scoop the core out with a small scoop, melon baller. or grapefruit spoon. Trim the bottoms to allow the pears to sit flat. Arrange the pears in a baking dish or on a small tray. Dress the fruit with the lemon juice, nutmeg, and a sprinkle of thyme leaves. Bake for 20 to 25 minutes, to heat and soften the pears a bit.

WHILE THE FRUIT IS STILL WARM, fill the cavity of each pear with a mound of Gorgonzola Dolce. Transfer the pears to a platter and drizzle liberally with honey. Scatter the walnuts evenly over the pears and cheese. Break the prosciutto in large bite-size pieces and stick a few chips popping up out of each mound of cheese. Snack on any extra pieces, which is why I bake 6 slices rather than 4.

6 slices of prosciutto di Parma

1 cup walnut halves, broken into generous pieces

½ cup acacia honey (light in color and flavor)

4 ripe Anjou or Bosc pears

Juice of 1 lemon

A little freshly grated nutmeg

About 1 tablespoon fresh thyme leaves, finely chopped

About 12 ounces Gorgonzola Dolce

7 The Lost Girls' Adventures in Italy

One fall, back in the mid-'90s, I took my mom on a trip to celebrate her sixtieth birthday. I wanted to go to the one place in the world she would most want to be: the town where her father was born, Gela, Sicily, where some of her cousins still live in the apartment that my grandpa, her dad, Emmanuel, was born in.

My grandpa was the eleventh of fourteen kids. The four youngest boys, including Emmanuel, went to America. They followed the Hudson River north through the state of New York and finally settled in Ticonderoga, near the top of Lake George, on the edge of Lake Champlain. At first, coming from a family that made its living largely as potters, they all worked as apprentices in a large pottery yard. Then, one horrible afternoon, a fire there claimed the life of one of the boys. Guided by Sicilian superstition, the three surviving brothers each felt forced to find a new trade. Emmanuel became a stonemason, joining many other immigrant men in the army of artisans it took to rebuild Fort Ticonderoga.

My grandpa was as strong as a whole team of oxen. (Lifting stones all day will do that.) He could hug a tree and suspend his body outright like a branch, parallel to the ground. His physical strength was matched only by the strength of his devotion to his family. After ten or more hours of back-breaking labor, he could return home and rally, staying up half the night to entertain and spend time with his kids or to tend to his gardens, even if he had to work by the light of the moon. He was also the head cook of the family (his wife was the seamstress and baker) and he would often rise early to prepare that night's dinner in advance, while it was still dark outside.

Emmanuel's garden was cut out of thick, muddy, rocky terrain, aided by the swing of his machete, the blade that he strapped to his side and would swing as an extension of his own arm. He'd sculpt, fertilize, burn, and turn the ground for the longest, most fertile growing season possible. After each one, he would dry his vines and burn them, turning their ashes into the soil. The nutrients would fortify the ground for the next season's crops. The garden fed his ten kids and helped to feed the community as well. My mom, being the firstborn, had many chores and responsibilities in the kitchen and gardens, where she worked alongside him.

I am lucky that Grandpa Emmanuel lived with us for the first several years of my life, so I, too, knew what it what like to grow up alongside him. Emmanuel Scuderi remains my mom's favorite person who ever lived after her more than eighty years on the planet. After my fifty, the two of them, Mom and Grandpa, are a two-way tie for me.

I carefully researched the trip with my mom for many months (this was years before online travel booking existed). She has very specific tastes (no blue décor in any room, 4 stars or higher, and only Alitalia for flights). On our tight budget I had to find the best values possible for hotels and a rental car (good luck finding an automatic in Italy twenty-plus years ago). Beyond what was prepaid and vouchered, our spending money was literally USD $40 each a day. (It was just a coincidence that I would eventually host a television show called *$40 a Day*.)

Flying to Italy twenty-four years ago was much different than traveling today. It was fabulous and fun. Everyone on the Alitalia plane was dressed for the occasion: men in sport coats or suits, ladies in smart-looking travel coats and slack sets or dresses. The sparkling wine and cocktails started flowing before takeoff. Upon takeoff and landing everyone cheered and clapped at the miracle of it, congratulating our captain and crew. In between, everyone mingled like they'd known each other for years, swapping their stories and cocktails and different brands of cigarettes. The staff had to work around the partygoers to serve the unending number of courses: hot and cold antipasti, a pasta course with multiple options, the meats and fish and sides, the dolci—a cart of sweets followed by fruits and cheeses and Italian digestifs. After a late supper we all slipped into slippers and passed out, briefly. Then in the darkened cabin the buzz of conversation grew again as we got our second wind, driven on by more wine, Parmigiano-Reggiano snacks, and chocolates.

When you arrive in Italy, you can't help but notice that the air is different, sweeter, with a restorative quality to it. La Dolce Vita, the sweet life, begins with the sweetness of the air. Regardless of your heritage, there's a mood to being in Italy. Everyone becomes at least a little bit Italian simply by being there.

Things matter both more and less in Italy. One becomes more emotional, volatile, and passionate about life and at the same time more relaxed and forgiving about things like schedules and time. To Italians, each day is a two-for-one: a few hours of work, commerce, and activity separated by a hearty meal and a long period of rest followed by a few more hours of work and activity. Then there's a universal twilight stroll-and-chat followed by cocktails, a late supper, and another long walk, all before collapsing into a bed of fresh linens, while deeply breathing the night air from the open windows. What a life!

Mom and I had studied Italian together in a small classroom in Clifton Park, New York, for several months before we left. Growing up, she and her brothers and sisters were supposed to speak only in Italian, but the kids wanted to be American. They each had an American name and an Italian name and it was clear which they wanted to identify with more. (Providenzia became Elsa. Her sister Salvatricia became Louis. I think they were going for *Lois* here.)

By the time we got to Italy, I could manage simple sentences in Italian, but Mom felt too self-conscious. Still, she was so proud to hear me buy stamps and tickets for the bus that she burst into tears.

We got lost every day in Rome, on purpose. (This is actually a technique my mom taught us kids on any day off she had during all of our young lives.) On each day we'd buy our tickets and take a bus to a different neighborhood, targeting one of Rome's seven hills. Then we'd use a series of maps to try to make the long walk home, back to our hotel on the Via Veneto. Every day we lived La Dolce Vita, two days in each one.

And then, we tried to drive. We tried to drive in Italy.

Mom's a great driver. Well, she's a great driver, in a way. Over the years Mom did have some driving *issues,* like an occasional temporary loss of her driver's license for speeding. But isn't that really a subjective thing: *speed limits?* Some people are excellent drivers and are capable of driving faster, safely. Right? Mom got us around just great and very fast, although parking—especially parallel parking—and following directions, maps, and signs were not exactly her strengths.

What a team! What a scene! Me barking orders off a map and Mom ignoring them, zipping in and out between Cinquecentos, Mini Coopers, and Vespas as we circled the train station twice before working our way into the outer lane of the traffic circle, then finally onto the A1. Phew! Next, exit 7, which would take us to the next highway, which would, eventually, lead us on our way south, then down along the coast to Messina and across the straits on the ferry to Sicily. It took three loops of the highways that surround Rome to figure out that we were looking for an exit that was under construction. So yup, that added a couple of hours.

The adventure really got interesting when we got out of Rome and headed south. We renamed the road along the Amalfi Coast "Oh My God Way." Each time we went around a death-wish hairpin turn, negotiating with the oncoming traffic solely by small, dental-tool-like mirrors protruding from cliffs that had winding roads with no shoulders, and we managed to live, we screamed, "Oh my God!" We'd pant to catch our breath, try to get our heart rates back down to normal, then a hundred bikers would come at us at thirty or forty miles an hour. Oh my God! Over and over again . . . "Oh my God! Oh my God! Oh, oh, ohhhhhh myyyyy Gooooddddd!!!"

At each hotel, I'd take over and park (Mom hates to do it and I love to). I aced my driving exam (second try), based on my parallel parking skills. I mastered the cramped lot of our Hotel Dei Cavalieri. So I couldn't navigate, but I could park that car like a pro.

During our time in Positano we fell in love with Hotel San Pietro. We couldn't afford to stay there but what a sight to see, literally carved into the side of the jagged cliffs, the edges gardened and terraced with lemon trees. The rooms hug the cliffs, each one different from the rest. The views from the terraces were spectacular; I daydreamed with Mom of brides (maybe even me one day) celebrating on the verandas. We took a boat launch out and, looking back, Positano appeared, appropriately enough, like a wedding

cake. We fell in love with lemon everything and mostly drank our day's $40 budget in limoncello.

If you're a fan of Dr. Seuss, then you might be able to picture a ferry to Sicily. In getting to it, Mom and I shared the driving and I pumped gas. We kept getting lost on the roundabouts, taking the wrong "about" from the "round." We finally found the ferry, and the contraption attached to it looked too sketchy to hold a donkey like Grandpa's Pepe, much less a car. I took the wheel and with every rickety bump of the way my heart skipped another beat, a river of sweat running down my back. Once on the boat, we parked, hovered over toilets, got coffee and lemon soda, and sat down to read. Seven minutes later, we were docking. Not exactly an odyssey at sea.

We then got lost on several more circles of directional roulette. Lather, rinse, repeat.

That said, the Lost Girls didn't waste a minute of the endless ride through the rugged green landscapes. Looking out on the countryside, we spoke endlessly about the generations of men and women who had literally carried the soil up and up and up, toward the sky, saturating the land and bedding the rocks to grow their gardens. Mom smelled the burning of the branches and vines and saw the smoke rising from it. We were traveling late in the fall to take advantage of off-season rates, so the time was right for that. Once the smell of the fires hit her nose, she began dictating all the memories of her childhood. I filled more than one hundred pages of my journal with notes and now those memories saturate my life and this book.

Eventually we got to Taormina, another towering, beautiful city that looked like a tiered cake. Every image of a fairy-tale, far-off land came to mind. The heart of Taormina sits between Greco-Roman theater ruins and a monastery that's now a fabulous hotel on the far side. We were in a hotel a tier lower than town and would walk up into it each day. Our favorite place to eat was a tiny but popular restaurant near the main church and the big town clock, Ristorante Il Duomo. We had Sicilian classics like orange and oregano salad and rolled breaded swordfish, salty pastas and lightly chilled red wines from black grapes.

Finally, the day had come to go and meet our family in Gela, which sits on the south end of Sicily. Once again the Lost Girls hit the road and the roundabouts. This day was worse than most because when we stopped for gas or advice, fewer people spoke English and my basic Italian was limited and frustrating to both me and anyone I tried to speak to. The countryside seemed so quiet and everyone seemed annoyed with us rather than accommodating—not the Italian way. Some seemed disturbed by our mere presence.

We were trying to get to Agrigento, to the Hotel Baglio Della Luna. The plan was to drop our luggage and meet our relatives and follow them to the

family apartment in Gela by twilight, just in time for dinner. Three hours into nightfall we finally pulled onto the long driveway, drying our tears of frustration. We were so late. Upon checking in, we were relieved to find our family there, waiting and worried. Once we explained the situation, they all started laughing and they, too, started crying, all of them talking too fast to follow in Italian. Eventually we got it. Our Italian cousins have a terrible sense of direction, too. They get lost, often. Apparently it's a family trait. We also discovered another important fact: We had been traveling on an Italian national holiday—a sabbath, which explained people's impatience. Oops!

I have no idea what time dinner finally began but the hour was of no matter. We all ate and drank and talked in broken languages well into the small hours of morning, and all in the apartment my grandpa was born in.

The next day, in the warm autumn sun, we walked on the beaches that Grandpa Emmanuel would sneak off to when he was a boy, leading his donkey Pepe. He'd go there to swim and play with sea turtles because that was much more appealing to him than working in a pottery yard. My mom walked the same sandy beaches and cried happy tears as she thought about her father and his childhood.

When we came home, I helped her unpack. The jacket she wore on the beach that day seemed heavy to me. Mom had filled her pockets with big handfuls of its sand.

Sicilian Orange and Fennel Salad with Oregano / SERVES 6 TO 8

6 to 8 oranges or blood oranges, peeled and cut into supremes

1 small red onion, peeled and very thinly sliced

1 small bulb fennel, quartered, cored, and very thinly sliced

2 to 3 ribs celery with leafy tops, very thinly sliced on the bias

1 cup loosely packed fresh flat-leaf parsley tops, coarsely chopped

2 tablespoons fresh oregano, chopped, or 2 teaspoons dried leaves

1 fat handful each of oil-cured black olives and buttery Cerignola or Castelvetrano green olives, pitted and coarsely chopped

Red or white wine vinegar, for drizzling (about 2 tablespoons)

About ⅓ cup EVOO

Salt and freshly ground black pepper

To turn this into a summer lunch or lightest of suppers, we add thinly sliced smoked tuna, which you should be able to buy wherever you get your smoked salmon.

/ / /

ARRANGE THE ORANGES, onion, fennel, celery, parsley, oregano, and olives on a platter and dress evenly with vinegar, then EVOO, salt, and pepper.

Swordfish Cutlets with Roasted Peppers Sauce / SERVES 4 TO 6

CUTLETS

2 to 2½ pounds very thin cut swordfish steaks, skin and bloodline trimmed away and gently pounded into ⅛- to ¼-inch cutlets

Salt and freshly ground black pepper

1½ cups plain breadcrumbs

½ cup panko

1½ teaspoons crushed red pepper flakes (½ scant palmful)

2 tablespoons fresh thyme leaves, stripped

2 lemons

1 fat handful of fresh flat-leaf parsley

2 cloves garlic, crushed

Olive oil or safflower oil, for shallow frying

Roasted Peppers Sauce (page 75)

In Sicily, swordfish spiedini are as common on a menu as a steak or a burger in America. *Spiedini* refers to skewers or cooking on a stick. For swordfish, the spiedini are often rolled and stuffed or coated in breadcrumbs. My mom and I enjoyed several swordfish bites, bits, and rolls in Sicily. We loved the texture and crunch, so at home, to maximize texture, I gently mallet out the swordfish into thin cutlets, then season breadcrumbs with gremolata (garlic, lemon, parsley, and red pepper flakes) and quickly shallow-fry them in safflower or olive oil. We top this light but satisfying version with raw tomato sauce or with a roasted pepper sauce, which also goes well with chicken, beef, pork, or eggplant Milanese/cutlets.

/ / /

PREHEAT THE OVEN to 275°F. Set two pans with a wire rack inserted in them, one for the breaded raw cutlets and one to warm the cooked cutlets on, in the oven. Place a large nonstick or stainless skillet on the stove for shallow frying.

SEASON THE THIN SWORDFISH cutlets lightly but evenly with salt and black pepper.

COMBINE THE BREADCRUMBS and panko on a plate and season with salt, red pepper flakes, and thyme.

TRIM THE ENDS of one lemon and cut it into wedges. Grate the zest of the remaining lemon—for about 2 tablespoons zest— onto a bed of the parsley. Add the crushed garlic to the parsley and lemon zest and finely chop the mixture to combine. Combine the gremolata with the breadcrumbs.

EVENLY AND FIRMLY PRESS each cutlet into the breadcrumbs on both sides and remove to a wire rack.

HEAT A SHALLOW LAYER of oil, about ⅛ inch, in a large frying pan over medium-high heat. Brown the fish cutlets for about 2 minutes on each side, until they are a deep, golden color, and transfer the fish to the other wire rack—lined pan, to keep warm in the hot oven.

PREHEAT THE BROILER to high and line a baking sheet with foil, matte side up. Arrange the peppers on the baking sheet and broil them for 15 to 20 minutes, turning them occasionally, until they are charred evenly all over. Be careful when opening the oven, as the steam will need to escape. Place the peppers in a bowl and cover until cool enough to handle, about 30 minutes.

ALTERNATIVELY, if you have a gas stove, peppers can be roasted directly on the grates over high heat in an open flame to char the skins evenly.

ONCE COOL, use paper towels to help clean off the charred skins; this helps to keep the bits from getting under your nails. Halve the peppers and remove the seeds and tops. Chop the peppers into bite-size pieces, ¾ to 1 inch. In a mixing bowl, combine chili paste with the vinegar, capers, and garlic and whisk in EVOO. Add the peppers, parsley, and mint. Stir to combine and season the peppers with salt to taste.

ROASTED PEPPERS SAUCE

2 large cubanelle peppers (light green mild Italian peppers)

3 large red field peppers (red rectangular peppers, sweet, similar to bell peppers)

1 tablespoon Calabrian chili paste, or 2 teaspoons crushed red pepper flakes

About 3 tablespoons red wine vinegar—eyeball it

About 3 rounded tablespoons Italian capers in brine

3 cloves garlic, finely chopped

About ⅓ cup EVOO

½ cup each of fresh flat-leaf parsley and fresh mint, chopped

Salt

Fried Calamari / SERVES 6

When I was a kid I'd pile calamari rings on my fingers like jewelry, then gnaw the rings off one by one. I love to make squid because it is so quick-cooking, and fried anything, if the oil is hot and the seasoning is right, is always a crowd pleaser. Soak the squid for at least an hour before frying—I use milk, because the lactic acid helps tenderize it. It makes a huge difference. Here I use Italian flavors in the seasoning, but another go-to for us is seasoning the flour simply with paprika or smoked paprika (pimentón) and salt. We most commonly serve calamari rings with lemon. If we make a sauce, it's simple, tomato-based, and hot or cold depending on the season. On the next page is a recipe for Sicilian Tomato Sauce (While your squid is having its milk bath, you can make this. It's delicious with fried seafood or seafood pasta, but we love long fusilli or chitarra—guitar string—square-cut spaghetti with it.) But Tomato-Basil Sauce (page 7), arrabiata (tomatoes with chili flakes), and Marinara (page 50) are all fine companions.

/ / /

RINSE THE SQUID and pat completely dry. Season with salt and pepper and place in glass or ceramic bowl, dress with the lemon juice, and cover with the milk. Refrigerate 1 to several hours.

IN A LARGE BOWL, whisk the flour with the fennel pollen, red pepper flakes, paprika, garlic, and salt.

FILL A LARGE DUTCH OVEN or other deep pot with the frying oil. (Make sure it's a few inches from the top of the pot to avoid splatter.) Over medium-high heat, heat the oil to between 350°F and 360°F, or to when the oil rapidly bubbles around the handle of a wooden spoon when inserted into it.

ARRANGE A BED OF CUT SHEETS of brown parchment paper on a cutting board or large serving platter.

DRAIN THE CALAMARI from the milk mixture. Working in batches, toss the rings and tentacles in the flour and shake off the excess, then fry them in the hot oil until evenly golden and crisp. Using a large spider or frying basket, remove the pieces from the oil to a wire rack–lined baking sheet. Stand back to fry

(recipe continues on page 78)

CALAMARI

1½ pounds cleaned squid, cut into ½-inch rings and tentacles

Salt and freshly ground black pepper

Juice of ½ lemon

About ½ cup whole milk, or enough to fully submerge the calamari

2 cups AP flour

1½ teaspoons fennel pollen (½ scant palmful) or 1 tablespoon fennel seeds, toasted and ground

1½ teaspoons ground or crushed red pepper flakes (½ scant palmful)

1½ teaspoons paprika

1½ teaspoons granulated garlic or garlic powder

2 teaspoons kosher salt

3 quarts frying oil, such as safflower oil

OPTIONAL GARNISH

Fried herbs such as rosemary and parsley leaves and very thinly sliced lemon

Lemon wedges, pits removed, for serving

SICILIAN-STYLE TOMATO SAUCE

About ¼ cup EVOO

1 yellow onion, finely chopped

Salt

1 large fresh bay leaf

3 to 4 large cloves garlic, very thinly sliced or chopped

2 teaspoons fennel seeds (about ⅔ scant palmful)

1 teaspoon crushed red pepper flakes, 1 teaspoon pepperoncini, or 1 scant tablespoon Calabrian chili paste

2 tablespoons sun-dried tomato paste or tomato paste

1 cup red or white wine (I use Nero d'Avola, a largely affordable and prized Sicilian red)

1 (28-ounce) can San Marzano tomatoes

2 cups passata or 1 (14-ounce) can tomato puree

A few leaves of fresh basil, torn

the herbs and lemon, if using, as they spatter. Pile the calamari and herbs high onto the parchment paper and tuck lemon wedges all around the pile.

MAKE THE SAUCE: In a Dutch oven or heavy-bottomed sauce pot over medium-low to medium heat, heat the EVOO, 4 turns of the pan. Add the onion and season with salt. Add the bay leaf and cook, partially covered, to sweat the onion, for 8 to 10 minutes, until the onion is tender. Add the garlic, fennel seeds, and red pepper flakes and raise the heat to medium. Stir the mixture for 3 to 4 minutes more, then add the tomato paste and stir to combine. Add the wine and reduce by half, then add the tomatoes and break them up with a wooden spoon. Add the passata or puree and wilt in the basil. Simmer at a low rolling bubble for about 30 minutes to combine the flavors and thicken the sauce. Adjust the salt. (The sauce may begin to splatter as it thickens. If yours does, partially cover it with a lid or use a splatter guard.)

Limoncello for Mammacello / MAKES ONE BOTTLE

John quickly won my mom over the first time she met him, but even more so after he made her one of her favorite Italian beverages that we drank on our trip.

/ / /

PLACE THE LEMON SKINS and vodka in a large Mason jar. Store for 7 to 14 days in a cool, dark place. Strain the liquor twice through a fine mesh metal strainer, then through a tea or coffee filter, and funnel into a bottle with a tight-fitting cork or lid.

IN A SMALL POT, heat sugar and water to dissolve the sugar at a low boil, then cool and funnel the syrup into bottle. Gently turn to combine the vodka with the syrup and store in the freezer.

Skins of 12 organic lemons—careful of the pith, yellow skin only

1 (750-milliliter) bottle of good-quality 100-proof vodka

1 cup sugar

1½ cups water

8 They Lived Happily (and Loudly) Ever After

I still have the first voicemail message my husband, John, ever left me. As I write this, that's about eighteen years ago. From the moment I saw his face (he says "among a sea of knees," as we were the two shorties in a room full of tall people), John and I have spoken on the phone or in person every single day of our lives.

I was new to Food Network and had made dozens of episodes of *30-Minute Meals* and a few of *$40 a Day* (a travel show that ran on the network from 2002 to 2006), but they hadn't premiered yet. I wasn't a person of celebrity at all, just a short girl at a tall party. John was a lawyer who worked for a film company. His real love was music and he had a band, played guitar onstage, and could play several other instruments as well.

We met at that party a few days before Christmas. We were guests of a mutual acquaintance, a beautiful woman who worked as a makeup artist but was also doing some modeling—or looked like it, as did all of her friends, male and female. She traveled in that stereotypical fast-lane world of bright lights and big parties, with other almost-famous beautiful people. She told

Carbonara: In prep; in process; in mouth; on sofa.

both of us a week or more before the party, which she was throwing for her birthday (she's a Christmas Eve baby), that we would be perfect for each other. Italian. Into music, film, and food. She was so foreign to me and lived such a glamorous life that I thought anyone who knew her would never go for me. John said he felt the same. But she was relentless and called me so many times beforehand that I felt I would be a real heel to not show up to the party, no matter how out of place I might feel.

I had no idea when I met John that he was the one she was talking about. We saw each other across the crowded room: Check. We introduced ourselves and went through our stats, job, interests, etc.: Check. When I told John that I worked in food, he told me what he'd made for supper the night before. Now, at this time, there was no such thing as Vice Munchies, and not all guys were self-described foodies and wannabe Bobby Flays. Back in my day, when straight guys told you they could cook, most often it was "a killer breakfast," because they wanted you to stay over until they made it, or they were the Master of Chili, or grilling meat. John said he made tilapia fillets

with warm tomatillo salsa, heavy on the lime and maque choux (New Orleans–style fancy corn) spilling out of a halved avocado. I knew he wasn't a chef, so I assumed he was gay. How many guys in the Northeast who don't work in food know what maque choux is? So, I did what anyone would do: I offered to fix him up with a guy I knew. With an amused expression on his face, John gently explained that, while it was a kind offer, he was straight. Check, please! Handsome, funny, lawyer, musician, cooks, loves his mom and dogs? Done. We spent more than half the night talking. (Yes, talking.)

We talked every day after we met, but he lived in New York City and I didn't. I lived, as I still do, in a cabin in the woods in Lake Luzerne, a four-hour drive north. Food Network put me up in a hotel in the city for a couple of weeks to film our first episodes of *30-Minute Meals,* and then again to help promote it. The next time I came to New York was in early January to take my mom and my Aunt Gloria (not a blood relative, but like family) to meet some friends of ours, including my publisher at the time (my books were still being sold "exclusively" in Albany grocery stores), at a café uptown that featured Italian food and performers from the Metropolitan Opera as singing waitstaff. John got grilled more than the swordfish and was a big hit. The wine and limoncello helped. Since my mom's favorite flavor is lemon, though she's not a big drinker, she can't say no to a good limoncello (or three). Mom's cheeks turned rosy and John coined the nickname "Mammacello," which stands to this day. John makes her his recipe for the lemon liqueur every year for Mother's Day and sometimes an extra batch at Christmas.

The first time John and I cooked together was at his apartment. It was a large living space with a tiny kitchen, a small bath and shower off that, and "the Stairs of Death." John's apartment had stairs that led you to a single bedroom and small closet—if you survived the climb. The stairs were so steep, they should have been referred to as a ladder. In fact, they reminded me of the ladder on the small balcony of my bedroom as a child in Cape Cod. I used to hang upside down from its rungs when my mom wasn't looking to clear my head when I was upset. But the appeal to John's "ladder of death"? It was the only way to access a coveted New York City find: outdoor space. John had a small deck on the roof, and he farmed the shit out of it! He had tomatoes, he grew herbs, he was an Urban Farmer before that was a thing.

John wore a Zara shirt, a bit too large, but he looked hot. He lit candle sconces against a long wall that begged for art. He had a lovely bistro dining situation out there, properly set, and an inviting, pillow-fluffed sofa. His kitchen was ridiculously small with a stove so narrow only one large pot could sit on it at a time. (A few years later this became the inspiration for the oval pasta pot and five-quart skillet that launched my kitchen line—they remain cornerstone pieces today.) He was playing Marvin Gaye when I walked in, "What's Going On." Even though the song is more political than romantic, we made out, then we made dinner. Chicken with rosemary and lemon and brown butter–balsamic ravioli. After dinner (John did the dishes—so sexy!), we watched the amazing, heartbreaking video of Jeff Buckley live in Chicago. We made out again.

Incidentally, the one thing a woman cannot fake is a love of bad music. John's band, The Cringe, is awesome and, as it turns out, he is a master musician. I don't have to fake anything with this guy. Read anything you like into that.

Another voicemail I saved from those early days was the first time John told me he loved me. Yup, it was on the phone, not in person. He was wandering around New York and it was cold and it was late and I'm sure there was another John involved—Johnnie Walker. We'd been dating awhile, and while I wasn't the type to think about who says "I love you" first, I knew it wasn't going to be me. I think it's an overused word, a misused word, and I like to protect it.

John calls me wandering around, stumbling around, and he sounds very, very angry. And he says, "I used to be an independent person. I was fine by myself and I dated lots of women!" And then he says, "But all of those women were inert. They had nothing going on, like they're inert on the inside. And, I don't know, but you're the opposite. You're so . . . *ert*. So I guess what I'm saying is, I love you." ERT is still our shorthand for "I love you"— it's engraved inside his wedding ring, and we sign every single letter and card and gift tag with it.

John and I make sense. We don't care *when* we eat. We care that we eat *together*, whether we talk or listen to music or watch a movie while we're doing it, or visit with old episodes of *Seinfeld* or *Law & Order*. We're both politicos and sports buffs and animal lovers, and we read a lot. That gives us a lot in common and it also gives us a *ton* to fight about. We love debating, and we are loud, and we don't trust people who are too quiet. We fight, but we get it out and we don't really care who wins. We get quiet together, too. And when that happens it's magical and we should do more of it.

This set of knives literally contains the history of the universe. They're handmade of meteorite and woolymammoth tooth, and John bought them for my fiftieth birthday. The inscription, *ERT,* is our way of saying "I love you."

The tabloids have reported that John and I have been "over" more than a few times throughout our relationship. I used to cry about it. Now I guess we're flattered they think people still care. And they've gotten so desperate in their phony stories, it's more laughable than sad. Life isn't always a fairy tale for any couple. But we've been together, this John and this Rachael, every day since the day we met. And that's something. It's a lot. And some days, it's everything. I love you, John. In *Spinal Tap* lingo, you turn me up to 11.

/ / /

Here are riffs on some recipes from the first time we cooked together, and others that just make me think of John.

Brown Butter–Balsamic Ravioli / SERVES 4

I am way into making my own pasta these days, but store-bought ravioli works great, too. And if you want to swap in Tomato-Basil Sauce (page 195) for the brown butter, go for it. Whatever parts of this you make, do it together! That's what date night's all about.

/ / /

MAKE THE PASTA: On a large work surface, mound the flour and season with salt, then use your hands to push the flour away from the center of the mound to form a well at the center. In a bowl, whip up the whole eggs, egg yolks, and EVOO and add to the well. Using a fork and working around the perimeter of the well, slowly combine the flour with the eggs and oil until they are incorporated and absorbed. Start to knead the shaggy dough once you get to the outside of the well. If the pasta dough will not come together, add 1 or 2 tablespoons of warm water. When the dough forms, place it in a bowl and then clean the bench or work surface. Knead the dough on a lightly floured surface in one direction, away from your body, forming a wave or shell out of the dough. Ball it up, knuckle-knead firmly, then repeat, turning the dough a 45-degree angle, then starting the knead all over again. Knead the dough for at least 15 minutes, until it is smooth and elastic. (It will look shaggy for a while—don't worry, it will get smooth! Just keep at it!) Cover the dough with a kitchen towel and let stand an hour or so, or wrap and chill it overnight, bringing it back to room temperature to prepare. Cut your dough into 4 equal pieces with a bench scraper. Keep the dough that you are not working with under a clean towel to keep it from drying out. Place your pasta maker on the widest setting and pass the dough through, then fold the dough over on itself in thirds and pass it through the pasta machine. Fold it in half and repeat three more times in total. Next, pass the dough through one time per notch on the machine until the dough is at the second-to-last setting, ¹⁄₁₆-inch-thick sheet. Cut the long sheet in half and place each sheet on a layer of flour-dusted parchment paper. Repeat this process with each piece of dough.

BASIC EGG PASTA
MAKES 4 SERVINGS OF FRESH PASTA, CUT OR FILLED

4 cups super-fine Italian flour or 3 cups AP flour, plus more for rolling

1 teaspoon kosher salt or fine sea salt

2 large eggs plus 3 large yolks, at room temperature

About 1 teaspoon EVOO

1 to 3 tablespoons warm water

BASIC CHEESE FILLING FOR PASTA

1 pound sheep's milk or cow's milk ricotta, drained

1 cup freshly grated Pecorino if using sheep's-milk ricotta, or Parmigiano-Reggiano if using cow's-milk ricotta

Salt and finely ground black pepper to taste

⅛ teaspoon freshly grated nutmeg

1 teaspoon lemon zest

Egg wash of 1 egg beaten with a splash of water, to seal pasta

(recipe continues on page 89)

TO HAND-ROLL, form a large pasta dough disc, then roll it out like pie dough, from the center outward, away from your body, on a lightly floured surface, turning the dough and continuing to roll until the pasta is very thin and almost transparent.

FOR MALTAGLIATI (hand-torn pasta typically made from scraps of pasta), I don't actually tear the pasta; I use a small sharp knife to cut irregular diamond shapes.

FOR TAGLIATELLE or other long, flat pasta, roll the sheets of pasta gently but fairly tightly from short end to short end, then slice ribbons between ¼ and 1½ inches wide. Separate the bundles into nests and cook in boiling water about 1½ to 2 minutes. Use a spider to carefully remove the pasta to a warm serving dish.

MAKE THE CHEESE FILLING: In a mixing bowl, place the ricotta, freshly grated Pecorino or Parmigiano-Reggiano, salt and pepper, nutmeg, and lemon zest. Stir to combine. Then place a sheet of pasta on the work surface and brush it with egg wash. Space small walnut-size mounds of filling 1 inch apart on the pasta sheet and cover it with a second sheet of dough. Press down around each mound to seal the dough. Cut with a furled-edge pasta cutter or sharp paring knife to separate the ravioli. Place them on flour-dusted parchment paper–lined baking sheets and cook in gently boiling salted water for 3 to 4 minutes, until floating and cooked through. Reserve about ½ cup cooking water for the brown butter and balsamic sauce. Ravioli freeze well. Freeze on baking sheets, then gather and place in large freezer bags, removing the air from the bag.

MAKE THE BROWN BUTTER and balsamic sauce: Heat a large skillet over medium heat. Add the butter in 1-tablespoon tabs and melt. Add the sage, if using, and cook the butter for 2 to 3 minutes, until nutty and deeply golden. Remove the sage to a paper towel–lined plate. Remove the butter from the heat and add the balsamic drizzle or reduced balsamic. Add the sauce and about ½ cup salty cooking water from the pasta to the ravioli to coat evenly. Top with nuts, if using, sage or parsley, and pass more cheese.

BROWN BUTTER–BALSAMIC SAUCE

You can use this simple sauce with cheese ravioli and add chopped toasted nuts or just grated cheese and parsley to serve. We love to serve it with crispy sage, browning the leaves in the bubbly butter.

6 tablespoons butter

Finely chopped fresh flat-leaf parsley or 16 sage leaves

2 tablespoons balsamic drizzle (or reduce ⅓ cup balsamic vinegar and 1 tablespoon (packed) light brown sugar down to 2 tablespoons thickened vinegar)

1 pound ravioli, homemade or store-bought (cheese, pumpkin, or mushroom)

Toasted pine nuts, chopped hazelnuts, or walnuts (optional)

Grated Pecorino or Parmigiano-Reggiano

Carbonara / SERVES 4, OR JOHN

About ¼ cup EVOO

⅓-pound chunk of meaty pancetta or guanciale, cut into ¼-inch dice

4 large cloves garlic, thinly sliced or chopped

1½ teaspoons coarsely ground black pepper

1 cup white wine

6 large egg yolks

1 cup grated Pecorino Romano, plus more to pass

1 cup grated Parmigiano-Reggiano, plus more to pass

Salt

1 pound bucatini or spaghetti

½ cup fresh flat-leaf parsley, finely chopped (a fat handful of leaves)

I didn't make this on our first date, but I had to include it since it's John's favorite. The first time I cooked it for him, on his birthday, I asked him what he wanted and listed offerings from Osso Buco and Veal Oscar (he told me he loved veal) to Lobster Thermidor. "I want Carbonara!" That's MY man! Pasta alla carbonara is a Roman dish, Coalminer's Pasta. It's simple, hearty, and blue collar all the way. Best of all, you can eat it twenty-four hours a day—spaghetti for breakfast is totally legit if it's made with bacon and eggs.

Many recipes for this dish include heavy cream. They may be delicious, but they're not authentic. The creamy consistency here comes from tempering the eggs and emulsifying them with oil, cheese, and cooking water.

Just before transferring the pasta to a pan with garlic, oil, and pancetta or guanciale, I add about 1¼ cups of boiling salty cooking water to a bowl of whipped egg yolks and cheese. This step keeps the eggs from scrambling into large curds when they're tossed with the pasta.

BRING A LARGE POT of water to a boil for the pasta.

IN A LARGE, DEEP SKILLET over medium heat, heat the EVOO, 4 turns of the pan. Add the pancetta or guanciale and render for about 3 minutes. Add the garlic and pepper and stir 1 minute more. Add the wine and reduce by half (about 7 minutes), then reduce the heat to low.

IN A MEDIUM BOWL, combine the egg yolks and grated cheeses. Add a liberal amount of salt to the boiling water. Add the pasta to the liberally salted boiling water and cook to 1 minute less than al dente per the package recommendation.

REMOVE ABOUT 1¼ CUPS of starchy cooking water from the pot and whisk it into the egg yolks in a steady stream to temper them. Reserve an extra ½ cup of starchy water just in case.

DRAIN THE PASTA or transfer it with a spider or tongs to the pan with the pancetta and garlic. Remove the pan from the heat and add the tempered egg yolks and parsley. Toss to combine. If the sauce seems too thin, return the heat to the lowest setting and, stirring constantly for 2 to 4 minutes, until the sauce thickens. Add salt to taste.

Roast Chicken with Whole Roasted Garlic / SERVES 4

We made garlic and rosemary chicken breasts for the first meal John and I cooked together, but we both prefer a whole roast chicken now that time and the size of our oven allow.

/ / /

PLACE THE CHICKEN in a shallow baking dish. Salt the chicken inside and out and place uncovered in the fridge overnight.

PREHEAT THE OVEN to 450°F.

PAT THE CHICKEN DRY and fill with the pierced whole lemon, thyme, and rosemary. Tie the legs up. Dress the bulbs of garlic with EVOO; season with salt and pepper. Arrange the garlic in the baking dish around the chicken. Rub the skin of the chicken with butter and season with pepper. Pour the wine into the bottom of the dish.

ROAST THE CHICKEN for 1 hour or until an instant-read thermometer inserted into the thickest part of the dark meat reads 165°F. Let the chicken stand for a few minutes on a carving board until just cool enough to handle. Carve the chicken, dividing the white and dark parts and slicing the breast meat on the bias. Arrange the chicken on plates or a platter and top with drippings, juices, and the juice from the remaining halved lemon. The garlic may get dark but it won't be charred. Serve in the skins or squeeze the paste from the skins with your knife and pass with a spoon to eat with the chicken or to slather on the warm chunks of bread.

1 (4-pound) chicken

Kosher salt

2 lemons, 1 pierced several times with the tines of a fork and 1 halved

A few sprigs each of thyme and rosemary

4 large bulbs garlic, 1 per person or portion, ends cut to expose the cloves (keep the hairy root end intact)

EVOO for drizzling

Freshly ground black pepper

3 tablespoons butter

1 cup white wine

Warm, crusty bread

Broccoli Rabe / SERVES 8

2 large bunches of broccoli rabe

Salt

1 cup sun-dried cherry tomatoes
or sun-dried (not in oil) tomatoes

¼ cup EVOO

1 small onion or 1 large shallot, chopped

4 cloves garlic, thinly sliced

1 tablespoon chili paste or 1 fresh,
long, hot red chili, finely chopped

Juice of 1 lemon

Freshly ground black pepper

TRIM THE BROCCOLI RABE of its tough ends and separate the stems into thin stalks.

IN A LARGE, DEEP SKILLET or pasta pot, bring 3 inches or so of water to a boil for the broccoli rabe. Salt the water liberally and add broccoli rabe. Cook for 3 to 4 minutes, until stems are not quite tender. Remove the broccoli rabe with a spider to a bowl of ice water and cool. Remove from the ice bath to kitchen towels and pat dry.

SOAK THE SUN-DRIED TOMATOES in boiling water in a bowl for 10 minutes. Drain and pat dry. Chop or thinly slice the tomatoes.

HEAT A LARGE SKILLET over medium heat and add the EVOO. Then add the onion, tomatoes, garlic, and chili paste and stir for 2 to 3 minutes. Add about ½ cup water and let it absorb. Add the broccoli rabe and toss to coat and combine. Add the lemon juice to finish. Season with salt and pepper and transfer to a platter.

Pink Champagne Spritz / MAKES ONE COCKTAIL

JOHN SAYS: Rachael loves a champagne cocktail—but not one that is too sweet. This cocktail, which is particularly delicious in spring and summer, is a riff on the classic but with pink champagne instead of white, lemon wheels instead of a twist, Peychaud's Bitters (which has a pretty red color) instead of Angostura Bitters, and elderflower liqueur, which is not quite as sweet as the traditional sugar cube and balances the drink nicely.

1½ ounces St. Germain elderflower liqueur

7 dashes Peychaud's Bitters

4 to 5 ounces rose or pink champagne

2 lemon wheels

/ / /

ADD ALL OF THE INGREDIENTS to a rocks-filled wine goblet. Stir gently and garnish with a straw.

9 Dogs Make You a Better Person

When I was twenty-six years old, my boyfriend and I were looking in the *Pennysaver* auto listings for a four-wheel-drive truck for me (that's life on a mountain in upstate New York). We didn't find a truck, but we did come across a letter, a plea, written by a mom-to-be of twins who explained that she had a two-year-old pit bull and didn't feel she could raise it properly with two babies on the way. She didn't want the dog to die, an almost certain fate for pit bulls taken to shelters (it's hard to get or keep home insurance if you adopt a pit bull, so no one did). We drove out the next night in search of the dog. Her name was Boots, referring to her socks, patches of white fur on her front paws. I fell in love with her at first sight and, in looking at her, I knew she was meant to be my girl. Her original family loved her, but Boots spent most of her days in a pen in the backyard, and when in the house, she was allowed only on the linoleum flooring in the kitchen area. She had spent time trying to get out of that pen so her paws were scarred and not so white anymore. They looked like my hands, scarred from years in the kitchen. She had big brown eyes and seemed to talk, literally—she had a deviated septum so she "spoke" in a series of grunts and snorts and deep sighs. She was a dramatic, tough girl. My girl. She came home with us that night and after a long shower and a home-cooked meal, her training began and she was no longer Boots. She was now my Boo.

In just a few weeks Boo learned so much! How to jump up on people and sofas, how to sleep in my bed, how to shower a face with big wet kisses, how to talk up a storm, and even how to sing and dance. She preferred to listen to rock in the car, her head out the window, drooling and crooning along with Zeppelin and Queen. But at home she loved jazz, Chet Baker, and Ella. After dinner each night I'd put on a disc and she'd put her paws on my shoulders and do the box step and the fox-trot with me. When we watched Turner Classic Movies I'd get a backache from sitting far enough forward in my big old chair for her to curl up and nestle behind me, her head on the arm, peeking out to watch along with me. She was what I most looked forward to after work, her sweet face and her kisses, those big eyes.

We make a cake for Izzy every year, but here's the one I was most scared of— "lucky number 13." What can I say? I'm a superstitious Sicilian mom.

She wasn't all ladylike, though—she snored, a lot, and loudly (sometimes I do, too). In her quieter moments, she'd nestle under the low branches of a fig tree in my entryway. When she got the leaves against her back just right, she'd stand frozen and meditate, releasing an occasional moan, sigh, or chant.

Over time Boo became my best friend and was there for me after that boyfriend left and the next one, too. She was my confidante and gave unconditional love. She lived to know John in her last years and he fell for her, too, oftentimes going for walks with her to get soft-serve or frozen yogurt. Grandma Elsa loved her, too, taking her for a spin and to the drive-thru at McDonald's for a plain burger and large water. The kids who worked there would run to the window to see her. Our whole town knew Boo.

What Boo taught me far outweighed what I taught her. She gave me a deeper understanding of compassion, empathy, and love. It seemed that she could read my mind: when my feelings were hurt or when I wasn't feeling well. She taught me to trust my own instincts more and eventually she even managed to teach me the value and the beauty of a nap. With her great sense of humor she made me laugh like a child again. She was the perfect companion and my pilot in command (PIC). I suppose the only complaint I ever had about Boo was that she was a picky eater with odd tastes. Her favorite food was butternut squash. She preferred it to a steak dinner and had me roasting it year-round. Weird dog.

Losing Boo was as hard on me as the loss of my grandpa, who would have loved her. He had a pit bull, when my mom was a little girl, who lived to be eighteen. Boo lived a little past thirteen, which is how old my Isaboo is now and that worries me deeply. When I lost Boo, I collapsed in the street. I bruised myself so badly, I couldn't button my clothes the next day from all the swelling.

Isaboo is so different and special. She is also freakishly like me in many (weird) ways. We both worry too much and are poor sleepers. We are both always concerned that we are missing out on something or feel that we should be doing something more important than sleeping. Moreover, we both get hives, we both have thyroid issues, and we both have bum knees and achy joints. Isaboo's name is a combination of my favorite name, Isabella, and Boo, in memory of my first dog. She truly is my daughter, my girl. John would say the same. Just looking at her fills my heart with joy. She is so sensitive and loving, and everyone loves her back. Her beauty is

inside and out. And her eyes, more human than dog, look deep into your soul.

When John and I aren't cooking for Isaboo, she proudly eats Nutrish, her own brand of food, tested by her (and me: I've tasted them all on the show and at events, to show our commitment to quality). Many years ago there was a dog and cat food scare in the United States due to lack of controls on imported animal food. Basically, we were poisoning our own animals. We decided to partner with Ainsworth/Dad's Pet Food at the time and started our own line of top-quality dog food; eventually we added cat food, too. The goal was not only to feed our animals well but to create funding for no-kill shelters, big and small, so we built that into the business model. To date we have given more than $30 million to animal rescue efforts. Smuckers is our partner now and they are just as committed to quality and the support of humane animal shelters until every animal finds a home. Our foods are as the name connotes: nutritious and delicious. I would just add a little more salt for my taste.

What can I say? I'm a sucker for animals. I get it from my mom, who always wanted to save every creature she met.

My friend Melanie Dunea is a photographer and the author of two books that combine her inventive portraits of chefs (or, in my case, a cook) with essays from each describing what their last meal would be. My answer that accompanied my portrait is as follows: "If I knew any meal were my last I would be too sad to eat. I enjoy living and eating here on earth. But if there is a heaven, I do know what my *first* meal there would be. I would have a bowl of salty spaghetti with lots of anchovies or sardines melted into the oil with lots of garlic and red pepper flakes. Then I would have a huge, roast butternut squash with just a little salt, nutmeg, and butter. Most importantly I will be dining with my Grandpa Emmanuel and my dog, Boo. Now that really would be heaven."

Isaboo's Birthday "Cake" / SERVES 6 HUMANS AND DOGS

1½ pounds ground beef or turkey

1 slice of soft wheat bread

¼ cup milk

1 large egg

1 large carrot, grated

¼ cup fresh flat-leaf parsley, finely chopped

A sprinkle of sea salt

Olive oil or canola spray

2 large potatoes, peeled and cubed

¼ cup chicken or beef stock

½ cup Greek yogurt

Every year on Isaboo's birthday I make her a cake with potato frosting. It's my favorite dog recipe, and that's saying something given that for thirteen years we've been publishing dog recipes in our magazine, *Rachael Ray Every Day*.

/ / /

PREHEAT THE OVEN to 375°F.

PLACE THE MEAT in a large mixing bowl. Crumble the bread and moisten it with a little milk. Add the bread to the meat along with the egg, carrot, parsley, and salt. Line a 6-inch springform pan with parchment paper and spray with cooking spray. Fill the pan with the meat mix and bake the cake for about 45 minutes, until an instant-read thermometer reads 165°F. Cool the cake to room temperature and remove it from the springform pan.

IN A LARGE SAUCEPAN, place potatoes with enough cold water to cover. Boil the potatoes for about 15 minutes, until tender. Drain well. Place them back in the hot pot and pass them through a food mill or ricer, then add a little stock and yogurt to combine. Cool the potato frosting, then spread it over the cake top, about 1½ inches thick.

Ditalini and Muttballs / SERVES 4

Here's an early popular recipe from the magazine, updated for a new generation of fur babies.

/ / /

IN A LARGE, DEEP SKILLET or saucepan, bring the broth to a boil, then salt it and reduce the heat to a simmer.

MEANWHILE, IN A LARGE BOWL, combine the ground meat, eggs, carrots, cheese, breadcrumbs, and parsley. Season with pepper. Form into 1-inch meatballs.

DROP THE MEATBALLS INTO THE BROTH and simmer for about 5 minutes, until cooked through. Stir in the pasta and cook until al dente, 6 to 7 minutes. Let cool before serving to your pooch! Season the humans' portions with salt, pepper, and Parmigiano-Reggiano.

6 cups chicken broth

Salt

¾ pound ground beef, pork, and veal

2 large eggs

⅓ cup chopped shredded carrots

⅓ cup grated Parmigiano-Reggiano, plus more for sprinkling for human portions

⅓ cup breadcrumbs

¼ cup finely chopped fresh flat-leaf parsley

Freshly ground black pepper

½ pound ditalini pasta

Summertime Strawberry-Banana Treats / MAKES 10 TO 12 CUBES

Because all dogs love ice cubes and yogurt, a nutrient-dense nibble for the dog days of summer.

/ / /

USING A BLENDER, puree all of the ingredients. Add enough water to make the mixture pourable. Pour into an ice cube tray and freeze for 4 to 5 hours, until solid. Give your pup one cube at a time, when he's been very, very good.

1 (8-ounce) container plain yogurt

1 cup strawberries, hulled

1 banana, peeled

2 teaspoons honey

10 Every Night Is Movie Night

When I was a little girl, I wasn't into playing with Barbie dolls or dress-up. What I did like was movies. Whether going to the local theater, a splashy New York City cinema, or watching on our TV at home, I was hooked. Film noir, Charlie Chan, cop dramas—these were my favorites. I loved the glitz and glamour of *Gilda*: a supper club, balanced with the excitement of fisticuffs and "Is that a gun? Oh no!"

I can remember Mom setting out my best dress to go to Radio City Music Hall to see big releases. The Rockettes would dance, the movie would play, and we'd get to share a giant, expensive Hershey Bar with Almonds at intermission. Between The Ziegfeld and Radio City, we met Lawrence of Arabia, Doctor Zhivago, and Auntie Mame, each of them dear friends to this day. Going to the movies was an event and to me, even if I'm watching from my sofa, it still is.

I'm also an Italian at heart, so that makes me a romantic. I want to live inside storybooks, snow globes, and the silver screen. I want our house to be Frank Capra's and I want every moment of life to be turned up to 11 like in *Spinal Tap*.

When I met John, he told me he was a lawyer. But he became more attractive to me when I found out he worked in the licensing and distribution of independent movies. He and I talked almost all night long that first night, and we have talked every day or night since then. Some of the many things we agreed on were our favorite films. The order or ranking varies between us a bit, but I knew he was The One when I said that one of my favorite comedies of all time was . . . he finished my sentence, *Defending Your Life*. Our first "alone" date (our actual first date involved my mom and others) was to see the latest film by my favorite foreign director, Pedro Almodóvar. The place was packed, so we ended up in standing room only and he fed me popcorn.

I'm a terrible sleeper. So is John, thankfully or cursedly. Movies help with the insomnia and to quiet our minds. Our familiar old friends, of which we have a catalog of roughly five hundred, are our bedtime stories. Books are for daytime and rainy days. For us, nights are for movies, familiar ones— voices we trust and sentences we've heard so many times, we can finish them ourselves.

Some of My Favorite Films—I cannot rank them and I can't even narrow it down to fewer than this and I have seen all of these films dozens of times or more, each.

The Godfather 1&2	*Jaws*
Citizen Kane	*The Exorcist*
The Third Man	*Murder on the Orient Express*
Lawrence of Arabia	*The Verdict*
Casablanca	*Witness for the Prosecution*
Network	*This Is Spinal Tap*
Double Indemnity	*Defending Your Life*
All the President's Men	*Groundhog Day*
North by Northwest	*An Affair to Remember*
Rear Window	*It's a Wonderful Life*
Psycho	

Here are John's Top Five Most-Watched Films

The Godfather and *The Godfather Part II*
(I count them as one movie, even though that's cheating)
This Is Spinal Tap
Jaws
The Exorcist
Groundhog Day

/ / /

And what are movies without popcorn? I've done a million toppings, but these are some of my biggest crowd faves.

My Top Three Flavored Popcorns / MAKES 10 CUPS SEASONED POPCORN EACH

Pop corn kernels in a plain brown paper sack for about 1½ to 2½ minutes on high in the microwave oven, no oil required. I put about ¼ cup in each lunch-size paper bag at a time. On the stovetop I use ½ cup corn to about 2 tablespoons safflower oil over medium heat.

Deviled Popcorn

10 cups popcorn

3 tablespoons melted butter

2 teaspoons Worcestershire sauce

1 tablespoon paprika (a palmful)

½ teaspoon cayenne

1½ teaspoons (½ palmful) each of pimentón/smoked paprika, granulated garlic, granulated onion, and mild dry mustard powder

Salt

Tabasco (optional)

PLACE THE POPCORN in a large bowl. Mix together the melted butter and the Worcestershire sauce. Drizzle over the popcorn in a slow, even stream. Combine the paprika, cayenne, pimentón, granulated garlic and onion, and dry mustard. Sprinkle over the corn, toss, and season with salt to taste. Sprinkle on a little Tabasco, if desired, "Some Like It Hot" style!

Dill and Cheddar Popcorn

10 cups popcorn

About 3 tablespoons melted butter

About ¼ cup white cheddar powder

2 tablespoons dried dill

1 teaspoon each of granulated garlic, granulated onion, celery seed, and dried lemon peel

Salt

PLACE THE POPCORN in a large bowl. Drizzle the melted butter evenly over the popcorn. Combine the powdered cheese, dill, granulated garlic and onion, celery seed, and dried lemon peel. Toss with the popcorn. Season the popcorn with salt to taste.

Za'atar Popcorn

10 cups popcorn

About 3 tablespoons melted butter

3 tablespoons each of dried dill, sumac, and toasted sesame seeds

1½ teaspoons dried lemon peel

1 tablespoon za'atar leaves, or 1½ teaspoons each of marjoram or oregano and thyme, combined

1 teaspoon each of granulated garlic and granulated onion

Salt

PLACE THE POPCORN in a large bowl. Drizzle the melted butter evenly over the popcorn. Combine the dill, sumac, toasted sesame seeds, lemon peel, za'atar, and granulated garlic and onion. Toss with the popcorn. Then season the popcorn with salt to taste.

Jalapeño Margarita / MAKES ONE DRINK

JOHN SAYS: A spicy margarita pairs nicely with any movie, and most flavored popcorns.

/ / /

MUDDLE THE JALAPEÑO AND CILANTRO at the bottom of a cocktail shaker. Add the tequila, elderflower liqueur, and lime juice. Shake well with ice and double strain into an ice-filled rocks glass. Garnish with a jalapeño slice and a cilantro sprig.

2 slices of fresh jalapeño, plus one for garnish

1 sprig of fresh cilantro, plus one for garnish

2 ounces tequila blanco

2 ounces St. Germain elderflower liqueur

2 ounces freshly squeezed lime juice

11 I Have a Black Thumb

There are three food-related things that I'm not allowed to do, because I'm terrible at them and I haven't improved after fifty years.

1. I cannot make a decent cup of coffee. It's piss light or like mud, even if I'm using a coffeemaker. I have the opposite of the Midas touch—I will break it or clog it or set off its alarm.

2. I cannot make toast. For years I have had a "stunt toaster" named Jeanette on the daytime show. I forget about bread and I've set it on fire at home and at work for years. I get this from my mother. She's a bread burner from way back.

3. I cannot garden. This one breaks my heart because my grandfather was such a wonderful gardener and my mother loves to landscape, too. Grandpa fed my mom and her nine sisters and brothers largely from what they grew. I guess because those roots run so deep in our family tree, I feel like a black sheep that I have a black thumb. If you're a dedicated and successful gardener, run when you see me coming.

A glimpse of our upstate gardens. My first dog, Boo, is buried here in her favorite spot in the sun. It's Izzy's turf now.

Why am I so bad at something I care so deeply for? Because I'm impatient. I overwater, overthink, and try to be the boss of plants. And they do not like it. I get angry at them for not getting with my program and then I end up fighting with them, sadly, often out loud.

I love watching others garden. One of my strongest memories of my first trip to Italy was of the smell and sight of men in their fields burning and turning their vines and plants back into the soil at the end of the growing season, to feed the earth for the next season. This made me cry, too, as it reminded me of Grandpa. I fell in love with my husband, John, the night I met him, but the first time I went to his tiny apartment I saw the most beautiful sight. John chose the place because it had a small deck space for him to plant. It was winter and the pots and planters were all covered, but I could see them in my head as he described his tomatoes and herbs to me. Swoon!

I think I'm a nurturing person but I have resigned myself to the role of cooking vegetables rather than growing them. Upstate my husband is the farmer. I can pick the stuff, and prepare it, but I'm not allowed near it while it's growing. (Not even the houseplants. My friend Susan even changes the water on my cut flowers. I don't go near them because I'm afraid I will wilt them.) John buys all of the seed from Italy, a gift "from Isaboo" each spring. Ironically, the one item that has failed in our yard more than any was my favorite as a child: sweet corn. But tomatoes, peppers, onions, kale, cabbage, lettuces, beans, beets, squash, celery, and eggplant are all right at home here. We grow so much food, it's hard to keep up with the cooking and canning of it, but it's fun to try. When harvesttime rolls around, our meals become filled with all that amazing, fresh stuff—and my hours become filled with round-the-clock cooking! I will cook obsessively all night long, eighteen-to-twenty-hour stretches, easily, in order not to waste. I cripple myself every September and early October from all that cooking. Zucchini can grow overnight. I can't keep up with the squash. I have a love-hate relationship with it; it grows so quickly and never stops. Kale is like a weed. I cut it and make kale everything—chips, stews, pesto, pastas. But it just keeps coming! Tomatoes—I wind up with five hundred thousand of them and I will not waste a single one. If you come to my house in late summer, I will not let you leave without taking a basket up the hill to the garden and filling it with as much as you can carry off. Many friends who have summer birthdays get special baskets filled with veggies as gifts, which we refill upon return until the growing season ends. It's the gift that keeps on giving.

So even though I can't grow stuff myself, I worked for over a decade with former mayor Bloomberg in New York City to improve children's access to some form of gardening. There's a lot you can grow in a classroom on the windowsill, or in egg cartons on a sunny counter at home. I've seen gardens grow up walls in kindergartens, on school rooftops, and in community plots. Watching kids with their hands in the dirt making their first connection between where food comes from and what they eat has brought me to tears. For city kids and for all of us, having a garden in your life is a game changer. Even if you're not allowed to tend it.

/ / /

Gardens grow your soul. Eat more veggies and go play in the dirt! And make these recipes with the fresh stuff you pull out of it.

Soba Primavera / SERVES 4

PREHEAT THE OVEN to 450°F. Pull the mushrooms into thin florets and combine with the shallots. Spray with cooking spray or drizzle with EVOO to coat the florets. Season with salt and pepper. Place the mushrooms on a rimmed baking sheet and roast for 20 to 25 minutes, until crispy, tossing and turning them midway.

IN A LARGE STOCK POT, heat about 4 quarts of water to a boil for the soba. Season the water with salt once it is boiling.

HEAT A LARGE NONSTICK SKILLET or wok over high heat. Add the oil, 3 turns of the pan. Add the carrots, squash, peppers, and asparagus and stir-fry for 2 to 3 minutes. Reduce the heat to medium or medium-high. Add the favas or peas, scallion whites, ginger, and garlic and toss for 1 or 2 minutes more. Add the vinegar or yuzu, mirin or sake, and soy sauce or substitute. Reduce the heat to a simmer.

COOK THE SOBA in the boiling water to 1 minute less than the package directions. Drain the soba and add it to the sauce and vegetables. Wilt in the greens. Drizzle the soba with the sesame oil. Toss with the scallion greens. Serve in bowls topped with crispy hen of woods mushrooms and shallots. Garnish with sesame seeds.

¾ pound hen of the woods mushrooms (a.k.a. maitake mushrooms)

2 shallots, thinly sliced

Nonaerosol cooking spray or EVOO for drizzling

Salt and freshly ground black pepper

3 tablespoons safflower or canola or peanut oil

2 carrots, thinly sliced on the bias

1 small green or yellow squash, thinly sliced on the bias (optional)

1 cup bell peppers or hot peppers or a combination of them, thinly sliced

1 small bundle of asparagus spears, trimmed and thinly sliced on the bias, tied with kitchen string

1 cup blanched and peeled fava beans or spring peas

1 bunch of scallions (white and green parts separated), sliced on the bias

1½-inch piece of ginger root, grated or finely chopped

4 cloves garlic, chopped

About 2 tablespoons rice wine vinegar or yuzu

About ¼ cup mirin or sake

About ¼ cup shoyu, soy sauce, or Bragg liquid aminos

1 (12-ounce) package soba noodles

1 bunch of rainbow chard or flat-leaf kale, stemmed and sliced into thin ribbons, or spring lettuces, thinly shredded

1 tablespoon toasted sesame oil

¼ cup toasted sesame seeds

Ribollita / SERVES 8 TO 10

BEANS

1½ cups dry beans—I use a mix of borlotti and either white beans (cannellini) or ceci (chickpeas) (Buon'Italia for beans and imported not domestic, please)

1 onion, halved

4 cloves garlic, crushed

2 large fresh bay leaves

1 small bundle of sage, tied with kitchen string

Salt

SOUP

About ¼ cup EVOO

3 carrots, chopped

4 ribs celery with leafy tops, chopped

2 onions, yellow or red, chopped

1 large leek, split lengthwise, washed and thinly sliced

1 zucchini, seeded and diced (optional)

4 large cloves garlic, sliced or chopped

Salt and freshly ground black pepper

1 bundle of rosemary and thyme, tied with kitchen string

1 bunch of lacinato or cavolo nero kale, stemmed and chopped or sliced

1 small savoy cabbage, chopped or sliced, or a small head of escarole, chopped

1 small bunch of Swiss chard, stemmed and chopped or sliced

About ¼ teaspoon freshly grated nutmeg

1 (28-ounce) can whole or diced tomatoes, or 4 vine-ripened tomatoes, peeled and diced

Minestra is an Italian soup and refers most basically to beans and greens cooked together. Minestrone is big soup of beans and many vegetables. Ribollita is a large vegetable, beans, and greens soup thickened with stale bread. "Ribollita" translates to "boil again."

The day after we serve ribollita, it becomes thick enough to literally fry up in a cast-iron pan, a crispy, delicious combination of the rich bread, plump with stock and flecked with vegetables. Once it's fried in olive oil, we top the dish with a fried or poached egg and serve it again.

/ / /

SOAK THE BEANS overnight. Rinse them and place them in a large pot. Cover by about 3 inches with water. Add the onion, garlic, bay leaves, and sage and bring to a boil. Reduce heat to a simmer, salt beans liberally, and cook for 40 to 50 minutes, until tender. Remove and discard the onion and bay leaves. Reserve the beans and what is left of the cooking liquid.

PREHEAT THE OVEN to 350°F.

HEAT A LARGE DUTCH OVEN over medium-high heat and add the EVOO, 4 turns of the pan. Add the carrots, celery, onions, leek, zucchini, and garlic and season with salt and pepper. Add the herb bundle. Partially cover the pot and sweat the vegetables for 15 to 20 minutes, until they soften. Add the greens, wilting them in stages. Season with nutmeg. Add the tomatoes, stock, and rind and simmer for 1 hour.

PLACE THE BREAD on a rimmed baking sheet. Toast it in the oven for 8 to 10 minutes, until deeply golden, nutty, and fragrant.

ADD THE BEANS AND BREAD to the soup and stir. Ribollita is done when the spoon stands upright in the pot.

SERVE THE SOUP in bowls topped with onion, EVOO, and cheese.

3 quarts chicken stock or beef stock—I combine them both (of course, for vegetarian preparation, use vegetable stock)

1 chunk of rind from Parmigiano-Reggiano

½ to ¾ pound stale white peasant-style bread or whole-wheat bread, torn into pieces

TO SERVE

Finely chopped white onion

Fruity EVOO, for drizzling

Grated Parmigiano-Reggiano

Bloody Gazpacho Maria / MAKES ONE COCKTAIL

JOHN SAYS: Rachael makes the best gazpacho I've ever had. This cocktail replicates the flavors in that chilled delicious soup and is light enough to serve during the day.

/ / /

MAKE THE TOMATO WATER: Puree the tomatoes, serrano pepper, cucumber, onion, and salt in a blender until smooth and pour the puree into a strainer lined with eight layers of cheesecloth. Place over an empty bowl and refrigerate overnight. Discard the leftover puree and reserve the clear tomato water in the bowl.

MAKE THE COCKTAIL: Muddle the cilantro leaves at the bottom of a cocktail glass. Add the tequila, lime juice, and tomato water. Shake well with ice and strain into a rocks-filled Collins glass. Garnish with the cilantro sprig, cherry tomato, lime wedge, and jalapeño slice.

TOMATO WATER

2 pounds tomatoes

½ serrano pepper

½ seedless cucumber, peeled

⅛ red onion, peeled and chopped

1 pinch of salt

COCKTAIL

1 tablespoon fresh cilantro leaves

1½ ounces tequila blanco

½ ounces fresh lime juice

4 ounces tomato water (recipe above)

Fresh cilantro sprig, cherry tomato, lime wedge, and fresh jalapeño slice, for garnish

2
friends

12 My Friend Jacques

The first time I met Jacques Pépin, it was around ten in the morning the day he was scheduled to appear on my show. I'd been a fan of his for pretty much forever and was thrilled he'd agreed to come on. I knocked on his dressing-room door and opened it to find him rubbing a dog's belly—I wasn't even sure whose it was; we always had "show dogs," colleagues' pets running around the studio—and the two of them playing tag on the sofa. On the table sat a glass of good French red wine. Love at first sight. J'adore!

Jacques is a singular man. A great chef, a passionate, gifted artist, and a devoted husband, father, and grandfather. He embodies the best of traits: humble, kind, gracious, and thoughtful (toward people and animals alike). To many of us, Jacques seems all-knowing, a master in the kitchen. But he certainly doesn't think this about himself. And he has a quality that there are no words for. It's evident in his eyes, and I know it because I've seen it before in my mother's eyes and her father's. There's a spark—some call it a twinkle—that can convey in a glance that life is wonderful and everything will be okay. See and enjoy the beauty of the world. Sit, eat, and drink. You are welcome here.

In Jacques's hands, three eggs and a pat of butter are the most mesmerizing entertainment. In one episode of our show he made back-to-back classic and country-style French omelets (the first is a simple oval made from egg and butter, and the second a fluffed, browned version, often with fillings). The entire audience was enthralled by his delicate technique and you could have heard a pin drop but for the applause in between the completed dishes. Then, in my favorite segment, he took a small knife he had brought with him (which was perfectly sharp but had been in his hand for many decades by the shape and size of it) and completely deboned a whole chicken, then stuffed and tied it, all in a less-than-seven-minute segment.

In honor of Jacques's eightieth birthday, we staged an hour of our show as a surprise birthday potluck. Friends popped up and cooked tribute dishes for the party, including a dear friend of JP's and another favorite guest of mine, Jacques Torres, handling the sweets. I made spaghetti cooked in red wine, which is a Tuscan technique. Given our mutual love of wine, I thought it a safe bet and Jacques complimented me in saying he had never seen this technique before (. . . really? WHOA!). More important, he twirled and ate it with gusto! He loved it! Success! This excised a demon of mine: The last time I made this dish was the most nerve-racking of my twenty years on TV, when I competed on *Iron Chef* (see page 260 for that story—it still gives me night sweats).

To thank Jacques for each appearance he's made over these last several years, I've tried to surprise him with something unique: handmade ceramic service pieces; VSWs (very special wines); elaborate bouquets combining flowers, herbs, and vegetables. All were fine but never felt personal or sincere enough. So I put myself out there a bit. I drew a picture and painted my friend a greeting card. Drawing for Jacques proved more nerve-racking than cooking for him! He is an accomplished artist, from his spectacular hand-lettered and hand-painted menus, to his endless numbers of prints and paintings. Super intimidating!

My own love of drawing began when I was a little girl. If I got up in the middle of the night, as I often did (bad sleeper, even back then), my mother would allow me to stay up as long as I did something that used my mind— reading, drawing, or constructing something with my Erector Set, all fine exercises that would help me "exhaust myself naturally," as my mother would say. (Sneaking out of bed to watch crime dramas or *Saturday Night Live*, as I did sometimes, was more frowned upon.) So while I often drew as a child, as an adult I haven't been able to find or make the time to practice as much as I would like.

I stared at the blank canvas of an off-white notecard made of fancy watercolor paper. I decided to relax and not pretend to be an artist, just have fun and make Jacques a card. What I ended up with I called a *Foodle*—a food doodle. It's a recipe in simple pictures inked in watercolor pens. I have done many since, but his was the first, a recipe for Swordfish Niçoise.

In late spring 2018, I was among a small group of people that Jacques sent the following note to, along with a large attachment of images.

> Dear Rachael,
>
> I have been blessed by life. I have been lucky in my professional life as well as my private life. I have a great family and many friends, and you are one of several who have supported and helped me to become who I am. For your kindness to me, I would like to gift you one of my paintings. I have added a list of photographs and an explanation to help you choose the paintings you like. I would appreciate your giving me your choices from one to five, with one being your first choice, as I do not know who will answer my email first. Of course, the first to answer will have first choice in the selection process.

My answer to this was that *any* of his works would be a cherished gift. How could I choose?

I live in a house in the Adirondacks, hidden among the trees, along the edge of a deep forest. The views from our home are rich, green, and dense. I have a painting of a barn hidden by trees under a rose-colored sky. It hangs in a sunlit corner of my cabin and, like the cabin itself, seems to have a life of its own. This painting is loved like a person, and it's a painting by my friend Jacques Pépin.

Swordfish Niçoise / SERVES 4

SEASON THE SWORDFISH with salt and pepper.

HEAT A CAST-IRON SKILLET over medium-high heat. Add 1 tablespoon EVOO, 1 turn of the pan. Add the steaks and cook for 3 minutes per side, until light golden and almost opaque through the steak. Douse with the lemon juice and transfer to a platter. Cover loosely with foil.

ADD 2 TABLESPOONS OF EVOO to the pan and melt the anchovies into the oil, breaking the anchovies up with a wooden spoon. Add the beans and lightly brown for about 3 minutes. Add the tomatoes, garlic, chili pepper, olives, and capers and toss for 2 minutes more. Douse the pan with the vermouth. Add the scallions and chopped tarragon.

PLACE THE SWORDFISH on plates and pile up the beans, spilling from the center of the steaks onto the plate. Top with the chopped eggs and a few additional whole leaves of tarragon.

4 swordfish steaks, 1 to 1¼ inch thick, trimmed of skin

Salt and freshly ground black pepper

About 3 tablespoons EVOO

Juice of 1 lemon

4 anchovy fillets

1 pound haricots verts, trimmed and blanched in salted water for 2 minutes, then cold shocked and dried

12 cherry tomatoes, halved

4 cloves garlic, thinly sliced

1 fresh red chili pepper, finely chopped, or 1 teaspoon crushed red pepper flakes

½ cup pitted Niçoise olives, coarsely chopped

3 tablespoons capers, drained

1 generous splash of dry vermouth

4 scallions (whites and green parts), thinly sliced on the bias

2 tablespoons fresh tarragon, chopped, plus a few whole leaves

2 hard-boiled large eggs, finely chopped

Classic French Omelet / SERVES 1

3 large eggs

Salt and freshly ground black pepper

1½ tablespoons butter

FILLING AND TOPPING SUGGESTIONS

- 3 dollops of fresh ricotta and a drizzle of acacia honey

- Crème fraîche, caviar, and minced chives

- 1 tablespoon melted butter for brushing, plus 2 tablespoons chopped fresh tarragon, fresh chives, and fresh flat-leaf parsley

Simple, but delicious. The key is to not let it brown—and to serve it with tangy, tasty cream and/or herbs.

/ / /

HEAT AN 8-INCH NONSTICK SKILLET over medium heat.

CRACK THE EGGS into a small mixing bowl and season with salt and pepper. Beat the eggs with a fork just until the whites are fully incorporated. If your pan is utensil-safe, you can use your fork as your only utensil; otherwise use a heat-safe rubber spatula for the pan.

MELT THE BUTTER in the pan and let it foam. When the foam subsides, add the eggs. Quickly scramble the eggs in small circles and shake the pan gently. When the eggs are soft-scrambled and wispy at the edges, allow the omelet to set but do not brown the eggs. Swirl the pan or remove it from the heat as soon as the eggs are dry enough to roll. If filling the omelet, add a few dollops of ricotta and a drizzle of honey. To serve, gently lift one edge of the omelet while tipping the pan to the opposite side to begin the roll. Turn the omelet out on to a plate.

TO SERVE WITH CRÈME FRAÎCHE, split the rolled omelet lengthwise down the center like a baked potato and fill with crème fraîche. Top with caviar and minced chives.

TO SERVE AN HERB OMELET, brush the rolled omelet with additional melted butter and top generously with chopped tarragon, chives, and parsley.

Crushed Crispy Potatoes

I learned this technique from reading and watching Jacques, yet in one of his most recent books he credits me for somehow improving on his recipe. I gently boil my potatoes in stock, then roast or pan-crisp the potatoes in fat, either olive oil or butter or, most usually, a combination of the two. I remain firm that the technique is his alone.

/ / /

TO ROAST THE POTATOES, position the oven rack one rung above the center and preheat the oven to 425°F to 450°F. For pan-roasting, heat a large cast-iron skillet over medium-high heat while the potatoes are boiling.

PLACE THE POTATOES in appropriate-size pot and cover the potatoes with stock and/or water to cover. Bring to a boil and reduce the heat to a medium rolling boil. Season the water or stock and water to taste with salt and cook the potatoes for 10 to 12 minutes, until just tender. Drain the potatoes and spread them on a parchment paper–lined baking sheet or arrange them in the preheated cast-iron large skillet. Gently and carefully crush each potato with a drinking glass to flatten it into a fat pancake about ½ inch thick. Brush both sides of the potatoes with fat and season with pepper. Roast in the oven or cook in the cast-iron skillet for 15 to 18 minutes, until very brown and crispy at the edges. Adjust the salt to taste.

½ pound small, thin potatoes, peeled, per person

Chicken stock and/or water to cover

Salt

Per ½ pound potatoes: 2 tablespoons fat total, such as olive oil or olive oil and melted butter combined—feel free to add crushed garlic and herbs such as rosemary or fresh bay leaves to flavor the fat

Freshly ground black pepper

SERVING SUGGESTIONS

- Pair the potatoes with a saucy dish such as Chicken with Tarragon (recipe follows).

- Pair with caviar and crème fraîche

- Pair with smoked salmon, thinly sliced shallots, crème fraîche, and capers

Chicken with Tarragon / SERVES 2 TO 3

1 (4-pound) chicken, or ask your butcher for 2 boneless skin-on breasts, 2 boneless skin-on thighs, and 2 drummers

Salt and freshly ground black pepper

2 tablespoons olive oil

1 tablespoon butter

1 large or 2 medium shallots, finely chopped (about ⅔ cup)

4 cloves garlic, chopped

1 cup white wine

1 cup chicken stock

1 teaspoon lemon zest

2 tablespoons freshly chopped tarragon, plus whole leaves to serve

½ cup crème fraîche

Juice of ½ lemon

Crusty bread or Crushed Crispy Potatoes (page 127), to serve

It's a French classic, and I share my version in honor of my friend Jacques.

/ / /

PLACE THE WHOLE CHICKEN breast-side down on a rubber board. Using poultry shears, remove the backbone of the chicken by cutting down either side; discard the backbone or reserve it for stock. Flip the chicken over and press down on the breastbone to flatten the bird. Remove the wings with shears and reserve them for stock. Using a sharp boning knife or chef knife, cut the thighs away at the joint, then feel for the leg joint and cut between the leg and thighs to separate. Following along each side of the breastbone, separate the breast meat and skin away from the bone. Using the tip of a boning knife or paring knife, remove the bones from the thighs, keeping skin intact. Leave the bones in the drummers. Season the chicken with salt and pepper.

HEAT A LARGE CAST-IRON SKILLET over medium-high to high heat, then add the olive oil, 2 turns of the pan, and brown the chicken on both sides, 8 to 10 minutes (the breasts may take longer than the thighs). Remove the chicken, reduce the heat to medium, and add the butter to the pan. When the foam subsides, add the shallots and garlic, season with salt and pepper, and stir for 2 minutes. Add the wine and reduce by half. Then add the stock, lemon zest, and chopped tarragon. Slide the chicken back into pan and cook at a low rolling simmer for 15 to 20 minutes, until the chicken is cooked through and no longer pink in the middle. Remove the chicken to a platter. Reduce the heat to low. Add the crème fraîche to the sauce and thicken the sauce a bit. Add the lemon juice and remove the pan from the heat. Bathe the chicken in the sauce and return it to a platter or transfer it to individual plates. Garnish with whole leaves of tarragon and serve with crusty bread or crispy potatoes.

Crispy-Skin Fish with Morels and Asparagus / SERVES 4

When I bring home asparagus, I hold a spear at each end and bend it—where it snaps away at the woody end is my guide to trim the bundle. Once trimmed, I keep the spears in fresh water in a deli tub until ready to use. For this dish I slice the asparagus on the bias in 2-inch pieces and separate the stems from the tops.

/ / /

PLACE THE FRESH MORELS in a bowl of salted cold water and let them soak for 15 minutes. Change the water and soak the mushrooms twice more, then let them dry on a kitchen towel and halve them lengthwise.

PLACE THE DRIED MUSHROOMS in a small pot with the stock and simmer to flavor the stock and plump the dried mushrooms.

PREHEAT THE OVEN to 200°F.

PAT THE FISH FILLETS very dry. Heat a medium cast-iron skillet or other heavy skillet over medium-high to high heat. Season the fish with salt and pepper on both sides and score the skin with a hash mark or two. Add oil to the pan, 2 turns of the pan. Working in batches, if necessary, place the fish in the pan skin-side down and press it with a spatula to prevent curling. Cook the skin-side down for 3 minutes, to a crisp. Turn the fish and cook 1 to 2 minutes more. Remove the fish to a platter and cover. Keep warm in the oven. Add the vermouth to the pan and melt in 2 tablespoons butter. Remove the pan from the heat and add the mustard and the juice of ½ lemon. Whisk to combine. Transfer the sauce to a small bowl and cover with foil.

RETURN THE PAN to the heat and add the remaining 3 tablespoons butter. When it foams, add the shallot and leek and cook for 2 to 3 minutes. Add the fresh morels to the pan and stir for 2 to 3 minutes more. Add the asparagus bottoms and toss for 1 to 2 minutes. Add the garlic and asparagus tops, and finally the softened dried morels and stock. Season with salt and pepper and add the juice of the remaining ½ lemon. Arrange the fish, skin-side up, on top of the mushrooms and asparagus. Spoon the sauce over the top of the fish and garnish with minced chives. Serve with crusty bread.

¾ pound fresh morel mushrooms (if you can't get fresh, then soak dried morels in simmering water for 20 minutes)

Salt

¾ cup dried morel mushrooms

1 cup chicken stock

4 (6- to 8-ounce) skin-on fillets of branzino, red snapper, or black cod

Freshly ground black pepper

2 tablespoons olive oil or safflower oil

½ cup white vermouth or white wine

5 tablespoons butter

1 tablespoon Dijon mustard

1 lemon

1 large shallot, finely chopped

1 leek, tough ends removed, quartered lengthwise, washed, and chopped into ¼-inch pieces

1 bundle of asparagus (about 1 pound), trimmed and cut on the bias in 2-inch pieces (see headnote)

4 cloves garlic, thinly sliced

About 3 tablespoons minced chives

Crusty bread, to serve

the political animal

My mom's vision has been deteriorating for some years now. It's very upsetting to her (and to me). And as a result, she has had to give up some of the things she loves, like driving her souped-up Mini Cooper—she was always a speed demon and lover of fast cars like her Triumph TR7s. These days Mom doesn't go on as many adventures as her heart longs for, but there was one recent one that wild horses couldn't keep her from. In December 2018 she and I headed to the Barclays Center in Brooklyn to see Michelle Obama.

My mom thinks of Barack and Michelle as her own children. She is so filled with love and pride, worry and interest in their lives, their family, and their plans for the future. It made my Christmas this year to see her eyes, cloudy though they may be, light up from within and glimmer like a child's when Michelle sat down next to her at a reception, whispered greetings, and gave her a hug. We were there to celebrate Michelle's memoir, *Becoming*. I'd been asked to stand up onstage before the event and say what I am "becoming," along with four wonder women (how was I included in this group?): a recognized Girl Scout who dreams of becoming a doctor, a Gold Star service woman and multigeneration military mom, Ina Garten, and the incomparable Alicia Keys. I said something like this . . .

I am Rachael Ray, a second-generation American, and I am becoming my mother's daughter. I am an advocate for my neighbors in need of food and clean water, for kids who want to live healthier lives or who live in fear of going hungry. I am a voice for the animals that fill our shelters longing for homes and for love. My mother is here tonight. Her name is Elsa Scuderi and I thank her for helping me become who I am today. And thank you, Michelle Obama. You will always be my First Lady.

I'd been asked to speak at the event because of my work with Michelle over the years to improve school food, to battle childhood obesity, and to get kids moving. My Yum-o! organization launched in 2007 with a three-part mission: Cook, Feed, Fund. Cook: to educate kids and their families about food and cooking. Feed: to help feed hungry kids in America. Fund: to offer scholarships for culinary or hospitality courses. We work with national partners under each umbrella, like Feed America and Share Our Strength/No Kid Hungry. We've helped rescue millions of pounds of fresh produce that would be thrown out or plowed under every year, to get it into sixty thousand soup kitchens. We've given more than two hundred scholarships to culinary students—from community college attendees to Johnson & Wales University and the Culinary Institute of America. But improving school food is really my number one goal. It's our best front on which to battle children's health issues and food insecurity. And this was the First Lady's cause, too. So we worked together throughout her husband's presidency to support Let's Move, her initiative to get kids more active, and her fight to improve school meals, lobbying on Capitol Hill for Child Nutrition Reauthorization in 2010. We have worked to provide hunger and water relief, scholarships to public school kids committed to work in food or nutrition, and lobbying and financial support for initiatives to improve public school food. School food programs are our only level front on which to battle children's health issues and food security.

Much of what I accomplished with Michelle and with the Clinton Foundation in the years before—President Clinton's Alliance for a Healthier Generation was an early partner of Yum-o!—has been lost or reversed since Barack left office. But I remain dedicated, and we find new partners every day to help us secure the health and welfare of American children. In addition, the world has saints among us like José Andrés, who has helped our organization find the path to feeding kids and families globally with some of our funds. José is my saint. I include him in my prayers often.

You might guess by now that I was raised as a Democrat. That said, I cried for the loss of John McCain and George H. W. Bush last year—I had deep respect and absolute admiration for both of them. The phrase *"They don't make them like they used to*" applies to these men, who led lives of service, principle, and sacrifice. Their memorials brought a flood of memories, and as I listened to the eulogies by their families, historians, and world leaders, the stories filled my soul and heart with hope and restored my faith in our country. An assembly of full-dress troops as far as the eye could see, lining the road and saluting and escorting President Bush to his final resting place, is an indelible memory that brought me to choking tears. It was a beautiful, deeply moving sight. I have spent time with many Republicans and Democrats, with Joe and Jill Biden, Laura Bush, Jenna Bush Hager, and other members of the Bush family, with Mitt and Ann Romney and some of their children. Bottom line, and for the record, I am a mix of conservative and liberal, of Red and Blue, and I think that's what it is to be an American. We can take each and every issue and every vote at face value and choose for ourselves our next step, our collective path. What a country, what a gift! I am proudly purple.

But, whatever the issue, I love to talk politics. And as with most other passions of mine—food, travel—I'm a complete romantic about it. I want to believe in statesmen and women, believe that seeking elected office is a noble pursuit. I want the people who represent us to be the best of us. I don't air my opinions on my TV show because I'm not a journalist or pundit. I'm a service professional who talks to people from all backgrounds and beliefs. I welcome them and treat them equally, always trying to listen and to learn.

13 Life Is a Mixtape

I think that part of the reason I've been on television for more than twenty years now is that I try to keep it real. I write all of my recipes myself and both *30-Minute Meals* and our daytime show are mostly unscripted. I like to have genuine conversations with our guests, and as for my food, I like people to see my mistakes as much as the dishes that come out perfectly. But even though I put my real self out there, I think that there are still parts of my life that people might be surprised about, like my borderline obsession with music.

As a child I was exposed to all types of music. My father was from Louisiana and he introduced me to jazz and opera and classical music. We moved to upstate New York when I was eight or nine and became supporting members of the Saratoga Performing Arts Center, a concert hall for rock and pop acts and the summer home of the New York City Ballet. We had a great hi-fi and we all collected records. My sister and I practically bankrupted my parents with the Columbia House Record Club. What a racket! As a teenager and young adult I frequented the clubs of New York, both famous and infamous, hanging out at Ludlow Street Café listening to ska and dragging my friends to see bands before anyone knew who they were.

The night John and I met, we talked about music literally until dawn. Today we have a collection of more than twenty-six hundred vinyl albums at our apartment in the city and a few hundred in our cabin in the woods. Next to our car and our properties, I think the possessions worth the most money in our homes are our record players and John's instruments and recording equipment. John plays piano and every type of keyboard, accordion, drums, guitars, mandolin, banjo, and even the trumpet. Show-off!

When John was a toddler he would sit and rock back and forth in front of a small portable record player. His favorite record was a mono pressing of the Beatles' *Sgt. Pepper's Lonely Hearts Club Band*. One afternoon his mom wanted him to come to the table and sit in his high chair for supper so she took the album off the turntable and started to put it away. Not so fast! John screeched "More!" and ripped the cover sleeve, throwing it in protest. (He's pretty much the same guy today.) Years later, at our daytime show, Ringo Starr came in to perform. Ringo was funny, fascinating, and he kindly sat with both John and me far past his allotted time. The highlight? Ringo signed a vintage copy of *Sgt. Pepper's* (something he typically does *not* do) John had bought at the record shop across the street years before. Ringo said, "I wish I'd known. I'd a brought ya a new one." Epic.

Feedback is a marriage of food and music, held every year in Austin during South by Southwest. Thirteen years ago, when we started it, I thought we'd be laughed out of town—and we almost were. But people showed up in droves, then and every year since. We've welcomed and fed hundreds of bands and thousands of fans.

The first big gift I gave John was a surprise weekend in Austin, Texas. I fell in love with Austin twenty years ago and I wanted John to love it, too. Austin is an almost utopian city, and one of the live-music capitals of the world. It was all about celebrating small, local businesses before that was a thing. They really do try to "Keep Austin Weird." So I'm a little mesmerized by Austin and now John is, too. It's our second-favorite American city.

My first memory of the city is seeing two men and their dogs. One man was in his twenties and had a gauge in one ear, a few tattoos, really skinny jeans, and a mixed-breed black dog at his side. The other man had gray hair, what was left of it, a generous smile, and an old Lab next to him. What I noticed was how much they seemed to enjoy each other's company. They eventually got up and walked in opposite directions, but I was impressed. There seems to be no ageism in Austin, and everybody has a dog. Cool.

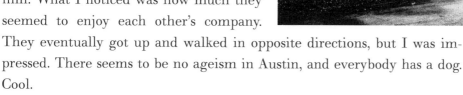

And the food in Austin—I could pretty much write an entire book just about that. It is world-class. We loved Austin so much, we wanted to give back to the city and be a part of the scene there in some way. So about thirteen years ago—with the help of my dear friends and colleagues Charlie Dougiello, who handles publicity for me, and Andrew Kaplan, my longtime producer who now manages my foundation, among about a hundred other things—we decided to throw a big, all-day party during the South by Southwest festival that happens in Austin every year in March. We wanted it to be free (we'd try to make some money back with sponsors) and we wanted to ensure that our guests were treated well and had a good time, so we made the following pledge: 1) Everyone who stands in line, some from as early as two in the morning the night before, will enjoy free food—which I write the recipes for and which caterers then produce thousands of portions of. 2) Everyone gets free drinks, thanks to our sponsors and John's gift for mixology.

3) We invite bands of every genre to perform—classic rock, pop, singer-songwriters, blues, country, rap, and hip-hop. Everyone is welcome, and after they hear their favorite band, they move on to make room for more fans to enter. Our lines make the nightly news and stretch more than a mile long. 4) There will be plenty of bathrooms.

We named the annual event Feedback, and it's like Christmas. It seems to bring out the best in everyone in attendance because we all believe in the power of music. It's been running for more than a decade and every show, each year, we turn to each other and say, "Wow! How can we ever top that?" Until the next year. The only two constant acts since year one are the Cringe, my husband's band, and Bob Schneider. If you don't know Bob Schneider, you should! He's worth a trip to Austin to catch a show, but he tours all over the country, too. Bob is Austin's favorite musical son and he has the awards to prove it. I remember the first time I heard him, he was on PBS's live-music show *Austin City Limits*. I stumbled out of bed in the middle of the night to find a pencil to write down his name. I bought his album the next day at my local Coconuts record shop in the Aviation Mall in Glens Falls, New York. We booked him that first year and we've been friends ever since.

But the best part is the surprises. You never know who you'll hear at a Feedback show: Green Day, Weezer, George Clinton and Parliament-Funkadelic, Blondie, Anderson Paak, Naughty by Nature, Salt-N-Pepa, Macklemore, The Record Company, Imagine Dragons, Lolo, Edward Sharp, Of Monsters and Men, Modern English . . . there's always something for everyone and everyone respects one another's work. One year we had the Eagles of Death Metal perform, and after their set they stood in the wings singing along as Kenny Loggins performed "Footloose." Seriously.

Feedback feeds my soul. Come join the party. It's the third Saturday in March.

///

We've cooked up one hundred thousand portions of food since Feedback began in 2007. Something spicy, something meaty, something veggie, always delicious. Here are a few highlights.

Upside-Down Frito Pie / SERVES 6

COMBINE THE MEAT with the baking soda and 2 tablespoons water. Let stand for 30 minutes. This will make the meat a deeper brown and crispier.

IN A SMALL SAUCEPAN over low heat, combine the anchos and the stock. Soak the anchos in the stock to reconstitute the peppers. Puree the mixture in a food processor.

HEAT A LARGE SOUP POT or Dutch oven over medium-high to high heat. Add the oil, 2 turns of the pan, and the bacon. Render the bacon for 1 to 2 minutes. Add the beef and brown and crumble until crispy and a deep brown. Add salt and pepper, cumin, coriander, paprika, allspice, and oregano and stir to toast them. Add the onion, garlic, and chipotle paste and cook for 7 to 8 minutes, to soften the onion. Add the tomato paste and stir. Then add the Worcestershire sauce, ancho puree, tomatoes, beans, and 2 cups water. Add the masa or cornmeal and simmer for 30 to 40 minutes, to thicken the sauce.

TO SERVE, open an individual-size bag of corn chips, add the toppings of your choice, such as white onion, pickled jalapeños, sour cream, and cheese, and top with chili. Serve in individual bags with a spoon.

CHILI

2 pounds ground sirloin

1 teaspoon baking soda

4 dried ancho chilies, seeded and stemmed

3 cups beef stock

2 tablespoons canola or olive oil

4 slices of meaty bacon or ¼-pound slab, finely diced

Salt and freshly ground black pepper

2 tablespoons cumin (a couple scant palmfuls)

1 tablespoon coriander (a scant palmful)

1 tablespoon sweet paprika

1 teaspoon allspice (⅓ palmful)

1 teaspoon dried oregano or marjoram (⅓ palmful)

1 large onion, finely diced

4 cloves garlic, chopped

2 tablespoons chipotle in adobo, pasted or finely chopped

2 tablespoons tomato paste

2 tablespoons Worcestershire sauce

2 (14-ounce) cans diced tomatoes with chilies

1 (15-ounce) can pinto beans or black beans, such as Jack's Quality Beans

2 tablespoons masa harina, polenta, grits, or tortilla crumbs

Corn chips, such as Fritos

TOPPINGS

Minced white onion

Pickled jalapeños

Sour cream

Shredded cheddar

Dozen-Spiced Fried Chicken Drumettes

WITH JALAPEÑO POPPER GRITS / SERVES 4

1 cup buttermilk

1 tablespoon chipotle-flavored hot sauce, plus some for serving

1 pound chicken drumettes (10 to 12 pieces)

Frying oil

1 cup flour

Salt and freshly ground black pepper

½ teaspoon granulated garlic

½ teaspoon granulated onion

½ teaspoon ground sage

½ teaspoon ground coriander

½ teaspoon ground ginger

½ teaspoon sweet paprika

⅛ teaspoon ground cloves

⅛ teaspoon freshly grated nutmeg

¼ teaspoon ground cardamom

½ teaspoon ground fennel

½ teaspoon cayenne pepper or hot paprika

½ teaspoon ground cumin

3 cups chicken stock

1 cup cornmeal/grits, medium to coarse

4 ounces cream cheese (half a brick)

2 jalapeños, red or green, finely chopped

1 cup grated Parmigiano-Reggiano

2 cloves garlic, minced or grated

Honey, for serving

Pretty much everything we've made at Feedback gets gobbled up (and washed down with a custom cocktail or beer). But these were an especially big hit. When it comes to wings, I'm all about the drumettes, but if you're into flats, they work here, too.

/ / /

COMBINE THE BUTTERMILK, hot sauce, and chicken to coat and let soak for at least 1 hour or overnight.

PLACE THE FRYING OIL, about 2 inches deep, in a large skillet or Dutch oven, or fill an electric tabletop fryer to the appropriate marking. Heat the oil to 360°F.

PREHEAT THE OVEN to 200°F.

COMBINE THE FLOUR with the salt, pepper, granulated garlic, granulated onion, sage, coriander, ginger, paprika, cloves, nutmeg, cardamom, fennel, cayenne, and cumin.

COAT CHICKEN DRUMETTES with the mixture, shake off the excess flour, and fry in batches for 10 to 12 minutes, until golden brown and cooked through. Season the drumettes with salt right when they come out of the oil. Place the fried chicken on a wire rack inserted into a rimmed baking sheet and keep warm in the oven.

MEANWHILE, HEAT THE STOCK in a medium sauce pot over medium to medium-high heat. Combine the cornmeal with 1 cup water and add the cornmeal to the hot stock. Stir frequently and let cook for 12 to 15 minutes. Stir in the cream cheese, jalapeños, Parmigiano-Reggiano, and garlic and season with salt and pepper.

SERVE THE POPPER GRITS topped with chicken drumettes and pass hot sauce and honey for topping the chicken.

7-Hour Smoked Brisket Sandwich / SERVES 8 WITH LEFTOVERS

WITH SMOKY BBQ SAUCE, SHARP CHEDDAR, RED CABBAGE SLAW, AND HORSERADISH SAUCE
(A.K.A. THE BEST SANDWICH I EVER MADE—AND MY HUSBAND EVER ATE)

MAKE THE RUB: In a small bowl, combine the salt, brown sugar, paprika, mustard seeds, garlic powder, coriander, cumin, ginger, and cayenne.

GENEROUSLY COAT THE BRISKET with lots of black pepper on all sides, then the spice rub, massaging the spices into the meat. Cover the meat with plastic wrap and let sit overnight in the fridge.

PREHEAT A SMOKER to 250°F and set up for cooking over indirect heat by placing coals and a couple of handfuls of wood chips to one side (apple or cherry chips are nice). Place the brisket fat-side up on the grate on the opposite side from the coals and cook for 4 hours.

REMOVE THE BRISKET from the smoker and slather with the grated onion. Using a double layer of foil, create a pouch/packet around the brisket. Add the apple juice and beer and tightly seal the foil pouch. Place the brisket back in the smoker for another 2 hours, adding a handful of chips and 12 or so coals. After 2 hours, open the lid and let the brisket sit in the packet for another hour.

WHILE THE BRISKET FINISHES COOKING, make the Smoky BBQ Sauce, Horseradish Sauce, and Red Cabbage Slaw (recipes follow).

THINLY SLICE THE BRISKET against the grain on a large cutting board. Add some BBQ sauce to the brisket slices and give everything a rough chop to combine.

PILE THE ROLL BOTTOMS with brisket and top with a sprinkle of cheddar and some slaw. Slather the roll tops with Horseradish Sauce and set the tops in place.

MAKE THE SMOKY BBQ SAUCE: Combine all of the ingredients in a small saucepan. Bring to a simmer and cook at a low bubble for 15 to 20 minutes.

(recipe continues on page 144)

SPICE RUB

3 tablespoons smoked sea salt or kosher salt

2 tablespoons light brown sugar

3 tablespoons sweet paprika

1 tablespoon mustard seeds

1 tablespoon garlic powder

2 teaspoons ground coriander

2 teaspoons ground cumin

2 teaspoons ground ginger

1½ teaspoons cayenne pepper

1 (8-pound) brisket, fat trimmed to ⅛ inch on top

Freshly ground black pepper

1 red onion, grated

½ cup apple juice or cider

½ cup lager beer, at room temperature

Smoky BBQ Sauce, Horseradish Sauce, and Red Cabbage Slaw (recipes follow)

8 seeded sourdough or kaiser rolls, split

Grated extra-sharp cheddar

SMOKY BBQ SAUCE
MAKES ABOUT 2 CUPS

1 cup good-quality ketchup, such as Heinz Organic

2 large cloves garlic, finely chopped

2 tablespoons (packed) dark brown sugar

2 tablespoons dark amber maple syrup

2 tablespoons Worcestershire sauce

1½ tablespoons cider vinegar

½ cup beef stock

1 teaspoon smoked sweet paprika

Coarsely ground black pepper

HORSERADISH SAUCE
MAKES ABOUT 1 CUP

1 cup sour cream

1 tablespoon heavy cream

1 tablespoon sliced chives

1 to 2 tablespoons prepared horseradish to taste

Kosher salt and freshly ground black pepper

RED CABBAGE SLAW
MAKES ABOUT 3 CUPS

2 cups packed shredded red cabbage

½ cup grated red onion (1 small onion or ½ medium onion)

1 Granny Smith apple, peeled and grated

3 tablespoons vegetable oil

2 tablespoons cider vinegar

1 teaspoon superfine sugar

Kosher salt and freshly ground black pepper

MAKE THE HORSERADISH SAUCE: In a small bowl, stir together all of the ingredients. Refrigerate until needed.

MAKE THE RED CABBAGE SLAW: Mix all of the ingredients together in a bowl until the cabbage is coated with dressing. Refrigerate until needed.

Lil' Veg-Head Corn Dogs / MAKES 20 TO 24 MINI (2- TO 3-INCH) CORN DOGS

HEAT 2½ INCHES of oil in a long or wide pot or pan or in a countertop fryer to 350°F degrees.

COMBINE THE FLOUR, sugar, baking powder, and salt. Sift the flour mixture together with the pepper, dry mustard, paprika, cayenne (if using), onion powder, and garlic powder into a bowl and stir in the cornmeal. In a separate bowl, whisk together the egg, milk, hot sauce (if using), and the remaining 2 tablespoons oil. Stir the wet ingredients into the dry ingredients with a wooden spoon until smooth.

PREHEAT THE OVEN TO 275°F. Place a wire rack over a rimmed baking sheet.

PAT THE HOT DOGS DRY and skewer them lengthwise. Dip the skewers into the flour-milk mixture to coat the corn dogs. Fry 2 or 3 corn dogs at a time in the hot oil for 4 to 5 minutes, until they are deep golden all over. Drain cooked corn dogs on the rack and keep them warm in the oven.

SERVE THE CORN DOGS garnished with drizzles of mustard or ketchup or a sauce of your choice.

Frying oil for frying the corn dogs, plus 2 tablespoons for the corn dog coating

1 cup flour

2 tablespoons superfine sugar

2 teaspoons baking powder

Salt and freshly ground black pepper

2 teaspoons Coleman's dry mustard

2 teaspoons paprika

1 teaspoon cayenne pepper, or 1 tablespoon hot sauce added with liquids (optional)

1 teaspoon onion powder or granulated onion

1 teaspoon garlic powder or granulated garlic

¾ cup cornmeal

1 large egg

1 cup milk

10 to 12 vegetarian hot dogs, cut in half

10 to 12 (4- to 6-inch) bamboo or wooden skewers, trimmed to fit in the pot or fryer

Garnishes: chipotle mustard and/or chipotle ketchup

Sweet 'n' Spicy Pickles / MAKES ABOUT 2 CUPS, OR ABOUT 80 SLICES

2 cups white balsamic or cider vinegar

½ cup sugar

2 teaspoons sea salt

1 large clove garlic, halved

½ small red onion, thinly sliced

4 Kirby cucumbers, sliced ⅛ to ¼ inch thick

1 small fresh red chili pepper, such as Fresno, sliced

2 dried bay leaves

A few sprigs of fresh dill

1 teaspoon coriander seeds

1 teaspoon mustard seeds

1 teaspoon black peppercorns

IN A SMALL SAUCEPAN, bring the vinegar, ⅔ cup water, the sugar, salt, and garlic to a low boil, stirring to dissolve the sugar and salt. Reduce the heat to low.

LAYER THE ONION, cucumbers, red chili pepper, bay leaves, dill, coriander seeds, mustard seeds, and peppercorns in a plastic or glass container in which they fit snugly.

POUR THE HOT BRINE over the cucumber mixture, cover tightly, and refrigerate for 24 hours or several days, stirring occasionally. The pickles will keep in the refrigerator for up to 1 month.

"Red 75" / MAKES ONE DRINK

1½ ounces grapefruit vodka, such as Deep Eddy Ruby Red

¼ ounce simple syrup (see page 249)

Sparkling wine

Red grapefruit twist, for garnish

2 dashes grapefruit bitters (optional)

JOHN SAYS: This one was a hit at Feedback 2018.

/ / /

MIX GRAPEFRUIT VODKA and simple syrup. Top with sparkling wine. Add bitters (if using) and serve on the rocks with a straw and garnish.

14 Awkward Celebrity Moments

I've been on TV, local and national, cable and broadcast, for more than two decades. I guess that makes me a "celebrity." Being famous on any level, being noticed for anything other than my work, makes me more uncomfortable than a trip to the dentist. (Sorry, Dr. Guido, I know I'm your worst patient ever!) I really hate having my picture taken, too. I feel so self-conscious that I stiffen up until I feel like a petrified tree with gnarly branches tangled around odd knots.

I work in front of cameras all day long, taping three hour-long shows a day at the daytime show, and I'm super comfortable there because I forget about the cameras. To me, I'm just hanging out with some guys and girls I know; they're not cameramen or stage managers, they're Veda and Cindy, Kevin and Trish, Jimmy and Manny, Britt and Ed, and dozens more. And I don't watch myself, ever. At the end of the day, I know I've worked my hardest and done my best, and when I leave the studio I leave behind who I am at work and go home to my private time and the things I love most: my husband and close friends, music, movies, books, cooking dinner, and my dog, Isaboo, in no particular order. (She doesn't like to watch me, either. It freaks her out if she hears me on TV. She thinks I'm trapped in it or behind it.)

Even though I'm a little claustrophobic, I love spending my days in front of a crowd (or three), chatting, meeting new people, and cooking several meals throughout the day. I'm a waitress at heart and a cook in my soul, so as long as I'm getting to know my customers and making them something good to eat, I'm happy. Like most of us, I strive for balance between the fullness of my workdays and the largely quiet nights at home. It's at the media events, photo shoots, parties, fund-raisers, and red carpets that I fall apart. Like wheels off the bus.

What follows are just a few of my countless awkward moments in that glitzy world. See if you can read them without shaking your head "No!" or putting your hand over your mouth in horror, embarrassed for me. At the very least, have a good laugh about it. I sure did (eventually).

John and I were invited to the last State Dinner at the White House in October 2016, hosted by the president and First Lady, Barack and Michelle Obama. It was in honor of the now former prime minister of Italy, Matteo Renzi. I chose a dress that had a sweeping skirt, a mosaic of falling leaves in autumn's color palette—gold, burgundy, and deep orange—and a simple black turtleneck sweater top. Issue number one: I failed to check the forecast. It was in the eighties in D.C. that day. Would have been good to know. On the walk from the car, through the gates and through the line and up the stairs, all in ridiculously high heels, the river of sweat that had run straight down my back was in my shoes, which resulted in an even less graceful stride. (Have I mentioned I'm no good at walking in heels?) As I attempted a flight of stone steps, I managed to hook the heel of my shoe through the crinoline from my skirt, tangling my foot in layers of netting. I had to wait at the check-in for the lovely woman receiving us to abandon her post briefly, retrieve scissors, and cut my foot free, discarding the ruins of my underpinnings. My makeup melted, and my hair dropped into my face and kinked and curled into cowlicks. A couple of hours later, after making it through security and the receiving line, we were escorted to our seats . . . at the head table. I was seated *next to Michelle*. OMG! But the second I saw her, sat and spoke with her, I remembered that it was so not about me. This was a moment, a wonderful night, and one that I eventually enjoyed beyond words. I am so humbled to have been included and it was magical, even after the moments of playing awkward duckling at the Super Prom.

Here's another one: I have been listening to Tony Bennett since I was born. He is a huge component in the soundtrack of my life. When I was working at Macy's Marketplace, I spent what to me was a small fortune at the time on two tickets, front row balcony, to hear Tony in person for my very first time at Carnegie Hall. The second seat was not for a date; it was for my coat and to allow myself the elbow room to lean forward and swoon as he serenaded me. He is a singular talent with a voice beyond compare.

So, to say I was nervous the first time he came to our apartment for dinner, about twenty years later, is a massive understatement. I was not nervous about my cooking. I vetted the menu with Tony and Susan, his beautiful and unbelievably approachable wife. I was nervous about Tony being comfortable in our odd, multilevel, treehouse apartment in the East Village. Could I make a place with little rooms worn and torn by humans and a sixty-pound pit bull clean enough for a man of refined taste? I polished the cutlery (not fine silver) and plates, washed and wiped every surface and glass. We polished, for the first time, every inch of our hardwood floors. When Tony and Susan arrived, they got the tour from John and then I showed them to a lounge room for snacks and champagne before our pasta course and entrée, osso buco. John poured the champagne and I made plates for them. I pulled out a chair and Tony went to sit. The floor had so much wax on it that the chair slipped out from under him and Tony fell and knocked his skull on a granite countertop behind him on the way down. He was literally down, on the floor. My life flashed before me. Gasp and horror! Did I kill my idol? Susan leapt up from her chair. "Just give him a moment. He'll be fine." Tony popped up like a cork. He picked up his champagne glass, gushed about dinner, and had two servings of everything.

After surviving my attempt on his life, Tony was the ideal dinner guest. Each time I left the table and returned, he stood for me. He sketched my husband in a pocket notebook of his. He left the sketch, and it hangs in our kitchen today, near that infamous counter/weapon.

The next time Tony was on the show I asked if I could tell the tale. I wanted to exorcise the demon. He said, "Sure. Just make sure they know it was your fault."

Not cringing yet? Try this: I'm a big fan of independent film and music. Years ago I was invited to help judge the documentary competition at Tribeca

Film Festival. I went to movies and filled out comment sheets and voted. When the awards ceremony night arrived, I was asked to go to the podium in front of the press pool to announce the winner of our group's category. I was wearing a black dress, any New Yorker's favorite color. The dress was rather low-cut, however, so a bra would be too obvious. Having a not-so-formidable rack, I felt okay going in with only "nips," sticky silicone petals to cover my nipples. As already established, under pressure and in high heels, I get nervous and I sweat, a lot. So I'm super nervous and holding on tightly to my card. I'm then placed in line behind Meg Ryan (never met her before or since). Really? I'm a fan of Meg all the way back to Betsy Stewart Andropoulos on *As the World Turns,* Goose's wife in *Top Gun,* Sally who met Harry! OMG! So, I sweat even more and the right nip falls off my breast and straight through my dress to the floor on the strip of carpet by my right pinky toe. What to do? Think. I cough, drop my card, bend to grab it, and plant my palm on the nip. It sticks! Thank God. I delivered my announcement with my right arm draped like Napoleon over my boob and scooted away as quickly as possible. I never got up the nerve to talk to Meg. For the best, I'm sure.

Then there is this fact: Over the last thirteen years and two thousand–plus episodes, I've had the chance to meet and interview several of my ce-

lebrity crushes in real life. My first crush goes way back, Tom Jones. The only person I would put on a dress for at age three. When Tom came on the show, I literally couldn't look him in the eye and keep a thought in my head. I had to keep asking questions while looking away from him. I went to work at 5:00 AM to make him rabbit cacciatore because I'd read he loves rabbit. Then I made him the same at dinner in our apartment! My husband went with it, but at the end of the night he asked if we could have Selma Hayek over sometime to balance the scales.

My biggest crush since Tom, though, has to go to 50 Cent, a.k.a. Curtis James Jackson III. Talk about a self-made man—and those dimples, that smile? OMG. I cannot. I have had many embarrassing moments with him and hope to have many more, too. He is gracious, beyond. He always leaves or presents thank-you notes and gifts and is so kind to everyone in the building. He deserves every success because he always moves forward without forgetting who he is and where he came from. He seems to set his bar higher and higher for himself. John is watching me write and I'm feeling guilty, so time to move on.

Except, well, we *are* here now, so . . . when it comes to crushes, laughter is often my biggest trigger. I simply get lost when I don't see the next laugh coming, so I get crushes on men and women who seem to crack us up without even trying. Denis Leary, you could make me wake up and laugh at my own funeral. Please do. Steve Carell, stop making me laugh and cry at the same time! I'm so confused and my eyes are puffy, too. Tina Fey, yes Ray is gay for Fey. Show-off! Is there anything you cannot do or write? And thanks again for that random shout-out in *Vogue* that I'm sure you totally don't remember. But I love you, forever. Alec Baldwin. I begged for years, literally. You came to the show. Run for anything, and you have my vote. Dick Van Dyke, we re-created your seminal show on our set, including *your* set. Mary Tyler Moore, the graceful, gracious, gleeful goddess that she was, came in and insisted on surprising you and "tripping" on the ottoman. I still dream, literally dream, of that day and sharing so many memories with both of you. Carol Burnett, you had an award named after you at the Golden Globes. You are the TV equivalent of Cecil B. DeMille! Your show in the seventies, as I've told you many times privately, brought everyone I love together (and shut them up), at least for an hour. You're limitless in your magical talents and powers, you're generous and a fountain of laughter, and I'm so glad we've shared time together.

I'm a goofy super-fan of so many of our show's guests, and if it's their first time on, I always worry whether they'll be comfortable with me, with our type of show. Looking back, there are many people who've filled my heart and made this awkward girl feel more comfortable in her high-heeled shoes. With a kind, honest eye, they have encouraged me and made me better at what I do. Michael J. Fox, you are the most massive amount of positive energy in a human body I've ever encountered. Period. Tracy Pollan, I love you, too, and I deeply appreciate your family's commitment to good, clean food. Julianne Moore, your talent as an actor is unsurpassed and as a person, you are thoughtful and genuine, and you have a gift for making people feel comfortable and at ease. You also make a hell of a key lime pie as well—or maybe your husband does? Lin-Manuel Miranda, you said when you came to the show for the first time "Puerto Ricans roll deep!" and brought thirty-seven family members with you! I got up at 4:30 AM to come in to work in time to make Tripletas for them all. I would do it every day; they're all extended family to me. Gwyneth Paltrow, you glow, inside and out. You're the real deal and a hands-on, hardworking, generous woman who can do so much so well, including cook. Billy Crudup, you're a genius actor, a generous guest, and truly a part of our family. Jake Gyllenhaal, I asked you to be our first guest ever. You couldn't make it, but you sent me flowers. Class act! Twelve years later, you finally came on and the experience of that visit was so worth the wait. Henry Winkler, who knew the Fonz runs so deep? Now, this girl does! Alan Alda, I'd watch *Four Seasons* all day and to be on your podcast—wow! What a thrill! Brain candy. Ringo Starr, a Beatle, loved my eggplant!

There are so many more: Kate Hudson, Patricia Heaton, Dame Julie Andrews, Hugh Jackman, Dustin Hoffmann . . . It's a beautiful experience to meet people who move you, make you laugh and cry and feel everything more deeply. It's a bonus when they turn out to be even more—more talented, more open, more kind—than you imagine them to be. To me, they're stars in a different sense. I'm an awkward celebrity compared to them all, but a grateful one.

Rabbit (or Chicken) Cacciatore / SERVES 4 TO 6

For Tom Jones.

Serve with buttery polenta, spiked and sweetened with honey and black pepper, or short pasta doused with the sauce and bathed in butter and cheese.

///

POSITION THE OVEN RACK in the center of the oven and preheat the oven to 350°F.

IN A SMALL POT over medium heat, simmer the dried mushrooms and the stock for 10 to 15 minutes to reconstitute the mushrooms and flavor the stock.

PAT THE CHICKEN or rabbit dry and season with salt and pepper.

IN A LARGE DUTCH OVEN over medium-high heat, heat the olive oil, 3 turns of the pan. Add 4 pieces of chicken or rabbit at a time and brown, skin-side down, then turn. Brown each batch for about 8 minutes, then remove from the pan and drain off any excess fat. Add the pancetta and stir for 2 minutes. Add the carrots, celery, onion, leek, garlic, chili paste, herb bundle, and bay leaves. Cook for 8 minutes more, to soften the vegetables. Add the juniper berries and then the tomato paste. Stir for 1 minute, then add the vermouth. Add the tomatoes and break them up with a wooden spoon. Add the passata and the mushrooms and stock, stir to combine, and nest the chicken or rabbit carefully in the pot. Bring the mixture to a boil, cover with a tight-fitting lid, and place in the oven for 1 hour.

PREPARE THE POLENTA or pasta, whichever you are using.

TRANSFER THE MEAT to a platter and cover with a little foil. Remove and discard the herb bundle and bay leaves from the sauce. Return the Dutch oven to the stove and bring the sauce to a simmer. Whisk the sauce to thicken and combine.

SERVE THE CHICKEN or rabbit topped with a bit more sauce alongside the pasta or polenta and a sprinkle of parsley. Pass cheese at the table.

1 ounce dried porcini mushrooms (about 1 cup)

About 2 cups chicken or beef stock

8 pieces of skin-on, bone-in chicken or rabbit

Salt and freshly ground black pepper

3 tablespoons olive oil

¼ pound meaty pancetta, chopped

2 carrots, peeled and chopped

2 ribs celery with leafy tops, chopped

1 onion, chopped

1 leek, quartered lengthwise and chopped

4 large cloves garlic, crushed and chopped

1 scant tablespoon red chili paste; or 1 fresh red chili, finely chopped; or 1 teaspoon crushed red pepper flakes

1 generous bundle of rosemary and thyme, tied with kitchen string

2 large fresh bay leaves

1 teaspoon juniper berries (⅓ palmful)

¼ cup sun-dried tomato paste or tomato paste

1 cup red vermouth or red wine

1 (28-ounce) can whole San Marzano tomatoes

1 (24-ounce) jar passata or tomato puree (about 3 cups)

Polenta or pasta, for serving

Chopped fresh flat-leaf parsley, to serve

Cheese, to serve

Osso Buco / SERVES 4 TO 6

2 cups chicken stock—I use 1 cup each chicken and beef stock

1 fat pinch of saffron threads (20 to 24 threads)

4 to 6 pieces veal shanks, 2½ to 3 inches thick, tied with kitchen string

3 tablespoons olive oil

Salt and freshly ground black pepper

1 orange

1 lemon

1 teaspoon fennel seeds

1 large carrot, peeled and chopped

2 or 3 small ribs celery with leafy tops, chopped

1 onion, chopped

1 bulb garlic, all but 2 cloves crushed and chopped; reserve the 2 whole garlic cloves

2 large fresh bay leaves

1 bundle of rosemary and thyme, tied with kitchen string

2 tablespoons tomato paste

2 tablespoons flour

1 cup dry white wine

½ teaspoon crushed red pepper flakes

1 (28-ounce) can Italian tomatoes plus their juices, the tomatoes crushed by hand

About ½ cup fresh flat-leaf parsley leaves

⅓ cup toasted pistachio nuts, finely chopped or processed into crumbs

Crusty bread, for mopping

For Tony Bennett.

PLACE THE STOCK and saffron in a small pot over low heat to steep.

BRING THE MEAT to room temperature.

PREHEAT THE OVEN to 325°F.

IN A LARGE, HEAVY DUTCH OVEN over high heat, heat 2 tablespoons olive oil, 2 turns of the pan. Season the shanks with salt and pepper, add to the hot pan, and cook for 10 minutes, turning the meat occasionally, until browned all over. Remove the meat to a large plate.

ZEST ABOUT 2 TEASPOONS each from the orange and the lemon and reserve the fruit.

REDUCE THE HEAT under the pot to medium. Add the remaining 1 tablespoon olive oil and the fennel seeds to the pot and stir for 1 minute. Add the carrot, celery, and onion to the pot, along with salt and pepper, and stir for 5 minutes. Then add the crushed and chopped garlic, bay leaves, and the rosemary-thyme bundle. Stir for 1 minute more. Add the tomato paste and sprinkle the flour over the vegetables. Stir for 1 minute more. Then add the wine and deglaze the pot, scraping and stirring for 1 minute. Stir in the saffron stock, red pepper flakes, tomatoes, and the juice of the orange to the sauce. Scrape down the pot and settle the meat into the pot. Cover with a tight-fitting lid and transfer to the oven. Cook for 2 hours, turning the meat once about halfway through.

WHEN THE MEAT IS ABOUT READY to come out of the oven, combine the orange zest, lemon zest, parsley, pistachios, and the remaining 2 cloves garlic and finely chop to combine.

REMOVE THE VEAL from the oven. Split the crusty bread and place it in the oven to warm through, along with the serving platter and dinner plates.

REMOVE THE SHANKS to the warm platter and cut off the kitchen string. Place the pot over medium heat, fish out the bay leaves and rosemary-thyme bundle from the sauce, and whisk to combine and thicken, 4 to 5 minutes. Turn off the heat and add the juice of 1 fat lemon wedge.

SERVE THE SHANKS in shallow bowls topped with chunky sauce and crusty bread for mopping up the sauce.

Eggplant Parm Steaks and Tomato Sauce with Pesto / SERVES 4

For Ringo.

MAKE THE EGGPLANT: Trim the tops and bottoms of the eggplants and slice them into ⅓- to ½-inch planks lengthwise. Salt both sides of the planks or steaks. Drain them on dish towels for 30 minutes. Press out the excess moisture.

SET UP A FRYING STATION in shallow dishes: flour; beaten eggs with salt and pepper; and breadcrumbs tossed with the lemon zest, oregano or marjoram, parsley, red pepper flakes, fennel pollen if using, granulated garlic, granulated onion, and cheese. Set the station near the stove. Heat a very wide, shallow 12- to 14-inch frying pan over medium to medium-high heat. Add a layer of frying oil about ¼ to ½ inch deep. Place a wire rack–lined baking sheet next to the frying pan. Line the pan with foil, paper towels, or parchment paper.

MAKE THE TOMATO SAUCE: Heat a large pot over medium heat. Add the butter. When it foams, add the garlic and stir it for 1 to 2 minutes. Add the tomatoes and break them up with a wooden spoon. Add ¼ cup basil and season the sauce with salt. Bring the sauce to a bubble, reduce the heat to low, and simmer for 30 minutes to break down the tomatoes.

ONCE THE RED SAUCE base is cooked down, pulse the remaining ¾ cup basil, lemon juice, pine nuts, and cheese to finely chop them. Stream in the EVOO. Add the herb paste to the tomato sauce, stir for 1 minute, and remove from the heat. Cover the sauce to keep it warm.

PREHEAT THE OVEN to 250°F.

BREAD THE EGGPLANT planks three at a time in the flour, egg, and breadcrumbs, pressing to set them. Cook the eggplant for 5 to 6 minutes per batch, until they are a deep golden color. Repeat until all of the eggplant is fried. If desired, you can keep the eggplant planks warm in the oven for 20 to 30 minutes.

TO SERVE, top the eggplant with the sauce or set the eggplant planks in a smooth pool of sauce. Top with shredded cheese, if using; you can broil the eggplant on a broiler pan and melt the cheese if you want the works. Toss extra sauce with a side of spaghetti cooked to al dente or use it for mopping with crusty bread, if desired.

EGGPLANT PARM

2 eggplants, heavy and firm

Salt

1 cup AP flour

4 eggs, beaten

Freshly ground black pepper

1½ to 2 cups breadcrumbs—eyeball it

1 tablespoon lemon zest

2 teaspoons dried oregano or marjoram

3 to 4 tablespoons fresh flat-leaf parsley, finely chopped (a handful)

2 scant teaspoons crushed red pepper flakes or ground red pepper (about ½ palmful)

About 1 teaspoon each fennel pollen (optional), granulated garlic, and granulated onion

1 cup grated Parmigiano-Reggiano

About 1½ cups refined olive oil or safflower oil, for frying

Shredded mozzarella or provolone (optional)

TOMATO SAUCE WITH PESTO

3 tablespoons butter

2 large cloves garlic, crushed

1 (28-ounce) can San Marzano tomatoes

1 cup basil, packed

Salt to taste

Juice of ½ lemon

½ cup pine nuts, lightly toasted

½ cup Parmigiano-Reggiano

¼ cup EVOO

Spaghetti, for serving (optional)

Crusty bread, for serving (optional)

The Green Garden / MAKES ONE DRINK

3 slices of fennel bulb, plus fronds for garnish

3 slices of seedless cucumber, peeled, plus one unpeeled slice for garnish

5 fresh sage leaves

1½ ounces vodka

1 ounce fresh lime juice

½ ounce simple syrup (see page 249)

JOHN SAYS: When we have dinner with our friend R.E.M. front man Michael Stipe, we start the meal with caviar and an ice-cold shot of good Russian vodka. Then, since I'm always inclined to make a mixed drink to begin the evening, I'll usually do something vodka-based, such as this crisp and verdant cocktail.

/ / /

ADD THE FENNEL SLICES to the bottom of a cocktail shaker and muddle well. Add the cucumber slices and muddle well. Add the sage leaves and muddle gently. Add the vodka, lime juice, and simple syrup, shake well with ice, and double strain into an ice-filled rocks glass. Garnish with the unpeeled cucumber slice and fennel fronds.

15 I Hate Paris in the Springtime

Some twenty years ago my mom drove me to JFK to catch a flight to Paris on assignment as the host of *$40 a Day*, a travel show on Food Network. I arrived curbside three hours ahead of my flight and was directed by an Air France representative to a very long line inside the terminal. Two hours later I'd finally arrived at the front of the line with my luggage in tow. I smiled wide and said "I made it!" and handed my passport over to the agent. She informed me that my flight was closed and my luggage could not be tagged, as it was now fifty-five minutes to flight time and luggage must be received no less than one hour prior to departure. Furthermore, she snarled, I'd been standing on the wrong line for my flight to Paris. I explained that I was directed to go there by one of their agents. I burst into tears and explained that this was my first foreign assignment for a new job and an entire crew was already in France waiting for me. Nothing. I don't know if the woman glaring back at me was American or French, but I have nightmares to this day remembering her stone-cold expression.

The next flight was not scheduled until the *next day*. I went home and spent the night staring into space, crying until my eyes were almost swollen shut. Let's just say this was the highlight of my trip. It managed to go downhill from there.

I finally arrived in Paris, and my crew of maybe half a dozen and I set off to uncover the hidden sides of Europe. The shoot included filming in Paris and Brussels. Over the course of the next week, our French-born cameraman, Frederic, got into physical fights with Parisians who would not honor our permits and let him film, we had our equipment stolen, we saw the inside of a police station, and we were denied access to multiple locations for our B roll. I studied French for seven years, yet no matter how hard I tried to speak in simple, clear sentences, I was met with that same cold stare I'd experienced at the Air France check-in counter, and everyone I spoke French with answered me *en Anglais*.

I had packed clothes—new clothes, clothes that I had charged, not yet paid for, and probably couldn't afford—based on what springtime in Paris looks like in the movies. *Everything* was too lightweight and totally inappropriate for the very, very cold and wet conditions—freezing rain, in fact, most of the time we were filming. I had to buy a long, black leather coat, which I also probably couldn't afford, just to keep from freezing to death while sitting on a frozen lawn, alone on camera, in front of the Eiffel Tower drinking inexpensive "but richly flavored Burgundy wine" and "enjoying a snack of crusty baguette and tangy, fragrant, herbaceous goat cheese." Why do I hate Paris in the springtime? The list was long. I swore I would never go back. Ever.

Never say never again! Or *jamais* say Jammet! In French, the word for "never" is *jamais*. Which happens to sound exactly like the surname of French friends of mine, the Jammets. André and Rita Jammet were the final owners (1988–2004) of the iconic La Caravelle, then New York's premier French restaurant (named for one of Christopher Columbus's triple-sail explorer ships, always in search of new possibilities and horizons). A colleague and close friend of mine, Cara Apotheker, married Patrick Jammet, one of Rita and André's handsome sons, and a grand romance was born . . . I fell in love with this family!

Rita and André carry on the spirit of the restaurant with their proprietary La Caravelle wines: Champagne Cuvée Niña, Champagne Rosé, and Champagne Blanc de Blancs. Their wines date back to late 1700s France and André's family, the former owners of Hotel Le Bristol, Paris, know their stuff. Rita is a force of nature, a singular woman. She is more than a sales-person and expert in the art of food, beverage, and service. Dining with Rita is like entering a room with Don Corleone. She knows every chef, somme-lier, and maître d' on the planet, and they all know and love her back. This family is the essence of Frenchness, so when the challenge came up in con-versation, could *they* make me love—or at least be open to learning to love—Paris? Well, what if you *do* only go around once? Don't die a hater! *Oui! On y va à Paris!*

Deciding to give it another try, about fifteen years after that last trip, I put on my positivity and headed to JFK airport with John, Cara and Patrick, and Rita and André. The trip started off perfectly, in the Air France First Class Lounge. Okay, I know what you're thinking. Duh, it went better if you flew first class. But a girl has to splurge now and then and I wanted to leave nothing to chance this time around. No surprise, the attentive staff was a wild leap from my previous experience . . . almost. Then, Patrick and Mini (Cara's nickname, because she is!) gave each of us the be-all and end-all of goodie bags. Cara got us a chilled glass of champagne and we opened our sacks to reveal happy-face plates and napkins with sunglasses on, José An-drés potato chips, individual squeeze bottles of crème fraîche, and tins of caviar, courtesy of Rita. Who finished the chips, caviar dip, and crème fraîche first? *J'avais faim!*

Paris itself, even though she made me cry, is a very beautiful woman with great bone structure. The wide boulevards, the lampposts that make her the city of lights, the bateaux à voiles, the grand bridges, Le Tour Eiffel, her star-like shape and star-studded city planning, the Arc de Triomphe de l'Étoile at its center . . . she is awe-strikingly beautiful and has influenced countless elements of our own still-young American cities, from Washing-ton, D.C., to Chicago to Brooklyn.

The coat of arms of Hotel Le Bristol, where we stayed, features unicorns. This is appropriate. The ivy-draped entrance feels mystical and the hotel was like a magical and surprisingly cozy castle with a lush, fecund courtyard at its heart. Our room was fairy-tale-esque, with a patio and terrace buzzing with happy bees and dripping with flowering bushes. Chilled rosé cham-pagne, fresh fruits, and a tower of macarons awaited our arrival. I get it. Cue Edith Piaf. For many this is simply the most romantic setting in the world.

When friends ask me to review my three days in Paris on this special weekend, an impressionist mural pops into my head, like those that used to fill La Caravelle. The three days were a colorful blur of happy faces, wine, and picture-perfect food that I still see, taste, smell, and feel. There were other moments, too. The ladies went shopping in Le Marais. John and Patrick went to see some world-class tennis at the French Open. We created lasting memories and truly enjoyed the endless hospitality of great chefs and teams of professionals at restaurants including L'Ami Jean, Clamato, Arpège, and La Bourse et la Vie.

All this said, Paris still intimidates me. Everything there is the biggest thing I've ever seen, and it made me feel tiny. I feel lost in things that are oversize. And it's so chic that I always feel underdressed no matter where I go or what I wear. The original is magnificent, but I feel safer in the knockoffs.

I am so fortunate to spend my working weeks in New York City, where I have access to the best French cuisine at places like Le Coucou, run by Daniel Rose, the same chef responsible for La Bourse et la Vie, not to mention La Mercerie, the café opened by his master chef wife, Chef Marie-Aude Rose. And because my home is in upstate New York, in the Adirondacks, I'm two hours by car to Montreal. It's an elegant and accessible sister city to beautiful Paris, with a personality and passion all its own.

Regardless, I love French food and have been cooking it my entire life. I'm known mostly for Italian, because that's what my grandfather exposed me to. But French was the food my mom taught me as a little girl. She was obsessed with Julia Child, learning basic French cooking from Julia's books and TV shows, all of which became the basis for many of her dishes and menus at her restaurants. So when I want to reminisce about great French or French-Canadian experiences, I don't need a fancy trip. I just cook some simple French-inspired dishes, à la Rachael.

/ / /

Here are a few of my favorite French classics, with a decidedly "me" twist.

Gougères / MAKES 20 TO 22 PUFFS

As much as I profess to dislike baking, I do enjoy making pâte à choux or pastry puffs, savory or sweet, because they're pretty foolproof. Plus: Cheese puffs make everyone happy on cold winter days.

/ / /

PREHEAT THE OVEN to 400°F.

IN A MEDIUM SAUCE POT over medium-high heat, combine 1 cup water, the butter, and the salt. Heat until the butter has melted and the water is boiling. Add the flour and cook, stirring constantly with a wooden spoon. Stir for about 2 minutes, until the mixture begins to create a dough ball in the center of the pot and the dough is completely pulling away from the sides of the pot.

TRANSFER THE MIXTURE to a large mixing bowl or the bowl of a stand mixer fitted with a paddle attachment. On low speed, add the eggs to the mixture one at a time, scraping the sides of the bowl well after each addition and beating until the bowl feels cool (the mixture should be very smooth and silky). Add the cheese and herbs, if using, to combine.

TRANSFER THE MIXTURE to a plastic food storage bag and cut ½ inch off one corner to create a pastry bag. On a baking sheet, secure parchment paper at the corners with a dot of dough. Squeeze the mixture into 1½- to 2-inch round balls spaced an inch apart. Dip your fingertip in the water and dot the tops of the pâte à choux to flatten the nubs from piping. Bake for 35 to 40 minutes, until golden brown and puffed. The pastry should look like it is sweating a bit.

SERVE THE GOUGÈRES warm in a cloth napkin–lined basket or dish.

6 tablespoons butter

½ teaspoon salt

1 cup flour

4 large eggs

1 cup shredded Gruyère

2 tablespoons minced fresh herbs such as rosemary or thyme (optional)

Fresh or Smoked Oysters
WITH LEMON-HORSERADISH MIGNONETTE

IN A SMALL BOWL combine the horseradish, shallot, lemon zest, lemon juice, pepper, sugar, thyme, and vinegar. Chill until ready to serve.

FOR RAW OYSTERS, unhinge and loosen the oysters from their shells, being careful not to lose the liquor, and arrange on a bed of salted crushed ice.

FOR SMOKED OYSTERS, prepare the smoker or stovetop smoker according to the directions and smoke for 15 to 20 minutes to unhinge the shells. For Oy-Ro, oyster roaster preparation, preheat the grill over a hardwood log fire while you soak burlap. Arrange the oysters on the griddle top and cover with wet burlap. Cook them for 20 to 25 minutes, until the oysters open. When I smoke oysters, I do batches of 50 to 60, and double my sauce.

2 tablespoons grated fresh horseradish

3 tablespoons finely chopped shallot

Zest and juice of 1 lemon

1 teaspoon coarsely ground black pepper

½ teaspoon superfine sugar or light-colored and light-flavored honey such as acacia

1 teaspoon finely chopped fresh thyme

¼ cup white balsamic vinegar or white wine vinegar

24 oysters, cleaned

Salade Haricots Verts / SERVES 4

IN A LARGE POT, bring a few inches of water to a boil. Salt the water liberally. Set up an ice-water bath in a large bowl. Cook the haricots for 3 minutes, then transfer the beans to the ice-water bath. Drain the beans and pat them dry.

IN A BOWL or shallow serving dish, combine the shallot, vinegar, garlic, and mustard, then whisk in the EVOO and pepper. Add the beans and herbs and toss to coat. Adjust the seasoning and serve chilled or at room temperature.

Salt

1 to 1½ pounds haricots verts, topped

1 shallot, finely chopped

About 2 tablespoons white wine or champagne vinegar

1 large clove garlic, grated or finely chopped and pasted

1 rounded tablespoon grainy Dijon mustard

About ¼ cup EVOO

Freshly ground black pepper to taste

About ¼ cup combined fresh dill, fresh flat-leaf parsley, and fresh chives, all finely chopped

Toast with Anchovies and Fennel Butter / SERVES 5 AS AN APP OR SNACK

1 pint heavy cream

½ teaspoon kosher salt

1 teaspoon fennel pollen

½ to ¾ teaspoon light-colored and light-flavored honey, such as acacia

15 baguette slices cut on a slight bias, ¼ to ½ inch thick, 3 slices per person per portion

30 Spanish or Italian best-quality anchovy fillets in oil, drained

Buy really great anchovies for this simple pleasure. My favorite version of this is served with vanilla butter at La Mercerie in New York City. I had to put my own twist on the dish, so I use fennel pollen, which is easily available online if your market doesn't carry it. Eat it any time of day—lunch, a snack, cocktail hour—all good.

/ / /

PLACE THE CREAM in the bowl of a food processor with the salt and pollen and turn machine on. Drizzle in the honey and process for 5 minutes, until butter forms and the buttermilk separates. Do not go too far or the buttermilk will reincorporate. Place the solid butter in a fine strainer and use a spatula to drain the rest of the liquid from the butter. Scrape the butter into a serving dish. If I make the butter a day ahead, I leave it wrapped in a paper coffee filter–lined or paper towel–lined small bowl to continue to drain.

BRING THE BUTTER to room temperature to serve. Smooth the top of the butter.

PREHEAT THE BROILER and toast each side of the sliced baguette to medium-deep golden brown. Serve warm.

SLATHER THE WARM BREAD with the butter and top with the anchovies, 2 fillets per toast.

Chicken and Mushroom Crepes / SERVES 4

HEAT A SMALL SKILLET over medium-high heat and add
2 tablespoons butter. Add the mushrooms and brown for 4 to
5 minutes. Add salt and the sherry and remove from the heat.

HEAT A 10-INCH SKILLET over medium heat, add the remaining
1 tablespoon butter, and swirl to melt. Add the shallot and stir
for 1 to 2 minutes, until softened. Add the wine and stir until
it evaporates. Add ½ cup stock and the cream and bring to a
bubble. Season with nutmeg, salt, and white pepper. Simmer for
10 to 15 minutes, reducing by about half. Stir in the mustard
and tarragon. Add the chicken to warm through.

IN A LARGE NONSTICK SKILLET over medium-low heat, warm
the crepes, flip them, and warm them for 30 seconds more.
Transfer the crepes to plates. Cover half a crepe with chicken,
mushrooms, and sauce. Fold the crepe over, then again, into a
triangle-shaped filled pancake. Top with chives and a sprig of
parsley or two.

3 tablespoons butter

¼ pound sliced cremini or pulled/sliced
maitake (hen of the woods) mushrooms

Salt to taste

2 tablespoons dry sherry

1 large shallot, finely chopped

⅓ cup white wine

About 1 cup chicken stock

¾ cup heavy cream

A little freshly grated nutmeg to taste

About ¼ teaspoon white pepper
or to taste

1 tablespoon grainy Dijon mustard

2 tablespoons tarragon, chopped,
or 2 teaspoons dried

3 cups pulled or thinly sliced white-meat
rotisserie chicken, or 2 small poached
boneless, skinless chicken breasts

8 Buckwheat Crepes (recipe follows)

Fresh chives and fresh flat-leaf parsley
leaves, to serve

Buckwheat Crepes / MAKES 8 TO 10 CREPES

My favorite crepes are served at La Mercerie in New York City. I've not
nearly as much practice, but my batter is easy to master and crepes
freeze beautifully if you want to make a double batch.

PLACE THE BUCKWHEAT flour and all-purpose flour in a mixing
bowl and add the eggs, milk, and salt. Whisk up until smooth.
Rest the batter for 30 minutes or refrigerate overnight. Bring to
room temperature to prepare, adding the melted butter or oil
when ready to make the crepes. Add milk as necessary to thin
the batter for cooking.

HEAT A CREPE PAN or 10-inch nonstick skillet over medium to
medium-high heat. Add ¼ cup batter at a time and swirl with
your wrist to coat the pan evenly to form a crepe, or use a
wooden crepe rake to spread the batter. Cook the crepe for
45 seconds or so. Turn the crepe with an offset spatula or a
sturdy toothpick to flick the crepe quickly. Cook for 30 seconds
more and transfer to a parchment paper–lined sheet. Crepes can
be held warm in a 175°F oven to fill and serve, or cooled and
wrapped between layers of parchment paper to freeze.

1 cup buckwheat flour

½ cup AP flour

2 large eggs

1 cup 2% milk, plus more if needed

½ teaspoon kosher salt

3 tablespoons melted butter or any
innocuous oil (light in color and flavor)

Farro Spaghetti in the Style of Pissaladière / SERVES 4

2 tablespoons EVOO

8 anchovy fillets

2 tablespoons butter

20 to 24 shallots, peeled, halved through the root, and thinly sliced lengthwise and then across

4 fat cloves garlic, grated on a wide tooth plane grater or very thinly sliced or chopped

2 tablespoons fresh thyme, chopped, or 2 teaspoons dried

½ cup Niçoise olives, pitted and coarsely chopped

1 cup dry white wine

About ½ teaspoon salt

About ½ teaspoon ground white pepper (or to taste)

About 1 teaspoon medium-coarse freshly ground black pepper (or to taste)

1 pound farro spaghetti

About ½ cup fresh flat-leaf parsley, finely chopped

1 cup combined freshly, finely grated Gruyère and Parmigiano-Reggiano

This is a twist on a recipe I've made for more than a dozen years—*That's Shallota Spaghetti.* The original was simple—basically a buttery sauce of twenty shallots, farro pasta, hazelnuts, parsley, and cheese. This is better. It incorporates all of the flavors, including olives and anchovies, of the classic French tart Pissaladière, but it's more fun to eat. Give it a twirl!

/ / /

BRING A LARGE POT of water to a boil for the pasta. Once at a rolling boil, reduce the heat to medium and cover until ready to cook the pasta.

IN A LARGE, DEEP SKILLET over medium heat, heat the EVOO, 2 turns of the pan. Add the anchovies and break them up with a wooden spoon. Cover the skillet and shake, then uncover the skillet and stir until the anchovies melt away into the oil. Add the butter and melt it into the oil. When the butter foams, add the shallots, garlic, and thyme. Cook for about 25 minutes, until medium-caramel in color. Add the olives, then the wine, and reduce for 1 minute. Add the salt, white pepper, and black pepper. Reduce the heat to low.

AFTER THE SHALLOTS have been cooking down for about 20 minutes, uncover the water for the pasta and bring it back to a full rolling boil. Salt the water generously. Cook the farro spaghetti for 8 to 9 minutes, 1 minute less than the package directions for al dente. Add 1 cup of the starchy cooking water to the sauce. Drain the pasta and transfer it to the sauce.

TURN OFF THE HEAT under the pasta. Toss the pasta with the sauce, ¼ cup parsley, and the grated cheeses. Adjust the salt and pepper, and place in shallow bowls. Top with the remaining ¼ cup parsley and serve.

Chicken Paillard Croque Madame / SERVES 4

Sometimes I layer thin blanched asparagus spears between the sauce and cheese, and other days I make a simple salad with vinaigrette to complete this plate.

/ / /

SEASON THE CHICKEN cutlets with salt, pepper, and herbes de Provence.

HEAT A LARGE NONSTICK SKILLET over medium-high heat. Add the EVOO, 2 turns of the pan. Cook 2 cutlets for 6 to 7 minutes, turning occasionally, and arrange on a baking sheet. Repeat with the remaining 2 cutlets.

IN A SAUCE POT or medium pan over medium heat, melt the butter. When the butter foams, whisk in the flour, then slowly add the milk. Thicken the sauce and season with salt, nutmeg, and white pepper. Reduce the heat to low.

SWITCH ON THE BROILER and position the oven rack at the center of the oven.

ASSEMBLE: On each piece of chicken, spread a layer of mustard. Top with 2 slices of ham lightly ruffled. Top the ham with the béchamel and top the sauce with an even layer of shredded Gruyère.

BROIL THE CHICKEN, ham, and cheese just until lightly browned and bubbly.

HEAT A NONSTICK PAN over medium heat. Melt the pats of butter and cook the 4 eggs, each a bit apart, sunny-side up, over easy, or fried. Cook 1 or 2 eggs at a time if the pan size dictates.

PLACE "CROQUE MONSIEUR" on plates and top each with an egg, turning them into Madames.

4 boneless, skinless chicken breasts, butterflied by cutting across but not through the breast, lightly pounded to 1/8 to 1/4 inch thick

Salt and freshly ground black pepper

About 1 teaspoon herbes de Provence

2 tablespoons EVOO

3 tablespoons butter plus 1 or 2 pats for the eggs

2 tablespoons flour
(Tip: for a gluten-free preparation, simply reduce the cream and season rather than making a roux)

1½ cups milk

Freshly grated nutmeg to taste

White pepper to taste

About ¼ cup Dijon mustard

8 thin slices of mild cooked ham—I buy French ham or prosciutto cotto

1½ to 2 cups Gruyère, shredded

4 large eggs

Bavette with Green Peppercorn Sauce Verte / SERVES 4

MAKE THE SAUCE VERTE: Place the parsley, tarragon, chives, capers, shallot, anchovies, garlic, lemon zest, lemon juice, and vinegar in the bowl of a food processor. Pulse to fine-chop the herbs, then turn on to stream in the EVOO. Transfer the sauce to a dish and stir in the green peppercorns. Cover with plastic wrap and chill, or serve immediately. If chilled, bring back to room temperature to serve. The sauce keeps in the refrigerator for 1 week.

MAKE THE STEAK: Bring the meat to room temperature, pat dry, and season generously with salt and pepper.

FOR THE GRILL or smoker, preheat the grill to 400°F to 500°F. For a smoky flavor, place a pouch of damp woodchips off to the side and open the pouch when you close the lid. Spray the grill with cooking spray and cook the steak for 8 minutes, turning occasionally, for medium rare. Rest the meat for 5 to 10 minutes. Slice against the grain.

FOR A CAST-IRON SKILLET, heat the pan over medium-high heat. Add olive oil to lightly coat the pan or coat the meat for outdoor grilling and cook the steak for 8 to 10 minutes for medium-rare meat, 10 to 12 minutes for medium-well, turning occasionally. The meat should be well browned and crusted. Rest the meat for 5 to 10 minutes before slicing against the grain.

GRILL OR GRIDDLE the halved lemon to caramelize it and get its juices flowing. Squeeze a little lemon juice over the sliced steaks.

ARRANGE THE SLICED MEAT in a fan and top with sauce verte.

SAUCE VERTE

1 cup fresh flat-leaf parsley tops, chopped

½ cup fresh tarragon leaves, chopped

¼ cup fresh chives, finely chopped

3 tablespoons nonpareil (small) capers in brine, drained

1 shallot, minced or grated

2 anchovy fillets in oil, drained and mashed

2 cloves garlic, grated or finely chopped

1 teaspoon zest plus juice of 1 small lemon

2 tablespoons white wine or champagne vinegar

½ to ⅔ cup EVOO

2 tablespoons green peppercorns in brine, drained and halved, coarsely chopped—run over them with a sharp knife once

Salt to taste

MEAT

2 to 2½ pounds flap sirloin steak, flank steak, or hanger steak

Kosher salt and coarsely ground black pepper

Cooking spray or olive oil for drizzling

1 lemon, halved

Laziest Boeuf Bourguignon / SERVES 6

3 pounds beef chuck, cut into large cubes of 2 to 2½ inches

Kosher salt and freshly ground black pepper

¼ cup olive oil

3 tablespoons butter

3 large onions, quartered and thinly sliced or chopped

4 large cloves garlic, crushed

1 bundle of fresh flat-leaf parsley, fresh thyme, and fresh bay leaf, tied with kitchen string

2 tablespoons flour

2 cups red Burgundy wine

¼ cup beef demi-glace, store-bought in the refrigerator or freezer section of the market

4 carrots and 4 ribs celery from the heart, cut into 2- to 3-inch pieces on the bias

I have cooked many versions of this recipe over the years, including, of course, Julia Child's, as well as Jacques Pépin's and Anthony Bourdain's—which cooks in just under 2 hours. Jacques was sous-chef to Pierre Franey and they created a Beef and Burgundy recipe for Howard Johnson's restaurants. I was a waitress there as a girl. I delivered hundreds of casseroles full of the stuff—the recipe came in boil-in-the-bag pouches so I guess *that* was the laziest, technically speaking. But if you have a good book to read, this recipe is pretty low maintenance, provides for lots of quiet time, and makes the house smell amazing all afternoon.

/ / /

BRING THE MEAT to room temperature and pat it dry. Season it liberally with salt and pepper.

PREHEAT THE OVEN to 325°F.

PREHEAT A LARGE DUTCH OVEN over medium-high heat. Add 2 turns of the pan of olive oil and brown half the meat—do not crowd the pot or the meat will sweat rather than develop a crust. Brown the meat for 8 minutes, until deeply brown, transferring the meat to a platter. Repeat with the remaining olive oil and meat. When all of the meat is brown, add the butter to the pan. When it foams, add the onions and season with salt and pepper. Partially cover the pot and sweat the onions for 5 minutes. Stir to lift up the meat bits from the bottom of the pan. Add the garlic and herbs and stir for 1 minute. Add the flour and stir for 1 minute more. Add the wine and bring to a bubble. Add the beef back to the pot and add just enough water to top the beef. Stir in the demi-glace. Cover the pot with a tight-fitting lid and place the pot in the oven. Braise the beef for 2 hours, stirring once after 1 hour. Add the carrots and celery to the beef and nest them in the sauce. Return the pot, covered, to the oven for the final hour. Uncover the pot and let it rest in the oven with the door ajar while you prepare the pearl onions and mushrooms.

MAKE THE ONIONS: In a medium skillet over medium to medium-high heat, heat 1 tablespoon EVOO. Add 3 tablespoons butter to the oil. When it foams, add the onions and season with salt and sugar. Cook the onions for 5 minutes, shaking the pan occasionally, until they are golden and tender. Sprinkle with 1 tablespoon parsley and remove from the heat.

MAKE THE MUSHROOMS: In a medium skillet over medium-high heat, heat the remaining 1 tablespoon EVOO. Add the remaining 2 tablespoons butter. When it foams, add the mushrooms and brown them for 7 to 8 minutes, then season with salt and pepper and deglaze the pan with the sherry. Sprinkle the remaining 1 tablespoon parsley on the mushrooms and remove from the heat.

SERVE THE BEEF in shallow bowls and top with pearl onions and mushrooms. Pass warm, crusty bread for mopping up the sauce.

TO SERVE

2 tablespoons EVOO

5 tablespoons butter

24 defrosted or blanched and peeled pearl onions

Salt

1 teaspoon sugar

2 tablespoons finely chopped fresh flat-leaf parsley

24 cremini mushroom caps, quartered

Freshly ground black pepper

¼ cup dry sherry or brandy

Crusty French bread

Sleep-on-It Coq au Vin / SERVES 4

MARINADE AND CHICKEN

4 chicken drummers, bone-in but skin removed

4 boneless, skinless chicken thighs

4 (6- to 8-ounce) pieces of chicken breast, 2 full breasts total, each breast cut in half on a slight bias

4 cloves garlic, crushed

1 bundle of fresh thyme, fresh flat-leaf parsley, and fresh bay leaves, tied with kitchen string

2 cups red wine such as Gamay or Syrah

1 cup beef stock

TO PREPARE

Salt and freshly ground black pepper

1 tablespoon olive oil

¼ pound slab meaty bacon, trimmed of tough skin and cut into lardons, small fat sticks, or cubed pancetta

¼ cup cognac or brandy

¼ cup (½ stick) butter

2 shallots, finely chopped

1 tablespoon tomato paste

3 tablespoons flour

2 tablespoons beef demi-glace

I marinate my chicken overnight in the wine. It brings a deeper color and a more developed taste. Otherwise, this recipe is a mash-up of great technique tips, including using mostly boneless chicken pieces for quicker cooking—thank you, Jacques Pépin—and all of the flavors present, including bacon and cognac—thank you, Julia Child.

/ / /

MAKE THE MARINADE: Place the chicken in a 2-gallon bag with the garlic, herbs, wine, and beef stock. Refrigerate on the lowest shelf overnight.

PREPARE THE CHICKEN: Pat the chicken dry but reserve the wine and herbs. Season the chicken with salt and pepper.

HEAT A LARGE DUTCH OVEN or deep cast-iron skillet over medium-high heat with the olive oil, 1 turn of the pan. Add the bacon and render it for 3 to 4 minutes, to crisp but not overcooked. Remove the bacon with a slotted spoon. Brown the chicken pieces in the pan in 2 batches. With the second batch, flame the chicken with cognac, then remove the chicken to a plate. Add the butter to the drippings and melt. Add the shallots and soften for 2 to 3 minutes while stirring. Add the tomato paste and stir to combine. Sprinkle in the flour and stir again. Add the reserved wine and herbs and whisk to lift up the pan drippings. Add the demi-glace, then slide in the dark-meat chicken and reduce the heat to medium-low for a rolling simmer. Cook for 15 minutes, then add the white meat and simmer for 15 minutes more.

MAKE THE ONIONS: Heat 1 tablespoon of EVOO over medium to medium-high heat in a small skillet. Add 3 tablespoons butter to the oil. When it foams, add the onions and season with salt and sugar. Cook the onions, shaking pan occasionally, until golden and tender. Sprinkle 1 tablespoon parsley on the onions and remove from the heat.

MAKE THE MUSHROOMS: Heat the remaining 1 tablespoon of EVOO in a medium skillet over medium-high heat. Add the remaining 2 tablespoons butter to the oil. When it foams, add the mushrooms and brown them for 7 to 8 minutes, then season with salt and pepper. Sprinkle the remaining 1 tablespoon of parsley on the mushrooms and remove from the heat.

SERVE THE COQ AU VIN—1 piece of breast, 1 piece of thigh, and 1 leg—in shallow bowls topped with sauce. Then nestle 2 croutons on the side of the dish for mopping up the sauce. Arrange a few onions and sliced mushrooms on top.

TO SERVE

2 tablespoons EVOO

5 tablespoons butter

12 defrosted or blanched and peeled pearl onions

Salt

1 teaspoon sugar

12 cremini or white mushroom caps, sliced

Freshly ground black pepper

2 tablespoons finely chopped fresh flat-leaf parsley

Charred or toasted bread, rubbed with garlic

Stone Fruit Galette with Nutty Pâte Brisée / SERVES 6

PÂTE BRISÉE (PIE DOUGH)

½ cup peeled, toasted hazelnuts
or lightly toasted pecans

1¼ cups AP flour

½ teaspoon salt

2 teaspoons sugar

About ⅛ teaspoon freshly
grated nutmeg

10 tablespoons (1 stick plus 2 tablespoons)
cold butter, cut into pieces

FILLING

3 cups firm, slightly underripe
stone fruit (plums, apricots, cherries),
pitted and sliced into ½-inch wedges

1 teaspoon lemon zest

2 tablespoons lemon juice

½ cup sugar

1 pinch of salt

3 tablespoons cornstarch

1 tablespoon cold butter, cut into pieces

Egg wash (1 egg, splash of water or milk)
or buttermilk, to brush the crust

About 3 tablespoons Demerara sugar,
for sprinkling

TO SERVE

Fresh basil leaves, mint leaves, or
purple basil leaves, torn

Freshly whipped cream

PLACE THE NUTS in the bowl of a food processor and blitz to finely chop. Add the flour, salt, sugar, nutmeg, and butter and pulse to combine the butter evenly with the flour into pieces the size of small peas. Pour ¼ cup water into a shaker over ice and shake. Pulse the processor and stream in the water until a chunky ball forms. If the dough is too dry to come together, shake the water and ice again and add another tablespoon of water. Knead the dough less than 1 minute to combine. Wrap it in plastic wrap and chill it for a minimum of 30 minutes.

PREHEAT THE OVEN to 350°F. Position the oven rack in the upper third of the oven.

ROLL OUT THE DOUGH to about 14 inches wide on lightly floured parchment paper and transfer to a baking sheet.

PLACE THE FRUIT in a large bowl and combine with lemon zest, lemon juice, sugar, salt, and cornstarch. Spread the fruit evenly on the dough, leaving a 2½-inch rim. Fold in the dough evenly around the edges in a rustic ruffle. Do not pile the fruit high—keep it in an even layer. Dot the fruit with bits of cold butter. Brush the ruffle of the dough with egg wash or buttermilk and sprinkle liberally with raw sugar. Bake for 35 to 40 minutes, until the dough is golden and the fruit is tender. Let sit for 10 minutes, then transfer to cool on a wire rack. To serve, top the galette with basil or mint. Pass the whipped cream at the table or serve alongside.

16 There's Always Room at the Inn

The holidays, Hanukkah through New Year's, have just come to a close. Seven families came to celebrate here with us, nestled in at our cabins in the woods. The timing stretched out from well before and went well beyond the twelve days of Christmas. It was more like twenty-five days—and we don't order out. I cook every meal. We call it "the Inn," and it's a scheduling nightmare and a heckuva lot of work, but it's worth it. This is our normal.

I found my little cabin in the woods when I left New York City some twenty-five years ago. I read an ad in the paper for a house, $575.00 a month, rent to own, on about 3½ acres. I fell in love with my neck of the woods in Lake Luzerne, not far from where I grew up. As my mom says, I really went far in life—ten miles!

Over the years I paid off my little cabin and we bought 199 more acres across the way, and on it we built a bigger cabin in the woods that sits across from the first. In time we added a third down the hill a bit, for guests. I've willed our land forever wild, inasmuch as it is possible to do so—trusts to fund taxes, etc.

The big cabin where we live full-time is framed in old beams from fallen barns, collected by Steve Colletti, the man who, over the years and with many men and women adding their talents, built our weird old-world-meets-new cabin on the hill. The design is based on my drawings. I tried to let architects and professionals bring it to life, but I wanted the house the way I saw it in my head. Steve worked hard to make that happen.

There's a huge fireplace in the middle of our great room, the stones cut from a mountain face in our backyard. It sits high in the room, with benches built into it on either side of the large glass doors. Its glow can be seen (and felt) through the whole house.

Our kitchen is always filled with music or the sound of a classic film, the smell of food cooking, and the gentle crackle of a fire, even on August nights. I have a wood-burning oven and huge butcherblock counters, so I can work everywhere and never miss a thing. This is where I spend my days, and it's my happy place.

Over our garage is a room with funny foam on every wall to corral the tone and strength of the music played in it. It holds a huge soundboard and dozens of instruments. There's a hallway that bridges the room to the rest of the house. That's the route you take to find John on any given day, surrounded by his keyboards, guitars, and drums.

We love being at home, in the country or in the city, more than anything. We love welcoming others to our space because it reflects who we are, what we love, and how we share. We are entertaining evenings, because as quiet as we are all day, ultimately we love an audience. A cook is only as happy as the last satisfied person she fed, and a musician, his last contented listener.

We throw a few big parties outside the house each year: our annual gathering in Italy for our anniversary, our collective office holiday party. These can range from 40 to 250 people, too big for either of our places. At home, we frequently host small groups of guests both in the country and in the city. And because we want to pay attention to each one and curate the food and the experience for them—I ask for menu requests from everyone who comes into my house and cater the meal to their desires—we keep it small.

I love homemaking. Except for the ironing, I guess, but I do plenty of it. I iron all the pillowcases and top sheets and clothes as needed. I fluff pillows constantly. Growing up, my mom never went to bed, even after a workday of twelve hours or more, with a dish in the sink or a pillow out of place. I'm definitely her daughter. I also love to decorate; I rather obsessively keep up with it, as I believe any space can be transformed into a wonderland, any room or home can come to life, if you show it some love.

Animals love our house, too! Beatrix Potter would have been in heaven. On our property upstate we have fat rabbits and squirrels and chipmunks. We have deer and moose, grouse and birds of every feather, and about fifty

FACT.

really happy, really big turkeys. We have feeders out there for everyone! Occasionally a mouse gets into the house. A few months ago, we had friends in the guest cabin and behind the pile of fresh towels in the closet they made quite a discovery: a tiny feather bed and several wrappers from Italian chocolates. I had a decorative set of angel's wings that hung on an old barn beam. The mouse gathered the feathers one by one and carried them to his space in the linen closet to build his bed. He snacked on the chocolates neatly wrapped in a dish and left the wrappers near his bed. On inspection of the record player's turntable, it appears he tried to jog off the chocolates on his "treadmill," and after he got his exercise in, he left a healthy pile of poop behind. This mouse was quite a little fella. I wish, like Beatrix, I could speak mouse, so a longer arrangement could have been worked out. Instead, we kindly asked him to relocate with the use of sonic devices and peppermint oil. No mice were harmed in the writing of this story.

There's always room at the Inn. In any season of any year and whether you are big or small, short or tall, human or feathered, fleeced or furry, get to our cabin. We'll all be waiting for you.

HOLIDAY MEALS 2018

Here's a list of the meals we cooked for friends and family during the parade of houseguests this past holiday season. Some are by request or to adhere to a special diet. Others are annual faves that we have to make or there'd be mutiny. Some also find their way onto the menu in Italy, so you'll find the recipes there.

ANCHOVY BREADCRUMB–STUFFED ARTICHOKES (SEE PAGE 193)

SHRIMP SCAMPI (SEE PAGE 287)

POACHED COD WITH TOMATOES (SEE PAGE 198)

FRIED CALAMARI (SEE PAGE 77)

PRIME RIB DINNER (SEE PAGE 37)

BUCATINI BOLOGNESE (SEE PAGE 42)

TUSCAN POT ROAST (SEE PAGE 201)

CHOU FARCI (STUFFED CABBAGE) (SEE PAGE 190)

ITALIAN ROAST CHICKEN AND POTATOES (SEE PAGE 199)

POTATO-PARSNIP PANCAKES WITH CRÈME FRAÎCHE SAUCE AND SALMON (SEE PAGE 186)

WHITE TRUFFLE PAPPARDELLE WITH BROWN BUTTER, SAGE, AND HAZELNUTS

PORCHETTA (SEE PAGE 229)

FRESH OR SMOKED OYSTERS WITH LEMON-HORSERADISH MIGNONETTE (SEE PAGE 167)

SHRIMP COCKTAIL (SEE PAGE 189) AND JONAH CRAB CLAWS WITH COCKTAIL SAUCE

BEEF RIBS WITH ALL THE TRIMMINGS (SEE PAGE 230)

3-MEAT WHITE CANNELLONI (SEE PAGE 196)

SPINACH AND RICOTTA CANNELLONI WITH TOMATO-BASIL SAUCE (SEE PAGE 195)

NEW YEAR'S DAY LENTILS WITH COTECHINO (SEE PAGE 202)

Potato-Parsnip Pancakes

WITH CRÈME FRAÎCHE SAUCE AND SALMON / SERVES 6 TO 8

3 parsnips, peeled and shredded into thin matchsticks on a mandoline or box grater

4 russet potatoes, peeled and shredded into thin matchsticks on a mandoline or box grater—place in a strainer and rinse well, then press to remove all of the liquid

1 bunch of scallions (white and green parts), finely chopped

Salt and freshly ground black pepper

2 large eggs, lightly beaten

About ¼ cup flour or matzo meal

About 3 cups neutral frying oil, such as safflower or vegetable oil

1 cup crème fraîche or sour cream

3 tablespoons capers, drained and chopped

1 lemon, halved

1 rounded tablespoon horseradish, freshly grated or prepared

½ cup combined finely chopped fresh flat-leaf parsley, fresh dill, and fresh chives

1½ pounds Scottish smoked salmon or gravlax

To serve: pulled dill fronds, additional whole capers, thinly sliced radishes, thinly sliced red onions or shallots, thinly sliced seedless cucumber

If you love latkes, you will LOVE this brunch. It's a guest favorite and often a request.

If not serving within thirty minutes of making the first potato pancakes, keep them crispy in a 300°F oven.

/ / /

PLACE A WIRE RACK inside a rimmed baking sheet lined with parchment paper.

PLACE THE PARSNIPS in a large mixing bowl with dried, rinsed potatoes. Combine with the scallions. Season with salt and pepper. Add the eggs and sprinkle in the flour and combine. In a large skillet over medium to medium-high heat, add oil to a depth of about ⅛ to ¼ inch and heat. When the oil ripples, add 6 piles of mixture and gently pat them into cakes. Cook until golden, flip with a thin spatula, then cook until golden on the opposite side, 6 to 7 minutes total per batch. Repeat with 2 more batches.

COMBINE THE CRÈME FRAÎCHE with the capers, juice of 1 lemon, horseradish, herbs, salt, and pepper.

ON A LARGE WOODEN BOARD or other serving surface, spread a few layers of cut brown parchment paper and arrange the parsnip-potato pancakes. Opposite the pancakes arrange the salmon and top with dill and capers. Down the center of the board arrange the radishes, onions or shallots, and cucumbers. Serve the sauce in a small bowl for dolloping.

Panettone French Toast / SERVES 8

CUSTARD

6 large eggs

½ teaspoon salt

1 cup half-and-half or heavy cream

1 teaspoon vanilla extract

1 teaspoon almond extract

2 tablespoons superfine sugar

About ⅛ teaspoon freshly grated nutmeg

TOAST

½ cup (1 stick) butter

1½ cups maple syrup or 1 cup honey

1 stick of cinnamon

8 thick-cut slices (about 4 x 5 inches) of panettone or brioche or challah bread

We make this on Christmas morning and as we buy and receive lots of candied citrus cake—panettone—we make it for guests over many holiday weekend brunches. The recipe is equally delicious prepared with thick-sliced brioche or challah bread. We serve this with a petite smoked ham, sausage patties, or bacon.

/ / /

IN A LARGE SHALLOW DISH, whisk up the eggs, salt, half-and-half, vanilla, almond extract, sugar, and nutmeg.

HEAT A LARGE GRIDDLE over medium heat.

IN A SMALL PAN, melt the butter. In a small pot, gently warm the syrup with the cinnamon.

PAINT THE GRIDDLE with the butter. Soak 4 slices of bread at a time in the egg mixture, turning and draining off the excess. Cook each slowly for 7 to 8 minutes, turning occasionally, until deeply golden. Remove to a wire rack–lined baking sheet and repeat with the remaining 4 slices of bread.

BRUSH THE TOAST with melted butter and serve, spooning the warm syrup over the top.

Shrimp Cocktail / SERVES 8 TO 10

MAKE THE BOUILLON: Place the herb bundle, onion, celery, carrot, garlic, wine, water, lemon, peppercorns, and bay leaves in a large pot and bring to a boil. Reduce the heat to maintain a low boil for 30 minutes. Add the shrimp and cook for 3 to 4 minutes. Drain the shrimp and cold-shock them in an ice-cold water bath. Drain them again and peel and devein them, but leave the tails intact.

MAKE THE COCKTAIL SAUCE: Combine all of the ingredients in a bowl and chill.

SERVE THE SHRIMP on ice with lemon wedges, caper berries, cocktail sauce, and saltines on a small tray alongside.

SHRIMP AND COURT BOUILLON

1 bundle of fresh flat-leaf parsley and fresh thyme, tied with kitchen string

1 onion, quartered

2 ribs celery, coarsely chopped

1 carrot, coarsely chopped

1 bulb garlic, halved across to expose cloves

1 cup white wine

2 quarts water

1 lemon, sliced

1 teaspoon black peppercorns

3 large bay leaves

3 pounds 8–10 or 10–12 count/per pound shrimp, in shell, 1 pound per every 3 adult guests

COCKTAIL SAUCE

1½ cups ketchup

About ½ cup minced celery and greens from the celery heart

Juice of 1 lemon

About 3 tablespoons freshly grated or prepared horseradish

About 1½ tablespoons Worcestershire sauce

About 1 tablespoon cayenne pepper sauce

½ tablespoon coarse black pepper

Chou Farci (Stuffed Cabbage) / SERVES 6 TO 8

SAUCE

2 tablespoons EVOO

2 tablespoons butter

2 bay leaves

1 onion, peeled and halved

2 cloves garlic, crushed and chopped or thinly sliced

1 (24- to 26-ounce) jar passata or tomato sauce

1 scant teaspoon sugar

Salt to taste

CABBAGE AND FILLING

1 cup loosely packed dried porcini mushrooms

2 cups chicken or beef stock, warmed

2 tablespoons EVOO

1 large or 2 medium carrots, grated or finely chopped

2 ribs celery, finely chopped

1 onion, finely chopped

1 leek, split, washed, and finely chopped (white and pale green parts only)

4 cloves garlic, finely chopped

2 tablespoons each finely chopped fresh thyme and fresh sage

Salt and freshly ground black pepper

½ cup white wine

MAKE THE SAUCE: In a large Dutch oven over medium heat, heat the EVOO, 2 turns of the pan. Add the butter to the oil. When it foams, add bay leaves, onion, and garlic. Then add the tomato sauce, sugar, and salt. Simmer, covered, at a low bubble, for 30 minutes. Remove and discard the onion.

MAKE THE CABBAGE AND FILLING: In a small pot, cover the mushrooms with the warm stock and reconstitute the mushrooms for about 30 minutes. Remove the mushrooms with a spoon and finely chop them. Add the stock to the tomato sauce. Heat a large pot of water to a boil for the cabbage. Heat a large skillet over medium to medium-high heat. Add the EVOO, then the carrots, celery, onion, and leek and sweat the vegetables for a few minutes. Add the garlic and herbs and season with salt and pepper. Cook until the vegetables are tender, stirring for another few minutes. Add the wine and let it absorb, 3 to 4 minutes. Cool the vegetables completely.

PLACE THE MEATS IN A BOWL. Season with salt and pepper and combine. Make a well in the meat mixture and fill it with the breadcrumbs moistened with milk. Add the beaten egg, cooled vegetables, chopped mushrooms, and the paprika, nutmeg, cumin, and allspice. Mix to combine.

PLACE THE CABBAGE in the boiling salted water and pull away the large leaves as they come free. (If the leaves are not coming loose, you can make small cuts around the core at the base of the leaves before placing the cabbage in the boiling water.) It will take 20 to 30 minutes total. Place the large leaves in layers on kitchen towels.

BOIL THE CORE for 15 minutes more. Drain, cool, cut in half. Finely chop it, along with 1 to 2 cups of cabbage, and mix it into the meat for more cabbage-y flavor.

PREHEAT THE OVEN to 350°F and position the oven rack in the lower third of the oven. Line a medium-large mixing bowl with cheesecloth and layer in the cabbage leaves carefully to reconstruct the outside of the cabbage with the largest leaves. Fold the leaves over the edge of the bowl to seal the filling on the bottom layer of meat later, making sure that the bottom of the bowl is also covered with a few cabbage leaves. Add one-third of the meat and press it into a flat layer. Cover with a few leaves and add one-third more meat, then repeat. Fold in the leaves over the filling and wrap the cheesecloth tightly to form a firm ball—a whole stuffed cabbage. Twist and tie the cheesecloth in the center with string. Place the cabbage in the sauce in the pot. Cover the pot with a tight-fitting lid and roast for 1½ to 2 hours, basting once. Remove the pot from the oven and carefully remove the cabbage to a board to cool enough to handle. Using scissors, trim away the cheesecloth carefully. Pour the sauce into a serving dish and set the whole stuffed cabbage into it. Slice the cabbage into wedges to serve.

¾ cup each ground beef, pork, and veal

1 cup breadcrumbs, saturated with ½ cup milk

1 large egg, beaten

1½ teaspoons paprika (⅓ palmful)

About ¼ cup freshly grated nutmeg

About ½ teaspoon ground cumin

About ⅛ teaspoon ground allspice

1 large savoy cabbage

Anchovy Breadcrumb-Stuffed Artichokes / SERVES 8

TRIM THE BOTTOMS and edges of the lower leaves of the artichokes and rub with 1 cut lemon. Fill a large pot of water and add the juice of 2 lemons. Bring the water to a boil, then reduce the heat to maintain a medium rolling boil. Add the salt. Add the artichokes and cook them for about 20 minutes in boiling water, until the leaves pull easily away. Drain on kitchen towels until cool enough to handle. Pull out the center leaves down to the hairy, fibrous choke. Scrape the choke out carefully with a small spoon. Clean all of the artichokes.

HEAT A LARGE SKILLET over medium heat and add the EVOO. Add the butter and melt it into the oil. When it foams, add the anchovies and melt them into the oil—they will dissipate as the heat works on them and become a natural, nutty salt flavoring for the oil and butter. Add the garlic, black pepper, and red pepper flakes and stir for 1 to 2 minutes. Add the breadcrumbs and toast for 5 to 7 minutes, until deeply golden. Remove the pan from the heat and cool the crumbs.

PLACE THE PARSLEY and mint in the bowl of a food processor and pulse to finely chop.

ADD THE PARSLEY and mint to the breadcrumbs. Add the zest of 1 lemon and stir in the cheeses.

PREHEAT THE OVEN to 400°F.

PLACE THE ARTICHOKES in a large baking dish. Fill the leaves from the outside into the heart with breadcrumbs, mounding a bit more at the center over the heart. Add water to a depth of ⅛ inch in the bottom of the dish and cover the dish with foil.

ROAST THE ARTICHOKES for about 20 minutes, until heated through. Uncover the dish and drizzle with more EVOO. Roast for another 20 minutes, until the tips of the leaves curl and brown and the stuffing is set. Douse the artichokes with the juice of 1 lemon and serve. Pull several leaves onto appetizer dishes per person and place 1 or 2 bowls on the table to collect the outer leaves. The hearts are first come, first served!

4 large male artichokes
(with pointed leaves)

4 lemons

About 2 tablespoons salt

About ½ cup EVOO, plus
some for drizzling

¼ cup (½ stick) butter, cut into pieces

About 16 anchovy fillets

10 cloves garlic, grated or finely chopped

1 tablespoon coarsely ground black
pepper

1 scant teaspoon crushed
red pepper flakes

8 cups breadcrumbs

1 large bundle of fresh flat-leaf parsley,
1½ to 2 cups packed leaves, picked

1 bunch of fresh mint, about
½ cup picked leaves

1 cup grated Parmigiano-Reggiano

½ cup grated Pecorino

Pappardelle with Robiola and Truffles / SERVES 6

½ cup whole milk

1 large clove garlic, crushed

9 ounces robiola rocchetta
(triple-milk soft cheese from Tuscany),
cut into 1-inch pieces

¼-pound chunk of Pecorino with truffles,
grated or thinly shredded

6 tablespoons butter

Salt and white pepper or finely
ground black pepper, to taste

1 pound (500 grams) egg pappardelle
or fettuccine

Fresh black or white truffle, grated,
or 2 ounces jarred shaved truffles

Minced fresh chives or minced
fresh flat-leaf parsley, to serve

PLACE 5 TO 6 QUARTS of water in a large pot to boil, for the pasta.

IN A SMALL PAN, warm the milk and garlic over medium heat. Steep the garlic in the milk for 5 minutes. Place the robiola in a large bowl and add the hot milk. Remove and discard the garlic. Add the grated cheese to the robiola. Place the butter in the small pan and return it to the stove over medium-high heat. Brown the butter for 5 to 7 minutes, until golden and nutty. Remove the butter from the heat and add it to the mixing bowl. Season the sauce with salt and white pepper or grind in a little fine black pepper.

SALT THE BOILING WATER for the pasta and cook the pappardelle or fettuccine 1 minute less than the package directions for al dente. Reserve ½ cup of the starchy water. Then drain the pasta and toss with the cheese sauce, adding in truffles to your taste. Use the cooking water as needed to thin the sauce to coat the pasta. Serve immediately, garnished with chives or parsley.

Spinach and Ricotta Cannelloni
WITH TOMATO-BASIL SAUCE / SERVES 6 TO 8

MAKE THE SAUCE: Heat a Dutch oven over medium heat and add EVOO, 2 turns of the pan. Add the butter and melt it into the oil. When it foams, add the onion, garlic, and bay leaf. Add the passata. Add the tomatoes and break them up with a wooden spoon. Season with salt and sugar and simmer for 30 minutes. Stir in the basil and wilt it into the sauce, then remove from the heat. Discard the onion, garlic, and bay leaf.

MAKE THE FILLING: Place the spinach in a large mixing bowl and loosen it with your fingers. Add the ricotta, provolone, Parmigiano-Reggiano, nutmeg, egg, salt and pepper, and parsley. Stir to combine.

TO ASSEMBLE: Heat a large pot of water to a boil and prepare an ice-water bath in a large mixing bowl. Pile up a few kitchen towels.

SALT THE BOILING WATER and add 7 or 8 sheets at a time to cook the lasagna for about 4 minutes. Transfer the cooked pasta with tongs or a spider to the ice bath to cold shock, then arrange them in a single layer on towels. Repeat until all of the pasta is cooked.

PREHEAT THE OVEN to 375°F.

TO A LARGE CASSEROLE DISH, add half of the remaining sauce. Place a few sheets of lasagna in front of you and mound about 4 to 5 tablespoons of filling into a log shape covering the width of the pasta. Roll to cover the filling and trim the end of the sheet. Place the cannelloni seam-side down in the sauce. The recipe will produce 14 to 16 rolls in a casserole, 2 rows of 7 or 8 rolls. Cover the cannelloni with the remaining sauce and top with an even layer of shredded mozzarella and an even sprinkle of Parmigiano-Reggiano.

BAKE FOR 30 MINUTES covered. Then uncover and bake for 15 to 20 minutes more, to brown the top. Sprinkle with parsley and serve.

TOMATO-BASIL SAUCE

2 tablespoons EVOO

2 tablespoons butter

1 small onion, peeled and halved

2 large cloves garlic, crushed

1 large bay leaf

1 jar passata or tomato puree (3 cups)

1 (28-ounce) can whole peeled San Marzano tomatoes

Salt

1 scant teaspoon sugar

1 handful of fresh basil leaves, torn

FILLING

1 (10-ounce) package chopped frozen organic spinach, defrosted in the microwave and wrung dry in a kitchen towel

1½ cups fresh ricotta

¼ pound provolone, finely diced

1 cup grated Parmigiano-Reggiano

About ⅛ teaspoon freshly grated nutmeg

1 large egg, lightly beaten

Salt and freshly ground black pepper

1 handful of fresh flat-leaf parsley, finely chopped

TO ASSEMBLE AND SERVE

14 to 16 dry flat egg lasagna sheets

½ pound fresh mozzarella, shredded

1 handful of grated Parmigiano-Reggiano

1 small handful of fresh flat-leaf parsley, finely chopped

3-Meat White Cannelloni / SERVES 6 TO 8

BESCIAMELLA

5 tablespoons butter

¼ cup flour

3 cups warm milk

Salt and ground white pepper, to taste

About ⅛ teaspoon freshly grated nutmeg

About ¼ cup grated Parmigiano-Reggiano

FILLING

3 tablespoons EVOO

1 pound ground veal

½ cup (5 ounces) ground chicken

1 onion, minced or finely chopped

3 cloves garlic, grated or finely chopped

2 tablespoons fresh sage, finely chopped

3 ounces of mousse pâté or leftover chicken liver, coarsely chopped

About ½ cup bone broth or chicken or beef stock

I roll cannelloni in egg lasagna sheets. For small cannelloni I use pre-cut squares, but they can be hard to find. For larger cannelloni, I trim each sheet as I roll, after par-boiling the sheets for a few minutes and cold shocking. I find my method much easier than filling dried tube pasta and quicker than making fresh sheets of pasta. It works in a time pinch. I can make the sauces, fillings, and a tray of each cannelloni, meat and spinach, in just about 2 hours total. Both of these fillings and sauces are great in stuffed shells, as well.

Often I add a little of my own leftover chicken liver in this dish, as I make lots of it around the holidays. If I don't have any on hand, I use store-bought mousse pâté of duck liver and pork, a thin slice or about 3 ounces. It makes this filling really rich and velvety.

MAKE THE BESCIAMELLA: In a medium sauce pot over medium heat, melt the butter. When it foams, whisk in the flour. When it bubbles, gradually pour in the warm milk. Season the sauce with salt, white pepper, and nutmeg. Whisk for about 5 minutes, to simmer and thicken, till it coats the back of a spoon. Stir in the cheese. Remove the pot from the heat and cover.

MAKE THE FILLING: Heat a large skillet over medium to medium-high heat and add the EVOO, 3 turns of the pan. Add the veal and chicken and cook for about 8 minutes, until lightly brown and finely crumbled. Add onions and cook for 5 to 6 minutes more, until the onions soften. Add the garlic, sage, pâté or chicken livers, and bone broth and combine. Stir in about 1 cup of besciamella sauce and remove from the heat to cool a bit.

TO ASSEMBLE: Heat a large pot of water to a boil and prepare a large ice-water bath in a large mixing bowl. Pile up a few kitchen towels.

SALT THE BOILING WATER and add 7 or 8 sheets of pasta at a time to cook the lasagna for about 4 minutes. Transfer the cooked pasta with tongs or a spider to the ice bath to cold shock, then arrange them in a single layer on towels. Repeat until all of the pasta is cooked.

PREHEAT THE OVEN to 375°F.

TO A LARGE CASSEROLE dish, add half of the remaining sauce. Place a few sheets of lasagna in front of you and mound about 3 to 5 tablespoons of filling into a log shape covering the width of the pasta. Roll to cover the filling and trim the end of the sheet. Place the cannelloni seam-side down in the sauce. The recipe will produce 14 to 16 rolls in a casserole, 2 rows of 7 or 8. Cover the cannelloni with the remaining sauce and top with small dots of butter and an even layer of sliced or shredded mozzarella and an even sprinkle of Parmigiano-Reggiano.

BAKE FOR 30 MINUTES covered. Then uncover and bake for 15 to 20 minutes more, to brown the top. Sprinkle with parsley and serve.

TO ASSEMBLE AND SERVE

14 to 16 dry flat egg lasagna sheets

A few tablespoons butter to dot the top of the cannelloni

½ pound fresh mozzarella, thinly sliced or grated

1 handful of grated Parmigiano-Reggiano

Finely chopped fresh flat-leaf parsley

Poached Cod with Tomatoes / SERVES 6 TO 8

About 2 tablespoons EVOO

2 tablespoons butter

1 bulb fennel, trimmed and sliced using a mandoline, plus a handful of fronds reserved for serving

3 ribs celery with leafy tops, thinly sliced on the bias

2 medium onions, halved and thinly sliced

1 bulb garlic, peeled and thinly sliced

Salt

1 teaspoon fennel pollen

2 large bay leaves

1 cup dry white vermouth

1 (28-ounce) can whole tomatoes, broken up with spoon, or 3 cups passata

1 handful of fresh tarragon leaves, chopped, or fresh basil leaves, torn

6 to 8 (6-ounce) pieces of cod, center-cut thick fillets

Juice of 1 lemon

Crusty bread, for mopping

IN A LARGE, DEEP SKILLET over medium heat, heat the EVOO, 2 turns of the pan. Add the butter and melt it into the oil. When it foams, add the fennel, celery, onions, and garlic. Season with salt, fennel pollen, and bay leaves. Cook the fennel and onions slowly for 12 to 15 minutes, until soft and sweet. Add the vermouth and reduce by half, about 3 minutes. Add the tomatoes and simmer for 15 minutes. Add the tarragon and cook for 10 to 15 minutes more.

DOUSE THE COD with the lemon juice and season with a little salt. Poach the cod in the sauce over medium-low heat, covered, until firm and opaque. Serve the fish in shallow bowls with lots of sauce, chopped fennel fronds on top, and bread for mopping up the sauce.

Italian Roast Chicken and Potatoes / SERVES 6 TO 8

PLACE THE CHICKEN in a bowl and dress with salt, black pepper, 3 tablespoons rosemary, the red pepper flakes, onion, fennel, oregano, chopped garlic, and sliced lemon. Toss to combine and transfer to a large plastic food storage bag. Leave in fridge for 24 to 48 hours.

PREHEAT THE OVEN to 425°F. Arrange the chicken in a large roasting pan. Add the wine and top with ¼ cup EVOO.

TOSS THE POTATOES with the remaining ¼ cup olive oil, the remaining 3 tablespoons rosemary, salt, black pepper, and granulated garlic. Arrange the potatoes on a parchment paper–lined baking sheet.

PLACE THE CHICKEN on the middle rack of the oven and the potatoes on the rack below the chicken. Roast until the chicken reaches 160°F to 165°F on an instant-read thermometer and the potatoes are golden. Douse the chicken with about ¼ cup brine from the chili peppers. Top the chicken with the chopped chili peppers. Arrange the chicken on a platter and top with some pan juices. Toss the potatoes in the remaining juices and serve alongside.

12 to 16 pieces of cut bone-in, skin-on chicken, breasts, legs, and thighs

Salt and freshly ground black pepper

6 tablespoons fresh rosemary leaves, chopped

1½ teaspoons (½ palmful) each: crushed red pepper flakes, granulated onion, fennel seeds and/or pollen combined, and dried oregano

6 cloves garlic, chopped, plus 2 teaspoons granulated

1 lemon, sliced

1 cup white wine

½ cup EVOO

6 medium potatoes, peeled and cut into bite-size pieces

½ cup hot red chili pepper rings, chopped, and their brine

Tuscan Pot Roast / SERVES 6 TO 8

PREHEAT THE OVEN to 325°F. Position the oven rack in the center of the oven or one rung below if necessary for your pot.

BRING THE ROAST to room temperature.

IN A LARGE DUTCH OVEN or a heavy braising pan over medium-high heat, heat the olive oil. Pat the meat dry and season with salt and pepper. Brown the meat on both sides and the edges—this will take about 10 minutes—and remove the meat to a platter or pan. Add the butter to the pot and melt it. When it foams, add the onions, celery, parsnips, carrots, garlic bulbs, rosemary, and bay leaves. Season with salt and pepper. Add the herb bundle and juniper berries. Reduce the heat to medium and partially cover the pot. Cook for 12 to 15 minutes to soften the vegetables, stirring occasionally. Stir in the tomato paste, then add the wine and bring to a bubble. Scrape up any brown bits on the bottom of the pot and add the beef back. Add stock enough to just come up to meat's edge. Cover the pot with a tight-fitting lid and place in oven. Roast for 2½ to 3½ hours, until the meat is tender.

REMOVE THE POT ROAST to a carving board and let it rest for 15 minutes. Then slice the meat against the grain. Remove and discard the bay leaves, herb bundle, garlic skins, and rosemary stems. Serve the sliced meat on a platter or in shallow bowls with vegetables alongside. Use the charred bread or roasted potatoes for mopping the sauce.

4 pounds meaty chuck roast, well trimmed, about 3 to 3½ inches thick

About 3 tablespoons olive oil

Salt and coarsely ground black pepper

¼ cup (½ stick) unsalted butter, cut into pieces

2 onions, red or yellow, root end intact, cut into wedges

3 ribs celery with leafy tops, thick cut on the bias

2 parsnips, thick cut on the bias (about 1 pound total)

4 medium carrots, thick cut on the bias (about 1 pound total)

2 bulbs garlic, ends cut off to expose the cloves

4 generous sprigs of rosemary

2 large, fresh bay leaves

1 small bundle of fresh thyme, fresh flat-leaf parsley, and carrot tops, tied with kitchen string

10 to 12 juniper berries (I use 12)

½ cup (about 1 tube) sun-dried tomato paste or tomato paste

½ bottle Italian red wine, such as Rosso di Montalcino

3 cups beef stock (I used RR's Stock-in-a-Box)

Charred bread or roasted potato wedges with olive oil and rosemary, crushed garlic, and salt

New Year's Day Lentils with Cotechino / SERVES 6

FARRO

Salt

1½ cups pearled farro

1 small onion, peeled and halved

1 large bay leaf

EVOO, for drizzling

LENTILS

1 (1- to 1¼-pound) cotechino sausage, casing pierced with the tip of a small knife or tines of a fork in a few places (optional; we prepare the cotechino sausage only on New Year's)

¼ cup EVOO

2 carrots, peeled and chopped

2 to 3 ribs celery with leafy tops, chopped

1 onion, finely chopped

1 leek, quartered, washed, and chopped

6 cloves garlic, crushed and chopped

Salt and freshly ground black pepper

6 ounces 'Nduja (salami paste)

2 cups lentils, such as lentils di Norcia or Puy lentils, rinsed

1 quart each chicken stock and beef bone stock

1 (15-ounce) can crushed or diced tomatoes (2 cups)

1 bunch of lacinato kale, stemmed and shredded or chopped

Cotechino is a large sausage served on New Year's Eve or New Year's Day to bring good luck. It is slow simmered and traditionally served with lentils, which signify coins or the ability to relieve creditors and provide for prosperity in the year ahead. It's a good-luck tradition that has served us pretty well so far.

These lentils are what I call a stoup—thicker than soup, thinner than stew, prepared with 'Nduja, a spicy salami paste. The soup is listed as a separate recipe to be served all winter long. I cook farro to mix into the lentils to make this dish heartier and to add a nutty flavor and texture.

The big finish is a basil-parsley-walnut paste that is stirred into each bowl.

/ / /

MAKE THE FARRO: In a large stock pot, bring about 2 quarts of water to a boil. Season the water with salt and add the farro. Then add the onion and bay leaf and cook for 20 minutes. Drain and transfer to a bowl. Remove and discard the bay leaf. Drizzle farro with EVOO, toss, and reserve.

MAKE THE LENTILS: Place the cotechino in a large pot. Cover by about 2 inches with cold water. Cover the pot with a tight-fitting lid and bring the water to a boil. Reduce the heat to low and simmer for 75 to 90 minutes, until warmed through and tender enough for slicing.

PLACE A DUTCH OVEN over medium to medium-high heat and add the EVOO, 4 turns of the pan. Add the carrots, celery, onion, leek, garlic, salt, and pepper. Stir and partially cover the pot. Cook for 5 to 6 minutes, until the vegetables soften. Stir in the 'Nduja and melt it. Add the lentils, chicken and beef stocks, and tomatoes. Simmer at a low bubble for 1 hour, then wilt in the kale.

MAKE THE HERB SAUCE: Combine basil and parsley in the bowl of a food processor. Add the walnuts, garlic, lemon juice, and cheese. Pulse to finely chop, then stream in the EVOO to form a thick sauce. Transfer to a bowl.

ASSEMBLE: Remove the cotechino from the water, then remove the casing and thinly slice the sausage.

ADD THE FARRO to the stew.

SERVE THE "STOUP" in shallow bowls and top with dollops of sauce and a few slices of cotechino.

HERB SAUCE

1 cup each fresh basil and fresh flat-leaf parsley tops

½ cup toasted walnuts

1 large clove garlic, crushed

Juice of 1 lemon

1 cup loosely packed grated Pecorino Romano (a few handfuls)

About ⅓ cup EVOO

Peppermint Pomegranate Cosmopolitan / MAKES ONE DRINK

JOHN SAYS: Smirnoff makes a seasonal vodka called Peppermint Twist, which basically tastes like a candy cane and is perfect for the holiday season. Alternatively, you could make your own version by crushing up a bunch of candy canes (maybe five to seven large ones or a dozen smaller ones), placing them in an airtight container with a bottle of your favorite vodka, letting it steep for four or five days, and then straining it back into the vodka bottle.

2 ounces pomegranate juice, plus enough to fill an ice cube tray

2 ounces Smirnoff Peppermint Twist vodka (or your own homemade candy-cane-flavored vodka)

1 small candy cane, for garnish

FILL AN ICE CUBE TRAY with pomegranate juice and freeze until solid.

ADD THE VODKA and pomegranate juice to an ice-filled cocktail shaker. Shake well and strain into a pomegranate ice–filled rocks glass. Garnish with a candy cane.

17 Golden Dreams of Tuscany

When I was a girl, my mom would always wish me sweet dreams at bedtime. In Italian, the expression for sweet dreams is *sogni d'oro,* dreams of gold. But even when I was a girl, my dreams seemed to be more sour than sweet, made up of moments in my day-to-day life that scared me, caused me stress, or provided general anxiety. Throughout my life, in my dreams, I'm just reliving my toughest moments, whether at school, at work, or at home. Like hitting replay, I keep trying to change or reinvent the outcomes of each event that bothered me. Ultimately, I'm working out my deep need to please people, to give them what they want. I'm still a waitress at heart, even in my sleep. I want everyone to be satisfied and happy. And to that end, sometimes I work so hard in my dreams that I wake up in a sweat. My dreams are not usually made of gold, but of dishwasher-safe stainless steel.

But there are a few nights a year in which I dream of Italy. These dreams are, in fact, *sogni d'oro.* In them I am falling from the sky, gently out into the Tuscan countryside. As my arms rise above my head and my foot touches the earth, I spring back up into the golden sky and I almost take flight, bounding and soaring out over the vineyards and olive groves, over the winding roads dotted with children, cats, and tiny three-wheeled farm trucks. I bounce back up and over the fields filled with the fragrances of herbs and mushrooms, of wild boar and game, of every vegetable and flower. Everything is beautiful, and the air is so rich it makes me cry. I swear I can experience this all with every one of my senses. I awake in tears, feeling overwhelmed by beauty.

I love Italy from the top of her boot to the bottom of her heel and I have a deep and special connection to Sicily, where part of my family is rooted. But for years now, I've only dreamt of Tuscany. I dream of it perhaps because its fertile environment grows the Sangiovese grapes that produce Brunello di Montalcino, my favorite wine if I had to choose. I dream of it because it is the first place I can remember spinning around in circles, dizzy from joy, the panoramic, 360-degree views of the vineyards leaving me breathless and awestruck. The tableau of Tuscany is my every fairy tale come to life, and I couldn't paint anything more saturated or beautiful with all my imagination. I dream of Tuscany because it's where I got married.

My mom found the castle in Montalcino where John and I were married while vacationing with my aunt. My family planned the wedding and it was breathtaking and very unusual. John and I registered for our marriage license in Florence, quite an adventure as we speak minimal Italian—finding

My beloved in-laws, Vicki and Andy Cusimano, stealing the show as usual on the dance floor (below). On the right we're cutting our wedding cake, a giant semifreddo that I actually never got to taste. I went to dance my ass off, and when I came back there was none left! Then ten years later (opposite) it happened again! Maybe I was too busy looking at fireworks and boogieing in a bathrobe.

the correct office was challenge enough, let alone getting there during the very limited hours they operate. (I don't think Italians put a lot of importance on paperwork.) The trouble was worth it, as our wedding day was absolutely beautiful. We held the ceremony on a sprawling lawn with low walls of stacked stone that enhanced the view by framing the endless vista of vineyards and groves. We walked down the aisle to Stevie Wonder's "You Are the Sunshine of My Life." We were married under what looked like a chuppah draped in flowers, grapes, and vines by an officiant who was technically Episcopalian dressed in a robe, rope belt, and sandals. The chuppah was set next to a large fountain with an obelisk at the center. We crushed a glass, for good luck. It was a Catholic-light, Jewish, Da Vinci Code wedding with a little something for everyone.

John planned the entertainment at the reception and a super group, Emporio, was born.

Of the hundred or so guests, about twenty played instruments, including the members of John's band, the Cringe. They were all invited to play for the reception. All the instruments and sound equipment were stamped EMPORIO for some reason, and so the new band was named.

After the wedding feast and the cake, a giant semifreddo that I never got a piece of, the musicians stayed dressed up in their wedding suits and dresses, while the guests and the bride changed into PJs, nighties, and bathrobes. A tradition was born. Emporio played until 4:00 AM and we all danced until the stone beneath our feet left us chafed, blistered, and in some cases bloody.

For ten years we returned to our castle and brought seventy or so people with us to celebrate our anniversary, our friends, great food and music, and life. Isaboo has made every trip, and on our tenth anniversary we were re-married in the same spot, with Isaboo walking me down the aisle.

For the last few years, we've scaled back a bit. Now we nest in a golden, windy, winding village-turned-villas and spa called Monteverdi. We bring a smaller gang, about forty friends, some who we see only on this annual pilgrimage. Our guests are mostly foodies/chefs and musicians, and all are close friends. They are there for a long weekend and many fly to Italy early or stay on after to tour on their own. I plan the menus weeks in advance and build elaborate shopping lists and sublists of how to execute the food. I review every recipe and list on the flight, and when we land at the small airport near Perugia I get a lot of attention and probably cause some annoyance. I'm walking a sixty-five-pound pit bull and toting dozens of bags and boxes of equipment and hard-to-find ingredients. I bring dozens of spices, in case I can't find what I need in the markets. I even reimport some (many) Italian goods, because I get very specific about every element of each dish. I know.

Isaboo walked me down the aisle for our tenth-anniversary vow renewal. Even she must've thought those shoes were ridiculous. What was I thinking??

Pazzo. Nuts. It's Italy—they have the best Italian ingredients available on the planet. But I like to be overprepared, so if the whole country runs out of juniper berries, I can still make my recipe for *cinghiale,* wild boar.

When we get to the villa, I go immediately into the kitchen to unpack, check the groceries that were delivered, organize the kitchen, and begin making my stocks and sauces. Not many people get what part of this story sounds like a vacation, but to cook in Italy, to look out at the exquisite vistas before me, and to smell that air and feel the beauty while preparing food for people I love, this is what I live for. Sharing beauty like this, and food and wine, time together with friends so far away from home but growing so close together—this is what I have worked for my whole life.

/ / /

On the following page are the full menus from this past year's anniversary celebration. I can't fit all the recipes in this book (or, at least, my editor won't let me). So here are some highlights from that magical weekend.

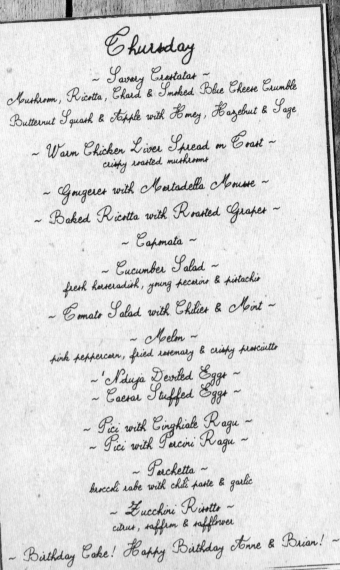

Thursday

~ Savory Crostatas ~
Mushroom, Ricotta, Chard & Smoked Blue Cheese Crumble
Butternut Squash & Apple with Honey, Hazelnut & Sage

~ Warm Chicken Liver Spread on Toast ~
crispy roasted mushrooms

~ Gougeres with Mortadella Mousse ~

~ Baked Ricotta with Roasted Grapes ~

~ Caponata ~

~ Cucumber Salad ~
fresh horseradish, young pecorino & pistachio

~ Tomato Salad with Chilies & Mint ~

~ Melon ~
pink peppercorn, fried rosemary & crispy prosciutto

~ 'Nduja Deviled Eggs ~
~ Caesar Stuffed Eggs ~

~ Pici with Cinghiale Ragu ~
~ Pici with Porcini Ragu ~

~ Porchetta ~
broccoli rabe with chili paste & garlic

~ Zucchini Risotto ~
citrus, saffron & safflower

~ Birthday Cake! Happy Birthday Anne & Brian! ~

Saturday

~ Black Oil Cured Olives with Chili & Orange ~

~ Calamari Fritti with Lemon & Herbs ~

~ Shrimp Scampi ~

~ Arancini ~

~ Zucchini Sticks with Tomato Basil Sauce ~

~ Raviolo with Chicken Liver & Black Truffle ~

~ Potato Tortelli with Porcini & Herbs ~

~ Tahini Caesar Salad with Romaine & Kale ~

~ Roast Beef Ribs ~
celery-portabella salad, cipollini agrodolce,
cracked green olives, toasted walnuts, arugula, salsa verde

~ Grilled Branzini ~
fennel slaw

~ Creamed Spinach with Taleggio ~

~ Dessert by Chef Anne Burrell ~
Fig Crostata with Gorgonzola Dolce

Brodo

When I land in Italy I go immediately from the airport to the kitchen—before I unpack a bag or settle in, I start roasting bones and vegetables for our broths and stocks. I use most of my stocks right up, but you can store them for up to a week in the fridge or six months in the freezer. Or, if you can vacuum pack them, they'll keep for up to a year in there!

/ / /

IN A LARGE STOCK POT, arrange the onion, leek, celery, carrots, lemon, and garlic. Season with salt and peppercorns and add the herb bundle, bay leaves, and chicken. Add the water and bring to a boil. Reduce the heat and simmer for 2 hours, turning the chicken occasionally. Cool the chicken for 1 hour in the stock, then strain and cool.

**BEEF STOCK
(PAGE 10)**

CHICKEN STOCK
MAKES 3 QUARTS

1 large onion, quartered

1 large leek, quartered and cleaned

2 large ribs celery with leafy tops, coarsely chopped

2 large carrots, coarsely chopped

1 lemon, sliced

1 bulb garlic, halved across to expose cloves

About 2 scant tablespoons salt (a couple of shallow palmfuls)

7 or 8 black peppercorns

1 bundle of fresh flat-leaf parsley, carrot tops, and fresh thyme, tied with kitchen string

2 large bay leaves

1 whole chicken or 5 pounds chicken legs and feet

6 quarts water

The menus from last year at Monteverdi. Yes, I cooked all that! On Friday, I took the night off.

Vegetable Stock with Porcini / MAKES 4 QUARTS

¼ cup EVOO

6 portabella mushrooms, trimmed, wiped clean, and coarsely chopped or thick-sliced

2 large onions cut into wedges, root ends attached

3 ribs celery with leafy tops, coarsely cut on the bias into thick slices

1 large carrot, coarsely chopped

1 large bulb garlic, halved across to expose cloves

3 tablespoons sun-dried tomato paste or tomato paste

1 rounded tablespoon salt

10 to 12 black peppercorns

1 cup loosely packed dried porcini mushrooms

1 bundle of fresh sage and carrot tops, tied with kitchen string

2 large bay leaves

7 quarts water

I use this stock in winter stews, with dark greens, in whole-wheat or farro pasta dishes, and with risottos prepared with mushrooms or truffles. See Brodo recipe (page 211) for storage suggestions.

/ / /

HEAT A LARGE STOCKPOT over medium-high heat and add the EVOO, 4 turns of the pan. Add the mushrooms and brown well, 5 to 7 minutes. Add the onions, celery, carrot, and garlic and brown for 8 to 10 minutes more. Stir in the tomato paste. Add the salt, peppercorns, porcini, herbs, and water. Bring to boil, then reduce the heat to low and simmer for 2 hours. Cool the stock, then strain.

VARIATION: VEGETABLE BROTH WITH PUMPKIN
MAKES 10 CUPS

I use this stock for light or citrusy vegetarian dishes from Moroccan food to rice pilaf to the Zucchini Risotto (page 222) and Arancini (page 222) listed in this section.

About ¼ cup EVOO

1 small pumpkin or 2-pound chunk or slab, coarsely chopped

2 large onions, quartered

About 1 tablespoon salt

3 carrots, coarsely chopped

2 large ribs celery with leafy tops, coarsely chopped

1 leek, coarsely chopped

1 bulb garlic, halved across to expose cloves

1 lemon, sliced

½ orange, sliced, with rind on

1 large bay leaf

1 bundle of fresh thyme, carrot tops, and fresh flat-leaf parsley, tied with kitchen string

About 1 tablespoon pink peppercorns

6 quarts water

HEAT A STOCKPOT over medium-high heat. Add the EVOO, 4 turns of the pan. Add the pumpkin and onions and cook for 12 to 15 minutes, until the pumpkin is browned and the onions soften. Add the salt, carrots, celery, leek, garlic, lemon, orange, bay leaf, herb bundle, peppercorns, and water. Bring the stock to a boil and reduce the heat to a simmer. Cook for 2 hours. Cool the stock, then strain.

Gougères with Mortadella Mousse / MAKES 24 GOUGÈRES

Cheese puffs, gougères, are a fairly quick, always popular gathering snack as is. The filling and pistachios take them to the next level for extra-special occasions.

/ / /

PLACE THE MORTADELLA, mascarpone, cream, nutmeg, pepper, and balsamic drizzle in the bowl of a food processor. Pulse-process to get the filling going, then process until smooth. Fill a pastry bag fitted with a plain tip or a large plastic food storage bag, trimming ½ inch off one corner for a makeshift pastry bag.

HALVE THE GOUGÈRES and fill with mortadella mousse; the filling once the top is in place should be about ½ to ¾ inch thick. Roll the sides of the stuffed pastry in pistachios and arrange on a serving dish.

GOUGÈRES (PAGE 165)

FILLING

1 pound mortadella, cut into chunks

1 cup mascarpone

½ cup heavy cream

⅛ to ¼ teaspoon freshly grated nutmeg

½ teaspoon ground white pepper

About 1 tablespoon balsamic drizzle (see note on page 214)

1 cup shelled pistachio nuts, preferably Sicilian, lightly toasted and then processed into coarse chips

Baked Ricotta and Roasted Grapes
WITH BALSAMIC DRIZZLE / MAKES 12 TO 16 SERVINGS

RICOTTA

2 tablespoons unsalted butter, melted, to brush the pan and put on top of the ricotta

2 bulbs roasted garlic, pasted*

2 tablespoons honey

2 tablespoons EVOO

2 large eggs

2 tablespoons fresh rosemary, finely chopped

Zest and juice of 1 small lemon

Salt and freshly ground black pepper

2 pounds fresh ricotta, well drained

1 cup grated Parmigiano-Reggiano

GRAPES

1½ pounds black grapes, Moon Drop grapes, or red seedless grapes—look for green stems and tightly packed grapes

About 3 tablespoons EVOO

2 to 3 sprigs fresh rosemary, leaves stripped

Salt and freshly ground black pepper

1 teaspoon fennel seeds

TO SERVE

Balsamic drizzle**

Toasted chopped pistachios

Fresh mint sprigs or leaves

Crostini/little toasts

This is a simple spread with gorgeous roasted grapes on top. Keep them on the vine for an extra pretty effect.

/ / /

MAKE THE RICOTTA: Line an 8-inch springform pan with parchment paper or butter a large 1½-quart ramekin and preheat the oven to 425°F.

IN A LARGE MIXING BOWL, whisk up the roasted garlic paste, honey, EVOO, eggs, rosemary, lemon zest, lemon juice, salt, and pepper. Stir in the ricotta and Parmigiano-Reggiano with a spatula and transfer the mixture to the prepared springform pan or baking dish. Bake for 40 to 45 minutes, until golden and set. Cool for 30 minutes.

MAKE THE ROASTED GRAPES: Raise the oven temperature to 475°F.

PLACE THE LARGE BUNCHES of grapes on a rimmed baking sheet and dress with olive oil, rosemary, salt, pepper, and fennel. Roast for 18 to 20 minutes on the center oven rack, till they slump and are heated through.

TO SERVE: Cool the grapes until they are cool enough to handle and arrange them on top of the ricotta. Drizzle the roasted grapes and baked cheese with balsamic and garnish with pistachios and mint. Serve with crostini.

* To roast garlic, cut the end off the garlic bulbs to expose the cloves. Drizzle with olive oil and season with a little salt and wrap in foil. Roast at 425°F for 40 to 45 minutes, until golden and soft. Cool the bulbs and squish the garlic from the skins. Mash the garlic into a paste.

** I make my own balsamic drizzle: Reduce 1 cup balsamic vinegar mixed with ¼ cup (packed) light or dark brown sugar in a small pan over high heat for about 20 minutes, until it's thick and coats the spoon. Cool.

Savory Butternut and Apple Crostata / MAKES 1 LARGE CROSTATA

IN THE BOWL of a food processor, combine the all-purpose flour, whole-wheat flour, salt, nutmeg, and sugar and sprinkle with the vinegar. Add the butter and pulse the processor until the mixture has the consistency of thick sand. With the food processor on, stream in the water until the dough comes together in mostly a ball. Remove the dough and pull it together on a cold board. Push it into the shape of a disc and wrap it tightly in plastic wrap. Chill the dough for a minimum of 30 minutes.

LET THE DOUGH soften slightly at room temperature, then roll it out on lightly floured parchment paper to a thickness of ⅛ inch or a bit less (it will hang over the parchment paper sheet on the edges). Transfer the parchment paper and dough to a baking sheet.

PREHEAT THE OVEN to 400°F. Position the oven rack in the center of the oven.

IN A LARGE SKILLET over medium-high heat, heat the EVOO, 3 turns of the pan. Add the squash and cook for 5 to 8 minutes, until it softens a bit. Add the apples and onion and season with salt, pepper, nutmeg, and thyme. Cook for 7 to 8 minutes more. Add the lemon juice to the squash and apples and cool for about 30 minutes before adding to the crust.

SCATTER HALF THE CHEESE on the rolled-out dough and top with the squash and apples, leaving a 2½-inch rim. Fold in and ruffle the crust.

IN A SMALL SKILLET over medium heat, melt the butter. When the foam subsides, add the sage. Crisp the sage leaves while the butter browns and becomes fragrant. Remove the sage leaves to a paper towel–lined plate.

BRUSH THE BROWN BUTTER over the filling and top with a scattering of the remaining cheese—if some gets on the crust edges, all the better. Brush the crust with egg wash and bake for 35 to 40 minutes, until the crust is golden. Cool a bit and top with the nuts and drizzled honey. Garnish with sage leaves and slice into 10 wedges or cut into 3-inch squares.

PIE DOUGH

¾ cup AP flour

¾ cup whole-wheat flour

1 teaspoon salt

About ⅛ teaspoon freshly grated nutmeg

2 teaspoons (packed) light brown sugar or granulated sugar

1 tablespoon apple cider vinegar or white balsamic vinegar

½ cup (1 stick) very cold butter, diced

4 to 5 tablespoons ice water

FILLING

3 tablespoons EVOO

1 pound butternut squash, from the neck only, peeled and quartered lengthwise, then thinly sliced ⅛ inch thick

2 apples, peeled and quartered, cored and sliced

1 red onion, quartered and thinly sliced

Salt and freshly ground black pepper

About ⅛ teaspoon freshly grated nutmeg

2 tablespoons fresh thyme, chopped

Juice of ½ lemon

2 cups (½ pound) shredded Fontina Val d'Aosta or Gruyère or Comté

¼ cup (½ stick) butter

12 fresh sage leaves

1 large egg, beaten with 2 teaspoons water

½ cup peeled hazelnuts, toasted and chopped

Acacia honey or other light-colored and light-flavored honey, to serve

Tahini Caesar Salad

WITH ROMAINE AND KALE / SERVES 8 TO 10

CROUTONS

3 tablespoons EVOO

3 tablespoons butter

2 cloves crushed garlic

1 teaspoon coarsely ground black pepper

3 cups cubed sesame semolina bread, or similar

½ cup each grated Romano and Parmigiano-Reggiano

2 tablespoons za'atar seasoning

DRESSING

About ½ cup tahini

3 cloves garlic

Juice of 2 lemons

1 tablespoon coarsely ground black pepper (scant palmful)

2 tablespoons Dijon mustard

About 1 tablespoon Worcestershire sauce (heads-up for vegetarians: Worcestershire sauce contains anchovies) (optional)

About ¾ cup EVOO

1 cup each Romano and Parmigiano-Reggiano, loosely packed

SALAD

1 large head romaine lettuce, coarsely chopped

1 bundle of lacinato kale, stemmed and coarsely chopped

You can make the croutons and dressing ahead. Just seal the croutons tightly; the dressing keeps in the fridge for a week.

/ / /

MAKE THE CROUTONS: Preheat the oven to 375°F. Line a rimmed baking sheet with parchment paper or foil. Heat a large skillet over medium heat. Add the EVOO, 3 turns of the pan. Melt the butter into the oil. When it foams, add the garlic and pepper and swirl for about 1 minute. Add the cubed bread and toss to coat. Transfer the croutons to the baking sheet. Sprinkle the cheeses over the bread and bake for 20 to 25 minutes, until deeply golden. Add the za'atar and toss while warm. Let cool. The croutons keep will keep in an airtight container for 7 to 10 days.

MAKE THE DRESSING: Place the tahini in the bowl of a food processor along with the garlic, lemon juice, pepper, mustard, and Worcestershire, if using. Turn the processor on and stream in ⅓ cup water to thin the paste a bit, then stream in the EVOO to form the dressing. It should be thick but pourable. Add the cheeses and pulse a few times to combine.

MAKE THE SALAD: Pile 10 to 12 cups of combined greens in a large bowl. Toss with enough dressing to coat generously. Top with the croutons and serve.

Cucumber Salad

DRESS SLICED CUCUMBERS, Persian or seedless, with lemon, EVOO, and salt. Arrange on a serving platter. Top with freshly grated horseradish (spicy) or parsley root (not). Top with grated Pecorino, finely chopped dill, parsley, and chopped pistachios or whole toasted pine nuts.

Tomato Salad with Chilies and Mint

TOP A PLATTER OF GREAT TOMATOES, sliced or chopped, with thinly sliced red and or green chilies (seed and finely chop for milder palates). Add chopped green or red onion if you like. Scatter lots of finely chopped fresh mint over the tomatoes and dress with fruity EVOO and salt.

Melon with Crispy Prosciutto

ARRANGE PROSCIUTTO in a single layer on parchment paper and roast at 400°F to crisp. Cool the slices. Arrange melon wedges/slices on a platter and top with pink peppercorns and some lime juice. Fry a few sprigs of rosemary in a little oil. Pile the crispy meat on the melon and scatter the fried rosemary, stemmed.

Portabella Salad with Celery / SERVES 8 TO 10

6 large portabella mushroom caps

Juice of 2 lemons

Salt and freshly ground black pepper

1 bunch of fresh flat-leaf parsley,
coarsely chopped

8 fat ribs celery with big, leafy tops,
thinly sliced on the bias

¼ cup EVOO

1 chunk of Parmigiano-Reggiano or
Pecorino, for shaving

GILL THE MUSHROOMS and wipe clean with a damp towel. Then slice the mushrooms very thinly. Dress the mushrooms with the lemon juice, salt, and pepper and let them set for 30 minutes. Add the parsley to the mushrooms. Add the celery to the salad. Dress the salad with EVOO. To serve, top with lots of shaved cheese and gently toss through the salad.

Creamed Spinach with Taleggio / SERVES 8

2 pounds mature, large-leaf spinach,
stemmed and coarsely chopped
(3 or 4 bunches)

2 tablespoons EVOO

3 tablespoons butter

3 shallots, finely chopped

4 cloves garlic, chopped

1 cup heavy cream

About ⅛ teaspoon freshly
grated nutmeg or to taste

Salt and freshly ground black pepper

1 pound Taleggio, the rind trimmed
and the cheese diced

Juice of ½ lemon

½ cup grated Parmigiano-Reggiano
(a couple of handfuls)

LINE A VERY LARGE STRAINER or colander with a large, clean kitchen towel. Fill the colander with spinach leaves and pour boiling water from a kettle over the spinach to wilt the leaves. When cool enough to handle, wrap up and twist the towel to wring out all excess liquid. Finely chop the drained spinach. (If you don't have a very large colander, you can do this in batches.)

HEAT A LARGE SKILLET over medium heat. Add the EVOO, 2 turns of the pan. Then add the butter. When the butter foams, add the shallots and garlic and cook for 3 minutes, until the shallots soften. Add the cream and season with the nutmeg, salt, and pepper. Melt in the Taleggio. Add the lemon juice and finish with the Parmigiano-Reggiano.

Zucchini Sticks and Tomato-Basil Sauce / SERVES 8 AS A STARTER OR SNACK

I use this same method and coating for two pounds of mozzarella sticks or provolone sticks as well.

/ / /

MAKE THE SAUCE: In a large sauce pot over medium heat, heat the EVOO, 2 turns of the pan. Add the butter and melt it into the oil. When it foams, add the garlic and stir for 1 to 2 minutes. Add the tomatoes and break them up with a wooden spoon, then add the passata and stir the sauce. Bring the sauce to a bubble. Stir in the basil and season with salt. Cook the sauce down for 30 minutes, then remove from the heat until ready to serve. When ready to serve, reheat the sauce over medium-low heat.

SET UP A BREADING STATION and place a wire rack over a parchment paper–lined large baking sheet or 2 small pans. The three sections of the breading station are 1) flour in a shallow dish, seasoned with salt and pepper, 2) eggs beaten in a shallow dish and seasoned with salt and pepper, and 3) breadcrumbs in a shallow dish with cheese, fennel pollen, red pepper flakes, granulated garlic, granulated onion, parsley, and lemon zest.

COAT THE ZUCCHINI in flour, then eggs, shaking off any excess, then evenly in the breadcrumb mixture. Place them on the wire rack–lined pans and chill for 1 hour.

HEAT THE FRYING OIL in a Dutch oven or tabletop fryer over medium to medium-high heat, about 350°F. Cook the sticks in small batches to avoid crowding, about 4 minutes per batch, until golden brown and crispy.

SERVE THE STICKS with lemon wedges and red sauce alongside for dipping.

TOMATO-BASIL SAUCE

2 tablespoons EVOO

2 tablespoons butter

3 cloves garlic, crushed

1 (28-ounce) can San Marzano tomatoes, or other canned tomatoes with a sprinkle of sugar added

1 (24-ounce) jar passata or 3 cups tomato puree

10 to 12 leaves of fresh basil, torn

Salt

ZUCCHINI STICKS

1½ cups AP flour

Salt and freshly ground black pepper

4 large eggs

2 cups breadcrumbs

About 1 cup grated Parmigiano-Reggiano (a few fat handfuls)

1½ teaspoons (½ palmful) each: fennel pollen or ground fennel seeds, crushed red pepper flakes or ground pepperoncini, granulated garlic, and granulated onion

About ½ cup fresh flat-leaf parsley tops, stemmed and then finely chopped

Zest of 1 small lemon

3 medium zucchini, halved and then seeded; if larger than medium size, cut into sticks about 3½ inches long and ½ to ¾ inch wide

2½ to 3 quarts frying oil

Lemon wedges and red sauce, to serve

Zucchini Risotto / SERVES 8 TO 10 (HALVE FOR 4 OR COUNT ON LEFTOVERS FOR ARANCINI

2 quarts vegetable stock, store-bought, or use Vegetable Broth with Pumpkin (page 212)

1½ to 2 teaspoons saffron threads

2 large curls each orange peel and lemon peel—remove the colored part of the peel only, not the white pith

6 tablespoons EVOO

2 small zucchini, firm, or 1 medium to large zucchini, finely chopped—if large, halve lengthwise and scrape the seeds away before chopping

Salt

1 tablespoon Calabrian chili paste, or ½ to 1 teaspoon crushed red pepper flakes

1 onion, finely chopped

4 cloves garlic, finely chopped

3 cups Arborio or Carnaroli rice

1½ cups white wine (⅓ bottle)

6 tablespoons butter, cut into small pieces

1½ cups freshly grated Parmigiano-Reggiano or Pecorino Romano or a combo

Juice of 1 lemon or juice of ½ orange

Fresh mint and finely chopped fresh flat-leaf parsley, to serve

IN A LARGE SAUCE POT over medium-low heat, warm the vegetable stock. Add the saffron, orange peel, and lemon peel.

HEAT A SKILLET over medium-high heat. Add 3 tablespoons EVOO, 3 turns of the pan. Then add the zucchini and cook for 2 to 3 minutes, until lightly browned and tender-crisp. Season with salt and add the chili paste to taste. Toss to combine and remove from the heat.

HEAT A LARGE, round-bottomed pan over medium-high heat. Add the remaining 3 tablespoons EVOO, 3 turns of the pan. Add the onion and sweat for 2 to 3 minutes, until softened. Add the garlic, stir in the rice, and cook for 1 minute more. Add the wine and let it get fully absorbed. Begin adding the stock a few ladles at a time, each time vigorously stirring with a wooden spoon or risotto spoon (hollow in the middle). Once you begin adding stock, the risotto will cook in about 18 to 20 minutes to al dente. In the last few minutes, after adding the last few ladles of stock, stir in the butter, cheese, and zucchini. Finish with the citrus juice. Season to taste with salt. Top with mint and parsley.

Zucchini Arancini

Arancini means "little oranges." I make a risotto every year of a different variety so I can literally roll the cold rice into balls to make the arancini for another meal.

Zucchini Arancini are what we did with the leftover risotto from Thursday's meal.

ROLL 2-INCH BALLS of cold Zucchini Risotto. Set up a breading station and coat the balls in flour, egg, and breadcrumbs mixed with some grated cheese, thyme, parsley, citrus zest, and a sprinkle of fennel pollen. Heat vegetable oil to 350°F and fry the risotto balls for 5 to 6 minutes, until deeply golden. Serve with lemon wedges and/or red sauce.

Raviolo with Chicken Livers and Truffles / SERVES 8

Mom's chicken livers are one of the recipes I do every year in Italy, due to popular demand. Not everyone likes to make their own pasta, but trust me, with this stuff it's more than worth it.

/ / /

CUT THE PASTA SHEETS into 2- or 3-inch circles for the ravioli and top with liver. Brush the edges with water and seal them. Cook the ravioli for about 3 minutes in salted and rapidly simmering water.

HEAT THE STOCK, lace it with brandy, and melt in the butter. Serve the ravioli with a little bit of stock in small, shallow bowls topped with chives.

Basic Egg Pasta (page 87)

1 pound of Elsa's Chicken (page 278)

3 cups chicken or beef stock

About 3 tablespoons brandy

3 tablespoons butter

Shaved truffle, black or white

Finely chopped chives, to serve

Toasted Cacio e Pepe / SERVES 4

Before and after the nights we feast there are simpler meals for a few rather than many. One night we had a pasta bar with three choices: spaghetti cooked in wine with beets (see page 262); beef and eggplant ragù, a John fave (page 281); and this dish, which was the biggest hit of the night and the simplest to make.

/ / /

IN A LARGE, DEEP SKILLET over medium to medium-high heat, heat the EVOO, 3 turns of the pan. I use my oval-shaped 5-quart skillet, but any 12- to 14-inch round pan will work really well. Add the butter to the oil. When it foams, add the pasta. Season the pasta with pepper and toast it for 4 to 5 minutes, until deeply golden in color and very nutty in its aroma. Add 1 quart water to the pan and bring to a boil, stirring occasionally and cooking for 8 to 10 minutes, until not quite al dente. Reserve 1 cup of the cooking water. Then drain the pasta. Return the pasta to the skillet, then add the cooking water and cheese. Stir for 1 to 2 minutes more, until the pasta is al dente. Serve in shallow bowls.

About 3 tablespoons EVOO

3 tablespoons salted butter

1 pound spaghetti

About 1 tablespoon coarsely ground black pepper (scant palmful)

About 2 cups finely grated Pecorino Romano

Potato Tortelli with Porcini / SERVES 8 AS AN APPETIZER

4 to 6 medium thin-skinned potatoes

Salt

2 cups loosely packed grated Pecorino

1 large egg

½ teaspoon ground white pepper

¼ teaspoon freshly grated nutmeg

1 recipe Basic Egg Pasta (page 87)

Semolina or flour, for dusting
the parchment paper

3 tablespoons EVOO

3 tablespoons butter

1½ pounds fresh porcini mushrooms
or mixed wild mushrooms, trimmed,
wiped clean, and thinly sliced

About 2 tablespoons each chopped
fresh rosemary and fresh thyme

4 cloves garlic, grated or finely chopped

Freshly ground black pepper

½ cup white wine

2 cups Vegetable Stock with Porcini
(page 212)

About 3 tablespoons finely chopped
fresh flat-leaf parsley, to serve

This one takes time and effort, but if you like fresh pasta and mushroom-umami flavor, it's oh so worth it.

/ / /

FILL A GOOD-SIZED POT with 4 to 5 quarts of cold water. Add the potatoes. Bring to a boil. Add the salt and cook the potatoes for about 35 minutes, until fork-tender. Cool the potatoes and peel them, then press through a food mill, fine sieve, or ricer. Combine the potatoes with cheese and egg and season with salt, white pepper, and nutmeg.

SPACE THE FILLING every couple of inches on a sheet of pasta. Brush the water around the small mounds of potato filling using a small brush. Set another sheet of pasta on top of the filling and seal gently but tightly with your fingertips. Cut the ravioli into squares using a small knife or fluted ravioli roller. Place the ravioli on rimmed baking sheets lined with parchment paper and dusted with semolina or flour.

HEAT A LARGE SKILLET over medium-high heat with EVOO, 3 turns of the pan. Melt the butter into the oil. When it foams, add the mushrooms and cook for 8 to 10 minutes, browning them. Add the rosemary, thyme, garlic, salt, and pepper. Stir for 2 to 3 minutes. Add the wine and cook for 3 minutes more, until the wine is absorbed. Add the stock to the pan and reduce the heat to low.

COOK THE RAVIOLI for 4 to 5 minutes in salted boiling water, then transfer with a spider to the mushrooms and sauce. Serve the pasta in shallow bowls and top with parsley.

Grilled Branzino with Fennel Salad / SERVES 6 TO 8

THIS IS MORE OF a method than a recipe. Branzino, sea bass, loup de mer, ragno—whatever name you call it—vary in size greatly between America and Italy. At home in New York City the branzino I get from my fishmonger are about 1½ pounds. In Tuscany the fish I get are 2½ to 4 pounds. To grill them, the fish should be scaled, gutted, and gilled, of course. Fill the cavity of the fish with sliced fennel, sliced lemon, sliced onion, crushed garlic, and herbs such as parsley and thyme sprigs and fennel fronds. Score the skin of the fish and coat with EVOO and season liberally with salt and pepper. Grill the fish over hot coals or medium-high heat for about 10 minutes per pound, turning occasionally. For example, a 2½-pound fish would take about 25 minutes.

IN A LARGE BOWL, combine the fennel and fronds, celery, onion, parsley, and tarragon. In a small bowl combine the garlic, fennel pollen, honey, lemon juice, and vinegar. Whisk in the EVOO and season the dressing with salt and pepper. Dress the salad and serve or refrigerate.

FENNEL SALAD

2 large or 3 medium bulbs fennel, halved, cored, and sliced using a mandoline or thinly sliced by hand, plus ½ cup fronds

4 large ribs celery with leafy tops, thinly sliced on the bias

1 small red onion, halved and thinly sliced or sliced using a mandoline

1 cup fresh flat-leaf parsley tops, coarsely chopped

½ cup tarragon leaves, stemmed and coarsely chopped (a bunch)

1 large clove garlic, grated or pasted

1 teaspoon fennel pollen (⅓ palmful)

1 tablespoon honey, such as acacia honey

Juice of 1 lemon

2 tablespoons white balsamic vinegar

About ⅓ cup EVOO

Salt and freshly ground black pepper

Porchetta / SERVES 10 TO 12

This is a go-to for a crowd at the holidays, John's b-day, on-and-off years, and a must crowd-pleaser for Italy, as well. You may need to order the meat from a specialty butcher, as most supermarkets don't carry these cuts. And you should prep your roast two days before cooking and take it out two hours before it goes in the oven, to get it first to room temp. The longer it sets, the better it gets.

FOR THE BELLY, make sure it's trimmed to the length of the loin and that it can wrap the loin—make sure the butcher is clear on your needs here. Next, trim one edge of the belly so that it is whittled down to skin to make a flap that encases the loin once wrapped. Use a boning or utility knife to trim that portion, about 3 inches wide. Tenderize the skin with the bumpy side of a meat mallet. Flip the pork belly back over and poke holes with the tip of a small knife into the fleshy side.

COVER THE LOIN all around with salt and pepper.

IN A SMALL PAN over low to medium heat, toast the fennel seeds and red pepper flakes for 2 to 3 minutes.

LAY THE BELLY OUT and rub with salt, garlic, fennel, red pepper flakes, sage, rosemary, orange zest, and lemon zest.

WRAP THE LOIN in the belly and tie tightly with string every 1 to 1½ inches. Rub the skin with baking soda and leave the roast uncovered in the fridge for 2 days. Place the roast on the lowest shelf, on a wire rack over a parchment paper–lined baking sheet. When ready to roast, bring to room temperature for 2 hours.

POSITION THE OVEN RACK in the center of the oven and preheat the oven to 500°F. Roast for 45 minutes, turning the baking sheet occasionally, then reduce the heat to 300°F and roast for 2 to 3½ hours, depending on the size of the roast. The larger the belly and loin, the longer it needs to roast. Roast the pork until an instant-read thermometer reads 145°F. Let the meat rest for 20 to 30 minutes and carve it with a serrated knife into ¼- to ½-inch-thick slices.

SERVE THE SLICED PORCHETTA with ciabatta rolls and lemon wedges, and arugula or broccoli rabe (see page 94).

1 (8- to 10-pound) meaty pork belly trimmed to fit the length of the pork loin used (see below)

Salt and freshly ground black pepper

1 (4- to 5-pound) pork loin, trimmed of all fat

1 bulb garlic (6 to 8 cloves), skinned and thinly sliced or chopped (about ¼ cup)

3 tablespoons fennel seeds or a half-and-half combo fennel seeds and fennel pollen (I use the half-and-half combo)

About 1 tablespoon crushed red pepper flakes or pepperoncini

12 sage leaves, stacked on top of each other and very thinly sliced

6 or 7 stems or sprigs of fresh rosemary, stripped and finely chopped

About 2 tablespoons orange zest (from 3 to 4 large oranges)

About 3 tablespoons lemon zest (from about 6 lemons)

1 tablespoon baking soda (about 1 scant palmful)

Roast Beef Ribs

WITH SALSA VERDE AND CIPOLLINI IN AGRODOLCE / SERVES 8 TO 10

6 large, meaty beef ribs, each
about 10 to 12 inches long
and about 10 to 12 pounds in weight

6 large cloves garlic, sliced,
plus 2 bulbs, the ends cut to
expose the cloves for roasting

1 gallon water

1 cup kosher salt, plus more for
seasoning the ribs

¼ cup superfine sugar

2 tablespoons juniper berries

1 tablespoon black peppercorns

1 tablespoon coriander seeds

1 onion, cut into thin wedges

1 lemon, sliced

4 bay leaves

Several stems of rosemary, bruised with
the back of your knife for the brine, plus
a few large stems to roast with the beef

Coarsely ground black pepper

About ¼ cup olive oil, plus more for
drizzling on the garlic bulbs

About 1½ cups white wine

This dish was served with a variety of sides, toppings, and condiments: Salsa Verde, Portabella Salad, Cipollini in Agrodolce, cracked green olives, toasted walnuts, and arugula. Plan ahead: You want to bring your beef to room temperature for at least twenty-four hours.

/ / /

CUT SMALL SLITS all over the beef and stuff with sliced garlic.

DOUBLE-BAG A 3-GALLON, plastic food storage bag. Fill it with a quart of water to dissolve the brining solution: salt, sugar, juniper berries, peppercorns, coriander seed, onion, lemon, bay leaves, and bruised rosemary. Add the ribs, then cover the ribs with the remaining 3 quarts water and carefully close the bags. Brine the meat for 24 to 48 hours.

PREHEAT THE OVEN to 325°F.

PAT THE RIBS DRY and season with salt and pepper. Heat a large roasting pan over medium-high heat using two burners. Add the olive oil to coat the pan and brown the ribs for about 15 minutes, being sure to brown the ribs on all sides. Add the wine to the pan and nest in the whole bulbs of garlic. Drizzle the garlic bulbs with oil and nest in a few stems of rosemary as well. Cover the beef with parchment paper, then tightly with foil, and roast for 3½ to 4 hours, until the meat is tender and barely falling off the bones. Remove the ribs from the oven and cool them enough to be able to handle. Gently remove the meat, separate the membrane, then cut the beef into 3 portions per rib. Drain and strain the drippings. Stack the meat neatly back onto the bones and pour the drippings over the top. Crisp the beef under the broiler for 5 to 10 minutes to heat it back up, then serve it with cracked olives, toasted walnuts, cipollini (see page 232), arugula, and portabella salad (see page 220).

(recipe continues on page 232)

SALSA VERDE
MAKES ABOUT 2 CUPS OF SAUCE

1 to 1½ large bunches of fresh flat-leaf
parsley tops (3½ to 4 cups)

1 large bunch of fresh mint leaves,
loosely packed (1½ cups)

2 large shallots, coarsely chopped

4 cloves garlic, crushed

4 anchovy fillets

Juice of 2 lemons

¼ cup red wine vinegar

About 2 tablespoons fresh horseradish

3 tablespoons capers

1 to 1¼ cups EVOO

1 scant teaspoon acacia honey

Salt and freshly ground black pepper

CIPOLLINI IN AGRODOLCE

2 pounds cipollini—small, flat-shaped
onions, yellow- or red-skinned

½ cup aged balsamic vinegar

2 tablespoons (packed) light
brown sugar

1 tablespoon kosher salt

¼ cup EVOO

1 tablespoon dried oregano

MAKE THE SALSA: Pulse-chop the parsley and mint together in the bowl of a food processor. Add the shallots, garlic, anchovies, lemon juice, vinegar, horseradish, and capers and continue pulsing for about 1 minute, until finely chopped and well combined. Scrape the mixture into a bowl and stir in the EVOO and a bit of honey. Season with salt and pepper to taste.

MAKE THE CIPOLLINI: Soak the onions for 15 minutes in water to loosen the skins. Peel and drain the onions. Add the onions to a wide, shallow pot or large, deep skillet (at least 2 inches high) and cover with about 2 quarts of water. Bring to a boil. Reduce the heat to a simmer and continue cooking for 15 minutes. Then add the vinegar, brown sugar, salt, EVOO, and oregano. Reduce the heat again, to medium-low to medium, and continue to cook for 45 minutes more, at a low boil, until the sauce is syrupy. (If the onions get too tender before the liquid turns to syrup, remove the onions until the syrup is reduced and then add the onions back in and toss.) Serve.

Rachael's Ragù alla Cinghiale / SERVES 8 TO 10

A common toast in Italy at special occasions is *Cent'anni,* or wishing someone or the group *100 years*. A friend of mine, Donna, a vegetarian as it happens, confused this expression with an animal hunted for food, commonly used when it's in season: *cinghiale,* or wild boar. One night Donna rises from the table to toast us and looks straight at me and cheers loudly, "Cinghiale!" (Luckily, we've been friends for more than twenty years now, so I let it pass that she was calling me a big, long-tusked, hairy pig at my own party.)

So, yes, this is sauce made of wild boar, which is in season in the fall, when we travel annually to Tuscany. This recipe and our chicken livers are a constant on my menu every year, by demand. There are a few farms that produce boar in America and there are purveyors who carry frozen, imported wild boar, but the same recipe can be prepared with pork shoulder. It marinates for at least a full day, so order and plan ahead.

/ / /

PREPARE THE MEAT: Trim the connective tissue, tendons, and fat and cube the meat to 1½-inch pieces—your yield will be about 3 to 3¼ pounds of trimmed meat.

MAKE THE MARINADE: Combine the wine, bay leaves, onion, celery, garlic, herb bundle, lemon, salt, peppercorns, and juniper berries in a large, nonreactive bowl. Set the meat in it and refrigerate for 24 to 48 hours. Remove the meat with a slotted spoon and drain very well. Pat dry. Strain the marinade and reserve it. Discard the solids.

MAKE THE RAGÙ: Place the mushrooms and broth in a large pot over medium heat and simmer for 8 to 10 minutes, to reduce by a third to a half. Then remove the mushrooms and chop them. Reserve 2 to 2½ cups of the infused stock.

IN A LARGE DUTCH OVEN or braising pot, heat the olive oil over medium-high heat. Season the meat with salt and pepper and brown well on all sides, working in batches if necessary to keep from crowding the pan. Deglaze and scrape up any brown bits with the brandy or Marsala and remove the meat to a platter.

(recipe continues on page 235)

1 (4- to 4½-pound) boar shoulder (about 2 kilos)

MARINADE

1 bottle of red wine

3 large fresh bay leaves

1 onion, quartered

2 to 3 ribs celery with leafy tops, coarsely chopped

1 bulb garlic, halved across to expose cloves

1 bundle of sage and rosemary, tied with kitchen string

1 lemon, sliced

1 tablespoon salt

1 to 10 black peppercorns

10 to 12 juniper berries

RAGÙ

1 cup dried porcini mushrooms

1 quart beef bone broth, store-bought or homemade (see page 10)

3 to 4 tablespoons olive oil

Salt and freshly ground black pepper

¼ cup brandy or ½ cup Marsala

3 tablespoons butter

2 carrots, chopped

2 medium onions, chopped

2 ribs celery with leafy tops, chopped

1 small bulb fennel, chopped

4 cloves garlic, chopped or sliced

2 tablespoons thinly sliced sage

2 tablespoons minced rosemary

(recipe continues on page 235)

Add the butter to the pot over medium heat. Add the carrots, onions, celery, and fennel and sear the vegetables. Cook them for 10 to 15 minutes, until they soften. Add salt and pepper, the garlic, then the sage, rosemary, and fennel. Stir in the strained wine marinade and simmer for 5 to 6 minutes, to reduce by half. Add the mushrooms, meat, stock, tomato paste, and passata. Cover with a tight-fitting lid and roast in a 300°F oven or on low simmer on the stove for 2½ to 3 hours, until the meat is very tender.

TOSS PICI or other rustic, hearty pasta with some starchy water, EVOO, or butter and the ragù. Top with additional ragù and serve with Parmigiano or Pecorino.

2 teaspoons fennel seeds or pollen

¼ cup sun-dried tomato paste or tomato paste

2 cups passata or tomato puree

VARIATION: PORCINI RAGÙ
SERVES 6 TO 8

This is a vegetarian alternative to the boar sauce.

1 cup dried porcini mushrooms

1 quart vegetable stock, store-bought or homemade (see page 212)

1½ pounds fresh mushrooms, such as cremini and hen of the woods/maitake

2 tablespoons EVOO

3 tablespoons butter

Salt and freshly ground black pepper

2 large shallots, peeled and finely chopped

1 carrot, finely chopped or grated

2 small ribs celery with leafy tops, finely chopped

4 cloves garlic, finely chopped or grated

2 tablespoons thinly sliced sage

2 tablespoons minced rosemary

¼ cup brandy or ½ cup Marsala

2 tablespoons sun-dried tomato paste

2 cups passata

IN A LARGE SAUCE POT, place the porcini and stock and bring to a low, rolling simmer. Reconstitute the mushrooms and concentrate the broth, reducing by about a third.

STEM THE MUSHROOMS and wipe with a damp cloth, then finely chop them. Pull apart the hen of the woods mushrooms into thin strips. Discard the very tough root ends that don't separate easily.

IN A DUTCH OVEN or braising pan over medium heat, heat the EVOO, 2 turns of the pan. Melt the butter into the oil. When it foams, add the fresh mushrooms and brown them for 12 to 15 minutes, until meaty in fragrance. Add salt and pepper, along with the shallots, carrot, and celery. Stir to soften them. Add the garlic, sage, and rosemary. Stir for 1 or 2 minutes more, then add the brandy to loosen the bits at the bottom of the pan. Remove the mushrooms from the stock with a slotted spoon. Add them to the vegetables. Add the tomato paste and passata and stir for 1 minute. Add the stock and pasta and simmer at lowest heat until ready to toss with starchy water, pasta, and cheese, as with ragù above.

Aperol Spritz / MAKES ONE DRINK

Orange wedge

2 ounces Aperol

2 ounces prosecco

JOHN SAYS: Campari—the famous Italian apéritif—is ubiquitous in Italy and often enjoyed in cocktails such as the Negroni. That said, Campari is a bit of an acquired taste. Imagine the most bitter grapefruit ever, but in a good way—and that's Campari. An excellent way to ease into Campari is to start out with Aperol, which is similar but lighter, slightly sweeter, and with about half the alcohol content. Rachael loves when I mix it with club soda for a crisp, refreshing summertime drink that we enjoy while playing ladder golf in our backyard (under the official rules of ladder golf, drinking is mandatory).

/ / /

SQUEEZE ORANGE WEDGE into a wine goblet. Add the Aperol. Fill the goblet with ice, top with prosecco, and stir gently. Garnish with a straw.

Classic Negroni / MAKES ONE DRINK

1½ ounces gin

1½ ounces Campari

¾ ounce red vermouth

2 dashes Angostura Bitters

1 orange wedge

1 lemon twist

Splash of club soda

JOHN SAYS: Rachael and I love Italy. I also love drinks that can be assembled easily and quickly in the glass, with no need for a cocktail shaker or strainer. As it turns out, the national cocktail of Italy—the Negroni—is just that kind of drink. If you're in Italy, you most likely will drink wine, but they do at least one cocktail and do it well.

/ / /

ADD THE GIN, Campari, vermouth, and bitters to a rocks glass. Squeeze in the orange wedge, add ice, and stir to chill. Garnish with a lemon twist and top with a splash of club soda.

work

3

18 The Girl with the Ice Cream Boobs

Ⅰf I were in charge of our country, working in restaurants would be a compulsory part of our education. And every participant would begin training as a DMO—Dish Machine Operator. Here they would learn invaluable life skills, beyond the ability to wash dishes and scrub pots: humility, patience, physical and mental endurance, organizational and spatial relationship skills, public relations, and a unique ability to clean disgusting things while controlling your gag reflex.

If life were a vinyl record, I might think about scratching it across the tracks for ages twelve to fourteen, so any time I played the album of my life I could just skip those years. What they felt like for me: acute paranoia, delusions of every kind, wild mood swings that turned on and off like a light switch—only I couldn't control the switch—oily and greasy everything, a general feeling of angst and its best friend, anger. When you feel and look your worst, and summer's coming up and you live in a resort town, what do you look forward to? Swimming and hiking with your friends? Joining summer theater groups? Listening to concerts in the park to cool off on hot summer nights? Nope. I wanted to go to work.

Mom had occasional babysitters for us kids, but she preferred to have eyes on us. She worked in restaurants for over fifty years, and for many of them she supervised all of the food, menus, and training for a multiple-restaurant chain that included a catering company, a large fine-dining-room steak house, a Tex-Mex place, and several franchise Howard Johnson's restaurants. As a girl I wanted to emulate my mom in every way. She could work eighty to one hundred hours a week. She taught training classes for hundreds of employees every summer. She drew her schedules and menus by hand on oversize Xerox paper. She was part tough boss and part mother hen. She was respected, and even feared by some. If an employee she cared about didn't show up, she'd go looking for them and get them in to work, but not before she'd stand over them as they pressed their uniform. If she had something to say to an employee who was taller than she was (which was most everyone, as she was only four foot eleven), she'd climb up on a milk crate to look them in the eye while directing them. She could expedite food for ten to twelve busloads of tourists a day up on that crate, a cloth draped around her to protect her clothes, pulling plates and shouting orders. To me, she looked like the Statue of Liberty come to life—a beacon in the chaos, guiding her team to shore and back to order.

To be like Mom you had to work like Mom, and no one worked harder. She wouldn't tell a bus person or line cook to clean the walk-in refrigerator

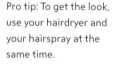

Pro tip: To get the look, use your hairdryer and your hairspray at the same time.

or freezer. She would show them how so there was no question of what she meant. She'd unload trucks, check in orders, inspect the toilets, and check the garbage cans for theft (employees over the years would steal whole filets of beef and hide them under the garbage bags in the cans). She'd cover breaks for any manager or kitchen staff member (no one knew or followed labor laws to the letter like she did), but if you *reminded* her it was time for yours, chances were she'd take your apron, for good.

The only way in to the restaurant business as I saw it was to listen, follow directions, and, upon my fourteenth birthday, get my working papers so I could start my career in food as a busgirl. My birthday falls in late August, so the summer I turned fourteen I had just a glimpse of my future as dish machine operator, which is how I would spend the following summer. Busgirls and busboys were mostly runners. We filled in breakfast buffets and salad bars, occasionally we helped the servers deliver large orders, and we cleared tables into bus buckets when servers were too busy. Not so bad, really. But dish machine operator was a whole other ball game.

The dish machine area ran about twenty degrees above the air temperature and was always 100 percent humidity. To work there felt like six-hour shifts in a wet hell. The thermometer that hung on the wall usually read well over 100°F. Hour after hour, buckets and trays of dishware and glasses and mountains of silverware just kept coming, pouring over you. Thousands of dollars of half-eaten eggs, pancakes, clam rolls, fried fish, hot dogs, and

I did make it to the top of the pyramid. But we had about fifty-four kids in our class, so landing the gig was not as competitive as you might think.

hamburgers—what ever happened to making kids clean their plates? After the first hour, if you walked away from The Machine to use the toilet or, God forbid, were sent into the dining room to help clear tables or clean the restrooms, you noticed immediately that you, in fact, stunk like wet rotten eggs and old milk. Nothing is cooler at fourteen than to have bad hair and bad skin, and to literally smell like garbage. Oh, except one thing . . . It's much cooler when your classmates come in for ice cream or Big Breakfast 1 or Big Breakfast 2 and see (and smell) you in all your glory. That is awesome! All of this for $3.35 an hour plus the couple of bucks in tips each server would share with you.

But, and I know this sounds really hard to believe, I was grateful and at the end of the day, each day, I was proud of myself. I took out garbage, cleared thousands of plates, cleaned bathrooms, carried boxes and buckets and racks of dishes and glasses till my legs swelled and my back ached, and I tried to keep a smile on while I did all of that. To this day, conquering hard work and managing stressful situations are what bring me peace.

At the end of my summer as dish machine operator, I got what at the time felt like the biggest promotion I would ever receive in my lifetime. I was made a Howard Johnson's Fountain Girl! Cue Disney birds circling my head and choirs of angels filling the air with song. A fountain girl didn't need to be eighteen, as liquor wasn't served on the fountain stools. This is where people came for milkshakes and ice cream. I don't eat sweets and never really cared about ice cream, but let me tell you I took this opportunity and seized it. I studied the recipe book for every drink and sundae on the menu. I mastered them all. I practiced the art of overfilling the conical ice cream scoop with the flat spade to ensure a proper hook-on to the side of the fountain glass for each ice cream soda and float. I could spray whipped cream rosettes to absolute perfection and always had an eye for cherry placement. The best part: I got a uniform. Beauty is in the eye of the beholder, and to me the orange-and-brown polyester zipper-back dress was like a prom gown. I did not have the same affection for L'eggs pantyhose and waitress shoes, but that's another matter.

Howard Johnson's had twenty-eight flavors, and each came in five-gallon buckets. They also had orange and lime sherbet and vanilla ice milk for shakes. The buckets were kept in a large coffin freezer that ran some twenty feet along the fountain counter. The syrups and sauces, the creamers we used in ice cream sodas, and, of course, the cherries, filled bins behind the freezers and under the counter. The scoops were kept in a cylinder-shaped dish rack that set into the freezer's edge, where water ran constantly for health-code compliance. I could upsell just about any fountain customer from single scoop to fancy dessert and the scoops flew under my watch, which meant a lot of empty ice cream tubs.

The one drawback of the job that I hadn't taken into consideration was my height. I'm on the shorter side. Once the ice cream level in a tub fell below the bottom third of the container, I could no longer reach it with a stretch of my arm. I would have to open two doors of the coffin chest and push up on the side of it and hurl myself over the side to get down into the last of the bucket, my feet dangling behind me. The problem was that the runoff of twenty-eight colors and flavors of ice cream dishwater flowed in a tiny river along the edge of the freezer, the runoff from the scoop-cleansing water. So, when I would turn around and present my sundaes and ice cream creations, I was also presenting myself in my precious orange polyester uniform with a line of melted ice cream, an ever-present stain of it, straight across the center of my chest. I became the girl with the ice cream boobs.

Humbling. However, I can still whip up a mean fountain drink. Only these days, I add liquor. These are all great "adult" shakes, but feel free to take the booze out—they work great either way.

Black and White Russian Root Beer Float / MAKES ONE DRINK

1½ ounces heavy cream or half-and-half (1 jigger)

1½ ounces Kahlúa or other coffee liqueur (1 jigger)

1½ ounces vodka (1 jigger)

6 ounces root beer, chilled

TO SERVE

Coffee ice cream

Real whipped cream in canister, homemade, or store-bought

Maraschino cherries

TO A TALL FOUNTAIN GLASS on a 6-inch under-liner plate, add the cream, Kahlúa, vodka, and root beer.

OVERFILL A CONICAL or round scoop with coffee ice cream and hook it on the side of the glass. Top with a whipped cream rosette and a Maraschino cherry.

SERVE WITH A LONG fountain spoon and straw.

Guinness and Jameson Float / MAKES ONE FLOAT (THAT'LL PUT HAIR ON YOUR CHEST)

1½ ounces Jameson whiskey (1 jigger)

A few dashes of chocolate bitters

Guinness Stout, 8 to 10 ounces, chilled

An overfilled conical scoop of French vanilla ice cream

Whipped cream and a cherry or shaved chocolate

TO A TALL FOUNTAIN GLASS or pint glass add the Jameson and chocolate bitters, and top with Guinness. Place the glass on a 6-inch under-liner plate. Hook a large scoop of French vanilla ice cream on the edge of the glass and top with a rosette of whipped cream and a cherry or shaved chocolate. Serve with a long fountain spoon.

Gianduja Milkshake / MAKES ONE SHAKE

½ cup milk

1½ ounces Frangelico hazelnut liqueur
(1 jigger)

3 tablespoons chocolate hazelnut
spread or paste

2 mounded scoops vanilla ice
cream or ice milk

1 mounded scoop chocolate sorbet
or ice cream

TO SERVE

Whipped cream from a canister,
homemade, or store-bought

Shaved milk chocolate or Gianduja
bar—hazelnut chocolate (optional)

BLEND ALL OF THE INGREDIENTS on medium speed, then switch to high speed to combine. Spoon into a tall fountain glass or pint glass. If the shake is too thick, add a splash more milk. Add a crown of whipped cream and shaved milk chocolate or hazelnut chocolate, if using. Grab a straw.

'Buca Milkshake / MAKES ONE SHAKE

½ cup cold strong coffee

1½ ounces heavy cream or half-and-half
(1 jigger)

1½ ounces Sambuca or other anise-
flavored liqueur (1 jigger)

2 mounded scoops vanilla ice cream or
ice milk

1 mounded scoop coffee sorbet or ice
cream

TO SERVE

Whipped cream from a canister,
homemade, or store-bought

Dark chocolate–covered espresso beans

BLEND THE COFFEE, cream, Sambuca, vanilla ice cream, and coffee sorbet on medium speed, then switch to high speed to combine. Spoon into a tall fountain glass or pint glass. If the shake is too thick, add a splash more cream or half-and-half. Add a crown of whipped cream and 3 chocolate-covered espresso beans. (When you bite on each, make a wish.) Grab a straw.

Negroni Freeze / MAKES 4 SLUSHES

These are the best happening of any hot summer day or night.

COMBINE THE GIN, campari, and vermouth and place in the freezer in an airtight container for 8 hours or overnight.

ADD FROZEN DRINK mix and orange juice to a blender with ice and blend until smooth and very thick and slushy. Spoon evenly into 4 chilled or frosted rocks glasses and garnish with sliced oranges. Grab 4 straws.

6 ounces gin such as Hendrick's, Plymouth, or Boodles (4 jiggers)

3 ounces Campari (2 jiggers)

3 ounces sweet vermouth such as Carpano Antica or Byrrh (pronounced "beer") Grand Quinquina Vermouth

TO SERVE

½ cup freshly squeezed blood orange juice or orange juice

4 cups ice cubes

4 slices of blood orange or navel orange

Frozen G&T / MAKES 4 FROZEN DRINKS

To make simple syrup, combine 1:1 ratio of water and sugar and heat to dissolve, cool, and place in a squeeze bottle. Store for 1 month in the fridge.

COMBINE THE GIN, syrup, bitters, and lime juice in an airtight container and store in the freezer for 8 hours or overnight.

FILL AN ICE CUBE TRAY with tonic and freeze for 8 hours or overnight.

IN A BLENDER, combine the frozen gin mixture, the tonic ice and plain ice cubes, and the sherbet or sorbet. Blend on medium speed, then on high speed to combine into a thick, frozen drink. Spoon into chilled or frosted rocks glasses to serve. Garnish with cucumbers and limes and serve with small spoons and straws.

7½ ounces gin such as Hendrick's, Plymouth, or Boodles (5 jiggers)

3 ounces simple syrup (2 jiggers)

5 to 6 dashes grapefruit bitters or orange bitters

Juice of 2 limes

Tonic water to fill a 12-cube tray

TO SERVE

12 ice cubes

1 scoop lime sherbet or sorbet

Thin slices of seedless cucumber

Slices of lime

19 How I Got to Carnegie Hall

When people come to our apartment, or our home way up in the woods, and are welcomed with a homemade meal I prepared, they often comment with something like, *"Wow, this is good!"* My husband, John, is always quick to reply with, "They don't give these jobs away, you know!" He's being cheeky and flip, but in a way he makes a good point. I worked hard to get to where I am.

A career is a funny combination platter of natural talent, the work you put in, accidents of plot, and dumb luck (good and bad). It seems that from birth I've lived and worked in and around food and in kitchens both industrial and home. For much of it, I've worked steady weeks of a hundred hours or more. I've washed dishes, loaded and unloaded trucks, and burned, bruised, and abused myself (body and psyche). I've also been mugged at gunpoint, twice. It hasn't been easy. But, with all of that, I wouldn't change a thing.

Because, just like in the game of Jenga, if you take out one strut, the whole thing collapses. It took being mugged for me to leave New York City.

It took leaving New York City and moving back upstate to meet Donna Carnevale, a boss who had faith in me and in my food, and who allowed me to teach a class called *30-Minute Meals* in her marketplace.

30-Minute Meals went on to become a local news segment, then a series of books produced by a one-woman powerhouse publisher, Lake Isle Press's Hiroko Kiiffner, who made a deal to sell my books in Price Chopper grocery stores. The books were a hit in Albany and the tristate area. They made me a local celebrity and got me an invitation as a last-minute guest on public radio. Yep, I cooked jambalaya on the radio, on a hot plate in a little sound studio.

One listener who liked what he heard told his friend Bob Tuschman, a VP at Food Network, to check me out. And someone gave Al Roker a copy of one of my cookbooks, *Comfort Foods: Rachael Ray's 30-Minute Meals*. Soon after, Al predicted "the storm of the century," and *Today* had a lot of guests cancel. So I got a call from Michelle, his producer, asking if I could fill in and do a food segment. My mom and I drove, white knuckled, out of the Adirondacks, where we got four feet of snow, to New York City (which got four inches). I carried my pots into *Today* in apple crates. I had to be dragged to makeup for powder—I was busy cooking and I didn't want Al to eat raw chicken and dumplings. I never watched the segment but I must've said "groovy" a lot because people stopped me for weeks after and said, "Hey, you cooked with Al! You're Groovy Girl!"

After the *Today* show, I was invited to Food Network, where I bluntly told them that I didn't belong there. I thought they'd been duped into believing I was a proper chef with a pedigree. I was a blue-collar cook. I was beer in a bottle and they were champagne. Apparently the Food Network wanted to drink more beer. They liked that I made simple food with the big promise of dinner in just thirty minutes. They liked that I didn't dress or look or talk like a chef. And even after I started a small fire on Emeril's set during the taping of my pilot, the brass there had faith and hired me.

The Food Network also gave me the opportunity to see the country and the world, all on a blue-collar budget. On local news upstate I'd taught thirty-minute meals, but I also did a small series of travel spots on things I could do within a hundred miles for less than $100, including jumping out of a plane. Food Network asked what I thought about a show they were working on, *Rich Man, Poor Man*. The concept was to give one host a huge budget and give a co-host a limited budget, and see what they could each experience in different cities and popular vacation destinations. I told them that in my experience waiting on the wealthy, the 5-star experience can look and feel much the same everywhere—fabulous but homogenized. The more interesting content is how rich life can be, even on a budget. I didn't get my old budget of $100, but I learned how to stretch *$40 a Day,* the name of my new travel show. We suffered for our art: dozens of canceled flights, scary hotel rooms, piles of luggage lost, food poisoning, chiggers, and even run-ins with the law. I still count most of those folks as friends.

Food Network let Hiroko sell my little books nationally, and for the first time in bookstores. We had several bestsellers together. The books and my work on Food Network got me an invitation to *The Oprah Winfrey Show.*

Okay, let me pause here to give you a sense of how I felt about Oprah. Back when I was offered my first TV show, the local one upstate, I was absolutely terrified. I just didn't think I was qualified and I was sure they'd figure that out and it would all end horribly. So my mom and I did what anyone would do: We wrote a letter to Oprah.

It's true. I had heard Oprah talk about how she'd been afraid to get her

OOOOOOOOO!!!!!!!
There are no words to explain how she changed the course of my life and the lives of everyone *in* my life. And there was no better way to celebrate my two-thousandth episode of television.

own local show in Chicago, and how she hadn't seen anyone like herself on TV and she didn't feel she belonged there. So I wrote her a letter saying how much I admired her and how scared I was. (I didn't get a response, for obvious reasons.)

So it's 2000-whatever and I'm on a book tour and they get me a connecting flight to Chicago to be on *Oprah*. But my flight was canceled. I was hysterical and spent most the night crying, wandering the halls of an airport trying to find another ride. I finally got to my hotel room at 3:45 AM and the car was coming for me at 6:00 AM, sharp. I pressed my skirt, tried to cool my face in ice water enough for the puffiness to go down. I pulled on my pantyhose, crammed my toes into fancy lady shoes, and off I went. On arrival I must have been a fright—the hair and makeup team looked at me with a great deal of pity. They curled my hair into big, long waves and did what they could for my still-puffy eyes. When I walked out on the stage to meet Oprah, I looked like a stalker trying to impersonate her. She was so cool, wearing jeans and a shirt. While cooking my vodka sauce, I felt overdressed, overexcited, overtired, and tongue-tied. Walking off set between segments, I thought I had bombed.

We went on break and they moved me to this chair setup where I'd sit with Oprah and have a chat. She sat down, and before the cameras started rolling again, she leaned over and took my hand, looked me in the eye, and said, in that way only Oprah

can, "I don't know what *it* is, but you have it. Let's have a nice talk." Everything around us melted. I went from feeling panic to joy. I didn't cry, miraculously. I just got filled up like I'd been driving on fumes and I made it to a gas station just in time. *Okay, you're here,* I thought. *Now just try to take a breath and talk.* It was a huge moment for me. I rediscovered myself, my belief in myself, in real time on her show! And I'm convinced I wouldn't have my *own* daytime show and all the opportunities that followed if I had not found the bravery to just keep trying things that terrify me like that show appearance, or that others might criticize me for and say I'm not up for. Oprah changed the course of my life and there's no way I can ever repay her.

I've never watched the clip of that episode. In fact, I've never watched myself on TV, ever, so I don't really know what happened, but I was invited

Every year for our anniversary, we return to the castle where we were married with a bunch of friends. One year it was under renovation. (It *has* been there a really long time, after all.) So Gloria Estefan and her family adopted us—a hundred people—and invited us to their place near Miami. This might've been our best anniversary ever because I didn't have to cook! Here's me with my feet in their pool.

back and kept going back. I did her show many times, and she joined me most recently for my two-thousandth episode.

Yes, for our two-thousandth, Oprah agreed to host *our* daytime show. Surprise guests that day also included my dear friend, the epic Tony Bennett, and my super-crush, the super-talented, super-successful 50 Cent. Curtis! I LOVE YOU! (I still apologize to my husband, also a guest that day, who was watching backstage when I accosted Curtis—awkward!) It was the most fun I've ever had at work. When Oprah hosts, you got nothing but net! She is a slam-dunk! It was a magic sparkler of a day that I can only half-remember because it all seemed a crazy dream, an absolute fantasia.

The most television I've ever produced in a year is 263 episodes. Whoa! What a ride it's been. I hope to share a few thousand more. I'm living proof that if you work hard, are grateful for it, and let that gratitude drive you, you can achieve more than you can imagine.

The first step to any great success is humility. It's finding respect for yourself through a hard day's work, no matter the job description. The ability to work at what you love usually starts with your willingness to work at anything. And work is a privilege, not a right. Working below your potential can be frustrating, but there is beauty and grace in most any job well done. I've had many bosses in my life, my mom included (she was the toughest). Without them, without any one of them, you wouldn't be reading this book and I would not be the same woman.

They don't give these jobs away, it's true. But if you hustle your ass off, you'll earn yours.

/ / /

A few recipes from memorable moments in my career.

Pancetta- or Prosciutto-Wrapped Shrimp

SERVES 4 AS AN ENTRÉE OR 6 TO 7 AS AN APPETIZER

This is a version of the first recipe I prepared at Food Network for the pilot of *30-Minute Meals*.

/ / /

PEEL AND DEVEIN THE SHRIMP, tails on. Rinse and pat them dry. Place the shrimp in a dish and dress with the zest of 1 lemon, salt, pepper, garlic, and EVOO, about 3 tablespoons or 3 turns of the bowl. Place a leaf of sage in the cavity of the back of each shrimp where it has been deveined. Wrap the shrimp with the pork in a tight, slightly overlapping layer covering the shrimp but not the tail.

HEAT A LARGE NONSTICK SKILLET over medium-high heat, add a turn of the pan of olive oil, using the remaining 1 tablespoon oil, and arrange the shrimp in the pan, well-nested and in a single layer. Cook for about 3 minutes, then turn and cook for about 3 minutes more. The shrimp should be firm and the pancetta or prosciutto crisp. Remove the shrimp to a platter. Add the wine and lemon juice to the pan, and swirl in the butter to melt. Spoon the sauce over the shrimp and serve.

20 very large shrimp, 6 to 8 count per pound, preferably, or 8 to 10 count

Zest and juice of 1 lemon

Salt and freshly ground black pepper

4 cloves garlic

About 4 tablespoons EVOO

20 large leaves of sage

20 slices of pancetta or Prosciutto di Parma

½ cup white wine or dry vermouth

2 tablespoons butter

Fettuccine alla Vodka / SERVES 4 TO 6

You Won't Be Single for Long Vodka Sauce was the first meal I made on *Oprah*. The show claimed the recipe requests jammed up their site for a bit, and the team might have just been polite to me, but it was popular, as over the years I've heard from many ladies that the promise worked and the sauce produced many proposals—most, I assume, for marriage.

/ / /

PLACE 4 TO 5 QUARTS of water in a big pot on the stove to boil for the pasta.

IN A LARGE, DEEP SKILLET over medium heat, place the EVOO, 2 turns of the pan. Add the butter, and when it foams, add the onion. Cook and stir for a few minutes, until the onion is softened. Add the garlic, season with salt, and stir in ½ teaspoon of chili paste or about ¼ teaspoon of red pepper flakes. Add the vodka and reduce by half, 2 to 3 minutes. Add the tomatoes and tear in a few leaves of basil. Reduce the heat and simmer the sauce for 10 minutes. Stir in the cream and reduce the heat to low.

SEASON THE PASTA WATER with a fat tablespoon of salt and add the fettuccine. Cook the pasta for 1 minute less than package directions, about 8 minutes for dried, 2 to 3 minutes for fresh. Have a mug or measuring cup on hand.

RESERVE ABOUT HALF A CUP of starchy, salty water and drain the pasta or transfer the pasta to the sauce with a spider. Toss the pasta with the sauce, grated cheese, and parsley, using water to loosen the sauce as necessary.

TRANSFER THE PASTA to a large serving bowl or to individual shallow bowls to serve. Pass additional cheese and top the pasta with more torn basil and chili paste or red pepper flakes.

2 tablespoons EVOO

2 tablespoons butter

1 small or medium onion, finely chopped

3 large cloves garlic, finely chopped or grated

Salt

1 teaspoon Calabrian chili paste, or ½ teaspoon crushed red pepper flakes

1 cup vodka

1 (28-ounce) can Italian crushed tomatoes

A few leaves of fresh basil, torn, plus a few whole leaves to serve

1 cup heavy cream

12 to 16 ounces fettuccine

1 handful of fresh flat-leaf parsley, finely chopped

1 generous handful of freshly grated Parmigiano-Reggiano, plus some to pass at the table

20 The Iron Cook

I was born into the food business. I was marked to be in a kitchen when I burnt my finger on an industrial stove at age two. Because I'm superstitious (as many Italians are), I believe it means something that my very first memory in life was in the kitchen. And even though it involved me getting hurt, I consider it a happy memory.

People approach their careers from different angles and for different reasons. Some become chefs to be the best in their field, the most accomplished and certified. For some, that kind of training and education is a part of who they are. It makes them feel safe. For me, being in industrial and home kitchens is my safe place, and I feel my own education in the kitchen, while not a formal one, is a journey that continues today. It was never my goal to go out and be the most accomplished or influential chef in the world. Instead, I wanted to be a great service professional. Here's my philosophy: A career is something that happens when you work as hard as possible at a job and consider the work itself the primary reward.

I can make a hell of a dinner and I can make just about anyone else believe (correctly) that they can, too. So as much as I value my gifts, I don't think that they raise me to the rank of Iron Chef. I don't put myself in a league with those folks. But I'd been doing *30-Minute Meals* for several years on Food Network, and they had asked me over and over again if I'd appear on their hit competition show. I'd always passed because, as I've said before, I'm a cook, not a chef. But they kept asking and, one fateful day in 2006, I finally agreed.

The night before the taping, I didn't sleep. I was turning over strategies in my head, mentally practicing my knife skills, and just generally panicking. My husband says he'd only ever seen me that nervous once before, the night before I was going to be throwing the first pitch at Fenway Park in Boston. But at least I'd spent three months preparing for that. (And I sent it right over the plate to Red Sox catcher Jason Varitek, who stayed in his crouch. Then I did the Toyota jump and watched my beloved Red Sox beat the Toronto Blue Jays.)

This was worse. I'd never felt more nervous or sick in my life. When I arrived at the studio, I looked white as a sheet. I couldn't eat anything, so all I had in my stomach was water, coffee, and vitamins. I was teamed up with Mario Batali, who arrived in a great mood, ready for the day. To Mario it's just food and we are here to play around and feed people. No biggie.

If you've never watched, the show works like this: Chefs are given some ingredients and a limited amount of time, and they compete in a cook-off to see who can make the best dish and be named "Iron Chef." Mario and I were a team, competing against Bobby Flay and Giada De Laurentiis. They are lovely, talented chefs who also happen to be really attractive. They arrived looking like central casting for "Successful Chefs in Top Physical Condition." Giada had an up-do that made her a statuesque beauty. She wore a tailored chef coat with floral embroidery and her name on it. I could practically see the Disney birds circling around her head. Meanwhile, I was in ten-year-old black jeans, work boots, and a white shirt from the Gap. I felt like the most uncool kid at prom. A marathon prom: It was an eighteen-hour day, no joke. In between visits to the bathroom to throw up (again, not kidding), I kept thinking, *What am I doing? Let me get this experiment over with and get out of here.*

I was cooking spaghetti in red wine, an ancient Tuscan technique I'd studied in a cookbook I'd been gifted. You cook the spaghetti literally in wine; it absorbs it and turns ruby red. And I had to use cranberries, our "secret ingredient," and combined them and the wine pasta with kale and sausage. I also remember that Mario assigned me the task of making lemon curd. Let me tell you, curd ain't my jam. To me it comes in a bottle and you put it in a hot water bath and done. To stand still for a half hour of whisking, well, I normally have a whole meal to show for that, not a tiny pot of custard.

Alton Brown was the host and seemed to come over every five minutes asking for comments. I had none. I was working as fast as possible but felt like I was frozen solid on the inside.

I would never have taken Vegas odds on it, but we won, and my dish was one of the favorites of the very long day. I "peaced out" and ran home, where I collapsed in a heap. It had been, honestly, one of the worst days of my life. I was terrified of letting down my partner and felt like I was pretending to be something I'm not, and what could be more exhausting than that?

Anytime anyone tries to call me "chef" I reject it. "I'm a cook" is my response. It's not a class thing, I just know where I don't belong. My lane is accessibility. My message is: You can do this if I can. That doesn't mean nothing I've ever made deserves a Michelin star. But that's not my audience, and it's not how I judge my life.

///

Here's my winning dish, with a few tweaks. It's a hit at the holidays, and I made it for Jacques Pépin on my show, who loved it. Can't ask for more than that!

Drunken Spaghetti with Roasted Beets / SERVES 4

Salt

1 bottle (750 ml) red wine, medium body, such as Rosso di Montalcino or Rosso di Montepulciano

1 pound spaghetti

ROASTED BEETS

2 large or 3 medium beets with abundant, leafy tops

2 tablespoons EVOO, plus more for drizzling

Salt

2 shallots, finely chopped

2 large cloves garlic, chopped

Freshly ground black pepper

A little freshly grated nutmeg

1 tablespoon balsamic drizzle or thick, aged balsamic vinegar (optional)

1 pound spaghetti cooked in red wine (see above)

Grated ricotta salata or Pecorino

½ cup chopped fresh flat-leaf parsley, or parsley and fresh mint combined

½ cup toasted, chopped pistachios—I use Sicilian, which are very bright green in color and available online from Kalustyan's

I call this "Drunken Spaghetti" for fun, but the point is the saturation of flavor and color. It marries with many ingredient choices and beets are one of my favorites, but be creative and adventurous with your own pairings. It's the technique that's fun to learn.

/ / /

BRING A LARGE POT of water to a boil for the pasta and salt it to taste.

POUR THE FULL BOTTLE of wine in a large skillet.

DROP THE PASTA in the boiling water and toss with tongs, then turn the heat under the wine to high and bring the wine to a full boil. Cook the pasta for 5 minutes, then drain it. Reserve ½ cup of the salty, starchy water just before draining.

ONCE THE WINE is boiling, reduce it for exactly 3 minutes, then add the drained pasta to it. Cook the pasta in the wine for 3 minutes, to al dente. Combine with sauce or added ingredients of choice, using the starchy water if necessary to combine.

PREHEAT THE OVEN to 425°F.

REMOVE THE BEET TOPS and stem them. Soak or rinse the beet tops and dry them. Shred them into 1-inch pieces.

TRIM THE BEETS and scrub them, then dry. Drizzle the beets with EVOO and season with salt. Place them in a tinfoil pouch and roast for 75 to 90 minutes, until tender. Cool the beets and rub off the skins with a paper towel. Shred on the large side of a box grater or with a wide-tooth Microplane.

IN A SAUTÉ PAN over medium heat, heat the 2 tablespoons EVOO, 2 turns of the pan. Add the shallots and garlic and season with salt and pepper. Stir for 3 minutes or so. Add the grated beets and heat through. Wilt the greens into the beets. Add a bit of nutmeg. Drizzle with vinegar, if using.

COMBINE THE BEETS and greens with the pasta and toss. Adjust the salt and pepper. Serve topped with cheese, herbs, and nuts.

VARIATIONS

DRUNKEN SPAGHETTI WITH SAUSAGE AND KALE
SERVES 4

2 tablespoons EVOO

1 pound sweet or hot Italian sausage or merguez lamb sausage, casings removed

2 large cloves garlic, chopped

1 bunch of lacinato kale, stemmed and sliced into 1-inch ribbons

1 pound spaghetti cooked in red wine

Grated Pecorino to toss and pass at the table

HEAT A LARGE SKILLET over medium-high heat. Add the EVOO, 2 turns of the pan. Add the sausage and brown and crumble. Add the garlic and sauté for about 2 minutes, until aromatic. Add the kale and wilt.

COMBINE THE SAUSAGE and kale with the pasta and add a fat handful of Pecorino. Serve in shallow bowls and top with more Pecorino.

DRUNKEN SPAGHETTI WITH MUSHROOMS AND CHARD
SERVES 4

1 ounce dried porcini mushrooms

1½ cups vegetable or chicken stock

3 tablespoons EVOO

¾ pound mushrooms such as hen of the woods, pulled into thin pieces, and cremini mushrooms, wiped clean and thinly sliced

Salt and freshly ground black pepper

2 tablespoons fresh thyme

1 large shallot, finely chopped

2 large cloves garlic, finely chopped

1 bunch of red Swiss chard, stemmed and sliced into 1-inch ribbons

A little freshly grated nutmeg

Juice of 1 small lemon

1 pound spaghetti cooked in red wine

Grated Parmigiano-Reggiano, for tossing and serving

½ cup peeled and toasted hazelnuts, chopped, to serve

IN A SMALL SAUCEPAN over medium heat, add the dried porcini mushrooms and stock. Simmer for 5 minutes to reconstitute the mushrooms. Remove them with a slotted spoon and chop them. Reserve the stock.

HEAT A LARGE SAUTÉ PAN over medium-high to high heat Add the EVOO, 3 turns of the pan. Add the fresh mushrooms and brown them for 12 to 14 minutes. Season the browned mushrooms with salt, pepper, and thyme. Add the shallot and garlic and stir 1 to 2 minutes more. Wilt in the greens and season them with a few grates of nutmeg. Add the lemon juice and remove the pan from the heat.

ADD THE SAUTÉED MUSHROOMS and porcinis to the pasta cooked in red wine, and use some of the porcini stock as needed to combine and keep the mixture moist and the pasta loose as you combine it with a fat handful of the grated Parmigiano-Reggiano. Serve the pasta in shallow bowls and top with more cheese and the hazelnuts.

#ihaterachaelray

Not everyone on the playground will like you. We all learn this early on, and if you're lucky, your parents at least tried to prepare you for it. If you've read this book, you know that I learned this lesson on the first day of kindergarten and am still aware of it as I write this in my fiftieth year.

That said, I don't know if anything could have prepared me for the tabloids or angry social media rants, or for a website literally dedicated to hating me—made up of a club of fanatics. It's an especially odd paradox that people would watch you every day, almost religiously, it seems, because of how deeply they hate you.

Kids can be cruel but grown-ups are worse, in that they're more practiced and precise with their cruelty. They've had years to perfect it.

So, let's clear up a few rumors and set the record straight.

For the record: I admire and appreciate the contributions of Martha Stewart to the world and our vocation. She's a forerunner, and without her, women like me might not have found our opportunities or received support in building our brands.

For the record: I deeply respected Anthony Bourdain and he remains my mother's favorite chef and television food personality. My heart breaks for the family and friends who miss him. I miss him, too.

For the record: Yes, I'm fifty and I chose not to have children of my own. I feel very fulfilled and I have worked hard to provide for my family and extended family and will continue to do so. But I didn't find my partner until thirty-seven, and if I had had a baby then it would have been considered a "geriatric pregnancy" with many elevated risks. That same year I brought home a dog, Isaboo, launched a magazine, and started a daytime TV show of 180 episodes a year while still making several series for Food Network. It would have been irresponsible to have a child then whom I could not devote myself to. And I never felt the biological clock that ticks in most women. I would never ask another woman about something so private, but I've been asked about this choice many times for decades. Asked and answered.

For the record: Rachel Roy is a designer and has always been very gracious to me. But my name is Rachael Ray. I'm a foot shorter than she is and far less glamorous. I have never met Beyoncé but I have seen her perform and she's a fierce force of a woman, very beautiful and talented. I have met Jay-Z and he was very polite, gracious. When I got caught up in their press due to a case of mistaken identity, I was shocked to be the focus of so much global hatred, and I'm allergic to bees, so all those stings from the "Beyhive" could have killed me. But, to be honest, it was kind of fun to imagine anyone thinking I'm cool enough to be hanging with any of those people on a regular basis. Most nights I'm home by six and shortly after that I'm cooking spaghetti in my pajamas and my King Kong slippers.

There are so many stories I could tell about the haters. I erased about two pages here of things people have said about me that really hurt—lies that have been told about me, my husband, my mother, and even our dog. But all that negative energy, negative words, written or spoken, have no larger purpose. Criticism is one thing; nobody's perfect. But hate for the sake of hate, spiteful and cruel, simply festers in the person who sends it into the world, rotting the mind, body, and spirit. No sense keeping it alive.

So how about we go the other way here, and instead of taking on the haters, honor the lovers?

Most of my colleagues—and I do consider them colleagues—treat me with great love. Emeril Lagasse once sang to my mom for her birthday, dripping with sweat in costume from the set of a Halloween show. I'm so honored to work with him, the master of it all, to this day on our show. Anne Burrell gave me the best time of my life with her *Worst Cooks*, and taught me that I, too, am a chef and teacher in my own right. I love you, Sparkle Horse. Guy Fieri gave me the gift of cooking with kids on TV (finally) and we turned out to be the biggest kids on set. Mario Batali nominated me to the *Time* 100. Bobby Flay taught a class for me in one of the last public school Home-Ec classes in

America down in Philly, and has cohosted some of our best shows. Mary Giuliani makes every day feel like a party. Sara Moulton gave me my smile in TV kitchens. Richard Blais has cooked thirteen meals in thirty minutes for us, no joke! Even Tony Bourdain changed his tune and started to throw love my way (most people don't know that, because the reconciliation never gets the same press as the supposed beef). Curtis Stone, Giada De Laurentiis, Graham Kerr, Josh Capon, Michael Symon, Michael Schlow, Kenny Oringer, Ryan "The Great" Scott, and on and on—there are so many who've made me believe in myself more. We all do the same thing, after all: teach people to make really good food for themselves and their families. And that's really all I want. To make life good for everyone.

When I think of all the cards and notes, letters, artwork, and, yes, food we've received at our offices, I'm overwhelmed. When I think of the families that came to be because of our show, colleagues who got married, careers that were launched, guests' lives that were improved, animals who found homes, or viewers who say I helped them get the confidence to start cooking, I'm filled with joy that no hater can take away. That I get to stand at kitchen islands every day—at the studio and at home—and do what I love for work and for play makes me feel more grateful than words can express.

21 I Never Lost a Nickel in the Restaurant Business

My feet were a size 7 through high school. Now they're an 8½, wide and callused. They look more Frodo-like than ladylike. I have a back that's strong like an ox, but it's crooked and compressing, shrinking up on me, at an alarming rate. My atlas, the top bone in my neck, sits out of alignment and pinches nerves so badly that when I'm stressed I curl inward like a turtle and cannot turn my head to the left. My right hand goes numb sometimes from carpal tunnel. Both hands are callused, like my feet, and covered with burns and scars, as are my forearms. I haven't worn polish on my fingernails in decades because I don't want to call attention to my hands.

Working in food preparation is hard on the body. But, if it's in you, in your blood, kitchens are your happy place and cooking is as good for your soul as it is for feeding any appetite. Every nick of the knife, every burn, and every ache and pain can go almost unnoticed and ultimately is more than worth it. At fifty, I could be better-looking but I couldn't be more fulfilled.

I love to wait on people. I want to give everyone more than what they've ordered. I like seeing a smile come over a person's face when I place a plate of food in front of them as they start to eat it with their eyes before it even hits their mouth. Then they take the perfect bite, close their eyes, and really taste the food. Their pleasure feeds *me*. It's exciting and addictive.

I grew up in restaurants, working in them long before I was old enough to hold working papers. My mom managed them, and she kept us with her as much as possible. One of my first memories in life is as a toddler hanging off my mother's hip while she called in orders on the wall phone of the industrial kitchen of The Carvery, our restaurant on Cape Cod, Massachusetts. One day Mom turned on the flattop grill before beginning her calls. She began "debating" prices with a purveyor and had gotten us all twisted up with the cord. She tried to hang up, then realized she'd have to unwind us first. Around we went in the opposite direction.

Often for lunch she would put slices of Swiss cheese on the flattop, letting them bubble; then she'd scrunch the cheese up with the spatula and pinch it in the middle. She'd pull them off and let them cool. Cheese bow ties. Yum! We'd have them with cups of tomato or onion soup.

Mom put me down while she finished her call. I looked up and saw the thick wooden handle of her spatula balancing on the sandwich board next to the griddle. I reached up over my head on my tippy-toes and tried to grab the handle. It was heavy and larger than I thought. I lost my grip and stumbled to the side and succeeded in grilling my thumb to the flattop grill. I can see the faded scar to this day. I consider it a mark of my destiny: working in food. I guess I did the Harry Potter scar thing long before it was cool.

Then again, maybe this event just marked me as accident prone. I did set Emeril Lagasse's kitchen on fire my first day of taping at Food Network kitchens. I was shooting a pilot for *30-Minute Meals* and I was nervous, so I kept asking questions, and I failed to notice the production staff preheating my pans for a really long time. BIG flames! I continued my luck and hacked off the tip of my left index finger on both my first day of taping *30-Minute Meals* and my daytime syndicated talk show. Both times we glued it back with Krazy Glue and liquid skin and carried on. As I've said far too many times, that finger is dead and I can stick it into a flame—and sometimes I do for a quick buck or a laugh.

Regardless, I have happily, if sometimes painfully, made a life for myself and my family by working in food. As a result, I've been asked countless times why I don't own or operate restaurants. The truth is, I've looked at more than a dozen scenarios: large and small, licensed or owned, full service to fast casual, but it never panned out.

The closest I've come to having a restaurant has been to guest chef for a night or two in someone else's. My close friends Ken Oringer of Toro NYC and Michael Schlow of The Riggsby in The Carlyle, in Washington, D.C., both asked me to guest chef at their restaurants. Both friends donated the proceeds of the event to our Yum-o! charitable organization. I've never lost a nickel in the restaurant business, but thanks to those guys I had two sold-out nights in it!

I wasn't trying for some grand plan with my menus these nights. Just started thinking about what people might want to eat, then once you write one recipe, you think about what complements it, and soon the recipes start writing themselves. Here are some highlights from what the staff and I cooked on those nights.

Guest Menu for Toro

SNACKS

Caesar Stuffed Eggs

Elsa's Chicken Liver

PRIMI

Beet Arancini

Spaghettini with Calamari in Squid Ink Ragù

ENTRÉE—SECONDI

Rolled Meatloaf with Broccoli Rabe,
Provolone, and Cherry Peppers

Garlicky Mashed Potatoes

Guest Menu for The Riggsby

SNACKS

'Nduja Deviled Eggs with Crispy Salami Bits

Sweet Onion and Roasted Garlic Dip with Potato Chips and
Green Onions

Elsa's Chicken Liver

ANTIPASTI

Roasted Lamb Meatballs in Spicy Tomato Sauce

Grilled or Roasted Artichokes with Capers and Charred Lemons

Anchovy Breadcrumb–Stuffed Roasted Peppers

PRIMI

Meze "Riggies" with Beef, Eggplant, and
Calabrian Chili Paste Ragù

Strozzapreti with Swordfish and Cherry Tomato Sauce

CONTORNI/SIDES

Escarole with Fava and Shaved Fennel

Green Tomato Salad

Roasted Broccolini and Fresh Cherry Peppers

SECONDI—ENTREES

Scottadito with Crispy Kale

Shrimp Scampi

'Nduja Deviled Eggs

WITH CRISPY SALAMI BITS / **MAKES 24 PIECES**

12 large eggs—I like Araucana blue shell because they have the brightest yolks

4 slices of deli-sliced hot soppressata

About ¼ pound 'Nduja

About ½ cup bufala ricotta or well-drained fresh ricotta

1 large clove garlic, pasted (chopped, sprinkled with a pinch of salt, and rubbed with the side of the knife to make a smooth paste)

1 teaspoon pimentón (smoked sweet paprika)

1 tablespoon EVOO

About 1½ teaspoons red wine vinegar

Salt to taste

Finely chopped celery tops

IN A LARGE SAUCEPAN, cover the eggs with cold water and bring to a full boil. Cover with a tight-fitting lid, remove from the heat, and let stand for 10 minutes. Fill a bowl with cold water. Crack the shells and let the eggs cool in the water. Peel and halve the eggs. Remove the cooked egg yolks from the whites.

PREHEAT THE OVEN to 350°F. Arrange the hot soppressata on a parchment paper–lined small baking sheet and bake for 10 to 12 minutes, until very crispy. Remove the salami and cool. Break or chop the salami into irregular bits.

CUT THE 'NDUJA into small pieces. Place the 'Nduja, hard-cooked egg yolks, ricotta, garlic, pimentón, EVOO, red wine vinegar, and salt to taste in the bowl of a food processor and pulse-process to form a mixture that is reddish orange in color and well combined.

SCRAPE THE EGG MIXTURE into a pastry bag, or use a plastic food storage bag and cut ½ inch off one corner to create a pastry bag. Fill the egg whites. Top the eggs with chopped celery greens and crispy salami bits.

Caesar Stuffed Eggs / MAKES 24 PIECES

CROUTON CRUMBS

3 tablespoons butter

1 tablespoon EVOO

1 clove garlic, crushed

1 cup homemade breadcrumbs from stale white peasant-style bread

½ cup grated Romano

Freshly ground black pepper

EGGS

12 large eggs plus 1 egg yolk

Juice of 1½ lemons

About 2 teaspoons Worcestershire sauce

About 2 teaspoons coarsely ground black pepper

About 2 teaspoons Dijon mustard

About ½ cup grated Pecorino Romano (a couple of handfuls)

1 fat clove garlic

6 anchovy fillets

About ½ cup EVOO

1 cup minced small inner leaves of romaine lettuce

PREHEAT THE OVEN to 375°F.

IN A SMALL SKILLET over medium heat, melt the butter. Add the EVOO and garlic and swirl for 1 minute. Add the breadcrumbs and toss to combine and evenly coat the bread. Arrange the breadcrumbs on a small rimmed baking sheet. Cover with cheese and season with pepper. Bake for 8 to 10 minutes, until the breadcrumbs are a deep golden and crispy.

IN A LARGE SAUCEPAN, cover the whole eggs with cold water and bring to a full boil. Cover with a tight-fitting lid and remove from the heat. Let stand for 10 minutes. Fill a bowl with cold water. Crack the shells and let the eggs cool in the water. Peel and halve the eggs.

PLACE THE EGG YOLK in the bowl of a food processor and add the lemon juice, Worcestershire, pepper, mustard, cheese, garlic, and anchovies. Pulse to combine, then turn on the processor and stream in the EVOO to form a thick Caesar dressing.

PLACE THE YOLKS from the hard-boiled eggs in a large bowl and break them up with a fork. Add half of the lettuce and about two-thirds of the dressing, adding in more to taste—the mixture should not be too wet.

SCRAPE THE EGG MIXTURE into a pastry bag, or use a plastic food storage bag and cut ½ inch off one corner to create a pastry bag. Fill the egg whites. Top the eggs with crispy breadcrumbs and the remaining finely chopped romaine.

Sweet Onion and Roasted Garlic Dip

WITH POTATO CHIPS AND GREEN ONIONS **/ MAKES ABOUT 3 ROUNDED CUPS**

PREHEAT THE OVEN to 400°F. Drizzle the cut end of the garlic bulb with olive oil and season with salt and pepper. Wrap the garlic in a foil pouch and roast for 35 to 40 minutes, until sweet and soft and caramelized. Cool the garlic, push the pulp from the jackets, and paste.

IN A 12-INCH SKILLET over medium-low heat, heat the 2 tablespoons olive oil, 2 turns of the pan. Add the onions and season with salt, the ground thyme, sugar, and white pepper. Cook the onions low and slow, stirring often, for about 35 minutes, to caramelize them. Add the vinegar and ½ cup water. Raise the heat to medium-high and allow the water to cook out. Cool the onions.

IN A BOWL COMBINE the onions, pasted garlic, and yogurt. Adjust the salt. Transfer to a serving dish and garnish with minced chives and petals of chive flowers. Serve with crispy potato chips and scallions.

1 large bulb garlic, halved across to expose cloves

2 tablespoons olive oil, plus more for drizzling

Salt and freshly ground black pepper

2 large Vidalia or other sweet onions, finely chopped

1 teaspoon ground thyme (not leaves or fresh)

1 teaspoon sugar

1 teaspoon white pepper

1 tablespoon apple cider vinegar

1½ cups Fage or other Greek yogurt

Minced chives and chive flowers to garnish

Crispy potato chips, sturdy enough for dipping

Trimmed scallions (white and light green parts), for dipping

Beet Arancini / MAKES 25 TO 30 RICE BALLS

PREHEAT THE OVEN to 425°F.

TRIM THE BEETS and place them on double layers of foil. Drizzle them with olive oil, season with salt and pepper, and form a foil pouch. Roast the beets for about 1 hour, until tender. Remove from the oven and let sit until cool enough to handle. Wipe the skins from the beets with paper towels and grate the beets on the widest holes of a box grater. Set aside. This makes approximately 2 cups of grated beets.

IN A MEDIUM SAUCE POT over low heat, warm the stock.

IN A ROUND-BOTTOMED PAN over medium-high heat, add and heat the 2 tablespoons olive oil, 2 turns of the pan. Then add the onion and garlic and soften for a few minutes while stirring with a wooden spoon or risotto spoon. Add the rice and season with salt, pepper, thyme, and allspice. Stir for 2 minutes more. Add the vermouth and let it absorb while stirring. Begin adding the stock a few ladles at a time. Stir vigorously to develop the starches. From the point at which the stock is added, the process for cooking the risotto should take 18 minutes to al dente. After about 15 minutes, before the final addition of stock, add the beets and stir for 1 minute. Add the butter and about 1 cup of grated cheese and stir for 1 minute more. Taste and, if needed, add the last ladle or two of liquid; if the rice is very creamy and starchy and cooked to al dente, do not add the last of the stock.

POUR THE RISOTTO onto a parchment paper–lined baking sheet to cool. Cool to room temperature, then chill to cool completely.

SET UP A BREADING STATION: flour; eggs; and breadcrumbs mixed with the remaining 1 cup grated cheese, salt and pepper, orange zest, and parsley.

HEAT THE FRYING OIL in a tabletop fryer or Dutch oven/frying pan to 350°F.

ROLL THE RISOTTO in 1½- to 2-inch balls and coat 5 or 6 at a time. Fry in batches for about 5 minutes, to a deep golden brown. Drain on a paper towel–lined plate or butcher paper, then serve warm or at room temperature.

2 medium beets

2 tablespoons EVOO, plus more for drizzling

Salt and freshly ground black pepper

6 cups vegetable stock

1 small onion, finely chopped

2 cloves garlic, finely chopped

1½ cups Arborio or Carnaroli rice

1 tablespoon fresh thyme leaves, finely chopped

About ¼ teaspoon ground allspice (a good pinch)

About ¾ cup red vermouth or fruity red wine

2 tablespoons butter

2 cups freshly grated Parmigiano-Reggiano

1 cup flour

4 eggs, lightly beaten

2 cups breadcrumbs

1 scant tablespoon dried orange zest (if you can't find this, zest 1 navel orange on a paper towel and microwave for 2 minutes, then lightly rub the zest between your fingers to break it up)

1 handful of fresh flat-leaf parsley, finely chopped

Enough frying oil per manufacturer's instructions for tabletop fryers, or 2 quarts oil for Dutch oven or cast-iron frying pan

Elsa's Chicken Liver / MAKES ABOUT 3 CUPS SPREAD

PER POUND OF CHICKEN LIVERS

½ cup (1 stick) butter

6 medium or 4 large yellow-skinned onions, sliced

2 large fresh bay leaves

1 teaspoon ground thyme

1 teaspoon ground white pepper

2 teaspoons coarsely ground black pepper

Salt

2 large cloves garlic, crushed

1 pound chicken livers, trimmed and patted dry

¼ cup brandy

1 cup white wine

TO SERVE

Toasted wheat or white bread rounds, rubbed with halved garlic cloves and drizzled with EVOO, or white and sprouted-wheat toast points, or whole-grain crispbreads. Allow a minimum of 4 toasts per person.

My mom, Elsa, taught me how to prepare chicken livers. Lots of butter and onions are the key, and a little ground thyme. These livers are most delicious as is, warm on toast. For showmanship sometimes I serve them topped with crispy roasted hen of the woods mushrooms and shallots on top or with raw, thinly sliced shallots, sliced cornichons, and fancy-flavored mustard such as Dijon with cassis. Leftover livers remain a delicious spread cold or warm but we warm through with a bit of chicken stock, to loosen it up enough to fill a pastry bag. We stuff large ravioli with livers (see Raviolo with Chicken Livers and Truffles, page 225).

/ / /

HEAT A LARGE SKILLET over medium heat and melt the butter. When the foam subsides, add the onions, bay leaves, thyme, white pepper, black pepper, and salt. Stir frequently for 15 minutes, until the onions soften. Add the garlic and cook for 15 to 20 minutes more, until the onions are soft and light caramel in color. Push the mixture to the sides of the skillet and raise the heat to medium-high. Add the livers to the center of the pan and season with salt and coarse black pepper. Cook the livers, tossing with tongs as needed, for 5 to 6 minutes, until browned and caramelized at the edges and cooked through. Douse the entire pan with the brandy and shake—it'll flame up a bit. Add the wine and let it absorb. Combine the onions and livers and remove and discard the bay leaves. Place the livers in the bowl of a food processor in 2 batches and grind until a few coarse bits of liver remain in a mostly smooth dip. Transfer to a serving bowl and mound the livers up.

Escarole with Fava and Shaved Fennel / SERVES 6 TO 8

SOAK THE ONION and fennel in ice-cold water until ready to use. Drain well.

REMOVE THE FAVA BEANS from their pods. Fill a medium saucepan with water, not quite to the top. Bring to a boil and add the favas. Boil for 3 minutes. Meanwhile, prepare an ice bath: Fill a large bowl with cold water and add a few ice cubes. Remove the beans with a spider and cold shock the beans in the ice bath. Drain the beans and remove their thin shells.

TOSS THE ESCAROLE with the onion, fennel, fennel fronds, favas, lemon juice, salt, pepper, cheese, and EVOO.

1 white onion, halved, peeled, and very thinly sliced

1 bulb fennel, quartered, cored, and very thinly sliced; reserve ½ cup fronds, coarsely chopped

1 cup fava beans

1 large head escarole, cleaned and coarsely chopped

Juice of 2 lemons

Salt and freshly ground black pepper

Shaved Parmigiano-Reggiano

¼ cup EVOO

Green Tomato Salad / SERVES 4

PLACE THE TOMATOES in a fine mesh strainer. Salt them and let them drain for 20 to 30 minutes.

IN A SHALLOW DISH, combine the tomatoes, cucumber, onion, parsley and mint, chili pepper, lime juice, and EVOO. Adjust the salt and add black pepper to taste.

3 large green tomatoes, cored, quartered, and thinly sliced

Salt

1 Persian cucumber or ⅓ seedless English cucumber, thinly sliced

½ white onion, thinly sliced

1 cup fresh flat-leaf parsley and fresh mint combined, chopped

1 large jalapeño or other green chili, seeded and thinly sliced

Juice of 2 limes

About ¼ cup EVOO

Freshly ground black pepper

Spaghettini with Calamari in Squid Ink Ragù / SERVES 6

3 tablespoons EVOO

1 small bulb fennel, quartered, cored, and finely chopped

1 small red onion, finely chopped

2 small ribs celery with leafy tops, finely chopped

6 cloves garlic, finely chopped or grated

Salt

1 tablespoon Calabrian chili paste, or 1½ teaspoons crushed red pepper flakes (scant ½ palmful)

3 tablespoons squid ink

1 cup dry vermouth

1 (14-ounce) can diced or crushed tomatoes

1 cup passata or tomato sauce

A few leaves of fresh basil, torn

1 pound spaghettini (thin spaghetti)

1 pound calamari, cleaned and cut into ¼-inch rings plus tentacles

¼ cup preserved lemon, chopped, plus 2 tablespoons juice

¼ cup fresh flat-leaf parsley, chopped

¼ cup Sicilian pistachios, toasted and chopped

Grated or shaved Pecorino (optional)

IN A LARGE POT, heat water to a boil for the pasta.

IN A LARGE, DEEP SKILLET over medium to medium-high heat, heat the EVOO, 3 turns of the pan. Add the fennel, onion, celery, and garlic. Season with salt and stir for 5 minutes, until the vegetables soften. Add the chili paste, squid ink, and vermouth and reduce by half, about 10 minutes. Add the tomatoes, passata, and basil. Reduce the heat to medium-low to medium.

SEASON THE PASTA WATER liberally with salt. Cook the pasta for about 1½ to 2 minutes less than the package directions, 5 to 6 minutes. Reserve a mug of starchy water and drain the pasta. Add the calamari to the sauce and cook for 5 minutes. Transfer the drained pasta to the sauce. Toss with half the lemon bits and their juice and half the parsley. Adjust the salt. Stir until the pasta is cooked to al dente, using the reserved pasta water to loosen the sauce as needed. Serve the pasta in shallow bowls topped with the remaining preserved lemon, the remaining parsley, and the pistachios. Pass the cheese, if serving.

Meze "Riggies" with Beef and Eggplant Ragù / SERVES 6

PEEL HALF THE SKIN in stripes from the eggplant and trim the ends. Cut into planks or steaks ¼ to ½ inch thick, then dice the planks. Salt the eggplant and drain in a strainer or on towels for 30 minutes, tossing occasionally.

IN A DUTCH OVEN over high heat, heat the olive oil, 3 turns of the pan. Add the beef and season with salt and pepper. Brown and crumble the beef until crispy at the edges. Add the garlic, fennel seeds, fennel pollen, oregano, and chili paste and stir to combine. Add the eggplant and cook for 5 to 6 minutes, until softened. Add the sun-dried tomato paste and stir for 1 minute more. Add the vermouth and let it absorb. Add the stock and tomatoes and break the tomatoes up a bit with a wooden spoon. Reduce the heat to low and stir in the basil.

SALT A LARGE POT OF BOILING WATER liberally and cook the pasta to 1 to 2 minutes shy of al dente. Reserve ½ to ¾ cup of the starchy water and transfer the drained pasta to a large skillet. Add a fat handful of cheese, some sauce, and pasta water as needed. Serve the pasta in shallow bowls topped with a generous amount of sauce, mint and parsley, and more cheese.

1 large, heavy, firm eggplant

Salt

3 tablespoons olive oil

1½ pounds ground beef, 80% lean

Freshly ground black pepper

4 cloves garlic, chopped or grated

1½ teaspoons fennel seeds

1 teaspoon fennel pollen

1½ teaspoons dried oregano leaves, lightly crushed (½ palmful)

1 rounded tablespoon Calabrian chili paste

3 tablespoons sun-dried tomato paste

1 cup red sweet vermouth

1 cup beef stock

1 (28-ounce) can San Marzano tomatoes

A few leaves of fresh basil, torn

1 pound meze rigatoni or other short-cut pasta

Freshly grated Pecorino Romano

Finely chopped fresh mint and fresh flat-leaf parsley combined

Strozzapreti with Swordfish and Cherry Tomato Sauce / SERVES 6

SAUCE

About ¼ cup EVOO

6 anchovy fillets

4 large cloves garlic, thinly sliced

1 tablespoon Calabrian chili paste

About 4 tablespoons Italian
capers in brine, drained

About 1 cup green Cerignola olives,
pitted and coarsely chopped

1 cup dry vermouth

3 packages of cherry tomatoes on
the vine or 1½ pints cherry tomatoes,
halved (about 5 cups total)

1 cup chopped fresh mint and
fresh flat-leaf parsley combined

PASTA AND SWORDFISH

1 pound fresh or dried strozzapreti pasta

4 thin swordfish steaks, each ¼ inch
thick and 1½ pounds before they are
trimmed of bloodline and skin and
diced into ¼-inch pieces

About 3 tablespoons olive oil

IN A LARGE SKILLET over medium heat, heat the EVOO, 4 turns of the pan. Melt the anchovies into the oil, breaking them up with a wooden spoon. Add the garlic, chili paste, capers, and olives and stir for 1 minute. Add the vermouth and reduce for 1 minute more. Add the tomatoes, cover the pan with a tight-fitting lid, and cook for 20 minutes, till the tomatoes slump. Add half the mint and parsley and reduce the heat to low or turn it off until ready to serve.

COOK THE PASTA in well-salted water. For dried pasta, reserve 1 cup of the salty water and then drain the pasta. Transfer it to the sauce 1 to 2 minutes shy of cooking time for al dente.

IN A NONSTICK SKILLET over medium-high to high heat, cook the swordfish in the olive oil for 2 to 3 minutes, until lightly browned. (You can cook the fish in batches; just cover the cooked swordfish to keep warm.)

TOSS THE PASTA with a little of its salty water (if using dried), the swordfish, and the sauce. Serve with the remaining mint and parsley on top.

Scottadito with Crispy Kale / SERVES 4

Leave time for the lamb to sit in the marinade overnight before preparation.

/ / /

USING A MEAT MALLET, pound each chop very thin, to ¼ inch. Season the chops with salt and pepper.

MAKE THE MARINADE: In the bowl of a food processor, combine the anchovies, capers, lemon zest, garlic, sage, and EVOO. Pulse the mixture to form a loose paste. Using a rubber spatula, transfer the mixture to a large plastic food storage bag or shallow dish. Add the lamb and coat evenly in the marinade. Place in the fridge overnight. Bring to room temperature before cooking.

MAKE THE KALE: Preheat the oven to 500°F. Position the oven rack one rung above the center. Place a wire rack inside a large rimmed baking sheet and arrange half the kale on the rack, filling the tray. Lightly spray the kale on each side and season with salt and pepper. Roast the kale for 4 to 5 minutes, until brown and crispy. Repeat with the second batch of kale. Line a large board or serving platter with brown parchment paper and loosely arrange the bed of crispy kale.

COOK THE LAMB: Preheat the grill to high and spray the grill rack with oil, or heat a cast-iron plancha or grill pan over high heat. Add the lamb and char, cooking for 4 minutes or so, then turn and cook until the chops are crisp at the edges. Char the lemon halves in a pan or on the grill for about 2 minutes, until caramelized and browned. The chops can also be broiled on high for about 10 minutes, turning once.

ARRANGE THE CHOPS on the bed of kale and douse them with the juice of the charred lemons.

12 frenched lamb rib chops

Salt and freshly ground black pepper

6 anchovy fillets

¼ cup capers in brine, drained

Zest of 2 lemons—after zesting, cut the lemons in half and reserve for grilling

4 cloves garlic, crushed

24 leaves of fresh sage, coarsely chopped

About ½ cup EVOO

1 large bundle of lacinato kale, stemmed, leaves left whole

Olive oil cooking spray

Rolled Meatloaf

WITH BROCCOLI RABE, PROVOLONE, AND CHERRY PEPPERS / SERVES 6

Salt

1 large bundle of broccoli rabe
or broccolini, trimmed

½-pound chunk of sharp provolone

1 pound ground beef

½ pound ground veal

1 pound bulk sweet Italian sausage

Freshly ground black pepper

1 cup coarse breadcrumbs

¼ cup whole milk

1 large egg, lightly beaten

1 cup grated Parmigiano-Reggiano

3 cloves garlic, grated or finely chopped

2 tablespoons finely chopped
fresh rosemary

About ½ cup pickled hot Italian
cherry peppers, sliced or whole,
drained and chopped

EVOO for liberal drizzling

SAUCE

3 tablespoons EVOO

1 small onion, finely chopped

1 rib celery, finely chopped

2 large cloves garlic, chopped or grated

Salt and freshly ground black pepper

2 tablespoons rosemary

¼ cup sun-dried tomato paste

1 cup sweet red vermouth or red wine

1 cup beef consommé or stock

1 (28-ounce) can San Marzano tomatoes

MAKE THE MEATLOAF: Preheat the oven to 375°F.

IN A LARGE SAUCEPAN, bring a few inches of water to a boil, salt the water, and add broccoli rabe or broccolini. Cook for 3 to 4 minutes, until just shy of tender. Drain well and chop into 1½-inch pieces.

SHRED THE PROVOLONE CHEESE on a coarse-tooth grater. Set aside.

COMBINE BEEF, veal, sausage, salt, pepper, breadcrumbs, milk, egg, Parmigiano-Reggiano, garlic, and rosemary in large bowl. Then roll out the meatloaf on a parchment paper–lined baking sheet to a ¾-inch-thick rectangle about 12 x 15 inches. Scatter the shredded provolone across the meat and top with the broccoli rabe or broccolini, then the cherry peppers. Stop a few inches short of the end of the rectangle. Roll the loaf and press the seam together to set. Smooth the roll of meatloaf and drizzle with EVOO. Roast for 1 hour, or until the internal temperature reaches 150°F to 155°F. Let rest for a few minutes before serving.

MAKE THE SAUCE: Meanwhile, in a sauce pot or Dutch oven over medium to medium-high heat, heat the EVOO, 3 turns of the pan. Add the onion and celery and stir for 3 minutes, until light golden and soft. Add the garlic and season with salt and pepper. Add the rosemary and tomato paste and stir for 1 minute more. Add the vermouth and combine. Then add the consommé and tomatoes, breaking the tomatoes up with a wooden spoon. Simmer the sauce for 30 minutes at a low bubble.

SLICE MEATLOAF and set each slice in a generous puddle of red wine sauce.

Shrimp Scampi / SERVES 4 AS AN ENTRÉE

IN A WIDE PAN over medium-high heat, toast the shrimp shells and heads in the EVOO, about 2 turns of the pan. Add leek, onion, lemon, garlic, peppercorns, bay leaf, and herb bundle. Sweat the vegetables for a few minutes. Add vermouth and reduce by half. Add the stock and bring to a boil. Reduce the heat to medium and simmer for 45 minutes. Strain the stock with a fine mesh strainer. Return the stock to the pan and bring to a boil. Reduce to about 1½ cups of concentrated stock.

IN A BOWL combine the garlic and EVOO. Add the shrimp and salt them, toss, and refrigerate for 1 hour uncovered before the preparation.

IN A LARGE PAN over medium-high to high heat, heat 2 tablespoons olive oil, 2 turns of the pan. Add the shrimp and sear for 2 to 3 minutes, then turn, season with salt and pepper, and cook for 1 minute more. Remove the shrimp from the pan. Add the remaining olive oil, another 2 turns of the pan. Add the minced celery and garlic and stir for 1 to 2 minutes. Add the chili paste, stir, then add the vermouth and let it absorb. Add the stock and let it bubble and reduce for 1 minute. Then add the butter and parsley and swirl the pan. Add the shrimp back to the pan and turn to coat. Cook the shrimp through 2 minutes more and douse with the lemon juice. Add the parsley.

TO SERVE, in each of 4 shallow bowls, place a charred slice of toast topped with 5 to 6 shrimp and a quarter of the sauce.

SHRIMP STOCK

Heads and shells of 20 to 24 jumbo shrimp or prawns

About 2 tablespoons EVOO

1 leek, quartered and cleaned

1 small onion, halved

1 lemon, sliced

1 bulb garlic, halved across

8 peppercorns

1 large bay leaf

1 small bundle of fresh flat-leaf parsley and fresh thyme, tied with kitchen string

1 cup dry vermouth

1 quart chicken stock

SHRIMP MARINADE

4 cloves garlic, grated or chopped

2 tablespoons EVOO

24 large shrimp, deveined, tails on (heads and peels reserved for the shrimp stock)

2 teaspoons kosher salt

SCAMPI

¼ cup olive oil

Salt and freshly ground black pepper

1 rib celery with leafy tops, finely chopped

4 cloves garlic, thinly sliced

2 scant tablespoons Calabrian chili paste

½ cup dry vermouth

¾ cup shrimp stock (recipe above)

3 tablespoons butter

1 handful of fresh flat-leaf parsley, finely chopped

Juice of 1 lemon

Charred bread, 1 slice per portion

22 What Chefs *Really* Eat

I'm a cook, not a chef, but I have lived and worked in kitchens all my life and many of my closest friends are chefs. Yes, people who work in food appreciate fine food, and we're lucky to sit at some of the world's best tables. When food people travel, it's no surprise, eating is often at the top of the list in making our plans. But, in my experience, chefs and cooks are not picky eaters. We eat standing up, out of buckets, or out of pots or pans with our fingers, scooping the last of something before sending the pan to the dishwasher. We mop up our messes with ends of bread, gulp down a slug of stock or soup or sauce and call it dinner. How many times have you seen the family cook in your home sit and eat almost nothing? That's because they've already eaten, sort of. Also, cooks and chefs are, by training, thrifty eaters, loath to waste any ingredient. We take pride in feasting on our scraps. I once watched Jacques Pépin take the rinds and scraps of eight cheeses, trim off the mold and dried-out, dead bits, then drop them in the food processor with white wine and garlic. A few pulses and it was the most delightful dip, served hot or cold. AKC: Always keep cheese. And always keep good bread in the freezer to eat it with.

When you work all day in the kitchen, part of your job is to taste and test every component of every dish, over and over again until each is just right. After a day and/or night, or both, of preparing food for others, the food you've been making loses its appeal. You're done with it, you want something else, something decidedly different, something for yourself. Often, you want something simple—scrambled eggs, a juicy, cheesy burger, hot or cold fried chicken. Carbonara works, too, and bacon and eggs spaghetti is a middle-of-the-night gem of a dish. Comfort foods. John and I always keep salami and cheeses and pickled vegetables on hand as well. Emergency provisions.

Years ago, I cocreated an event with my friend Lee Brian Schrager for the Wine & Food Festival, first in South Beach and later in New York City. I wanted people to get to know some of the world's finest chefs, so I challenged them to come to even ground, to come to the bun and place their mad skills into *their* idea of the perfect burger. The American economy has had some bumpy roads over the last few decades, and when it got shaky and people were eating out less, fine-dining chefs won them back by making their food more affordable and accessible. Food trucks, as well as fast-casual and takeaway restaurants, became the new norm, and these food formats were being led by some of the world's finest chefs and restaurateurs. Burgers started popping up everywhere, friendly, unassuming, unpretentious, and you can eat them with your hands. And chefs and restaurateurs LOVE them. Danny Meyer is the best example: He has many fine-dining restaurants to his credit, but none as successful as his main street chain Shake Shack (which will be arriving in your town soon, if it hasn't already), with its classic griddled burgers, bacon cheese fries, and shakes.

I cocreated the Burger Bash, a charity cook-off in South Beach and New York City, because what's more fun than hot buns? Thanks to the chefs for their happy patties. I flip for all of them.

We called our event Burger Bash and the chefs ate it up—Michael Schlow, Michael Symon, Bobby Flay. Together we've slung enough patties to donate millions of dollars to support culinary education and fight hunger, and celebs like Neil Patrick Harris and Chrissy Teigen have joined the fun. I hope it goes on forever, because it's a bunch of patties, and a party, that really stack up. Wanna eat like a chef? Belly up to a good burger.

Here are a few things that I crave after a long, hard day at work.

Fried Onion S'mack Burgers / SERVES 4

SAUCE

½ cup sour cream, Greek yogurt, or Fabanaise or mayonnaise

¼ cup ketchup

3 tablespoons pickle relish

About 2 teaspoons Worcestershire sauce

BURGERS

2 medium onions, peeled and sliced using a mandoline

1½ pounds ground beef, 80% lean

About 1 tablespoon canola or peanut or other neutral oil

8 slices of American cheese

4 large, soft burger rolls, plain or sesame

Sliced dill/gherkin pickles

Chopped iceberg lettuce

You smack these burgers down, literally, with a burger spatula to "seal the deal" between the beef and the onions, but smack also refers to the sauce that makes these patties taste a little like a Big Mac—and you'll be smacking your lips for sure! Fried onion burgers, a.k.a. Oklahoma-style burgers, are all about how thin you can shave the onion. You need a mandoline. Mandolines, if you don't have one, are inexpensive and you can get one delivered from Amazon by tomorrow morning.

/ / /

MAKE THE SAUCE: Combine the sour cream, ketchup, pickle relish, and Worcestershire in a small bowl.

MAKE THE BURGERS: Heat a large cast-iron skillet or griddle over medium-high heat.

SLICE THE ONIONS on the thinnest blade setting of a mandoline, carefully.

PLACE THE BEEF in a bowl and score to separate into 4 portions. Roll the beef into balls.

DRIZZLE THE OIL in the pan or over the meat balls and place the meat in the pan with 3 inches separating each portion. Top each ball with a quarter of the onions and press the meat into flat patties, bonding the onions to the meat. Cook the beef for 3 to 4 minutes and flip, cook, and press for 2 minutes. Add the cheese, 2 slices per burger, and cook for 2 minutes more, 7 to 8 minutes total between both sides.

CONSTRUCT THE HAMBURGERS: bottom of bun, 2 tablespoons sauce, pickles, lettuce, patty, 1 tablespoon sauce, and top of bun.

Steak 'n' Frico Eggs / SERVES 4

PREHEAT A CAST-IRON SKILLET over medium-high to high heat. Season the steaks with salt and pepper on both sides.

MAKE THE SALSA VERDE: In the bowl of a food processor, combine the shallot, garlic, parsley tops, mixed herbs, salt and pepper, capers, anchovies if you have, lemon juice, and vinegar. Pulse-process to combine. Then stream in the EVOO and transfer the sauce to a small bowl.

MAKE THE CHEESE CRISPS AND EGGS: Heat a small nonstick skillet over medium heat. Add ¼ cup of the Parmigiano-Reggiano to coat the bottom of the pan. When the cheese begins to melt, top with 1 large egg and cover the pan with a lid or foil. Cook until the cheese is golden and crispy at the edges and the yolk is at the desired doneness. Cool the egg and frico for 1 minute or so, then remove from the skillet. Repeat with the other 3 eggs.

MAKE THE STEAKS: Cook the steaks in the cast-iron skillet for about 3 minutes per side, then rest for 5 minutes.

SERVE THE STEAKS next to the frico eggs and top with the salsa verde. Garnish the plates with hot pickled cherry peppers.

4 (6-ounce) portions of flank or skirt steak

Salt and freshly ground black pepper

1 shallot, coarsely chopped

2 cloves garlic, crushed

1 cup packed fresh flat-leaf parsley tops

½ cup packed mixed herbs of choice— combine any of tarragon, basil, mint, and cilantro

2 tablespoons capers, drained

2 or 3 anchovy fillets, if you have on hand

Juice of 1 lemon

2 tablespoons white or wine vinegar

About ½ cup EVOO

About 1 cup grated Parmigiano-Reggiano

4 large eggs

Italian pickled cherry peppers, sliced

Fried Chicken Sandwiches / SERVES 4 TO 6

About 3 cups frying oil, such as safflower or canola

1½ cups flour

Salt and freshly ground black pepper

2 teaspoons white pepper (⅔ palmful)

2 teaspoons ground cumin (⅔ palmful)

2 teaspoons smoked paprika (pimentón) or paprika (⅔ palmful)

1 cup buttermilk

2 to 3 boneless, skinless chicken breasts, halved horizontally into 4 to 6 cutlets, or boneless thighs, well-trimmed

TO SERVE

Soft burger buns, finely chopped white onions, chopped iceberg lettuce, bread-and-butter pickles, hot sauce and/or honey or store-bought hot honey

PREHEAT THE OVEN to 300°F.

POUR ABOUT 2 INCHES of oil into a large cast-iron skillet or a Dutch oven. Heat the oil over medium-high heat to about 360°F for frying. Place a wire rack inside a rimmed baking sheet lined with foil next to the frying pan or pot.

COMBINE THE FLOUR with the salt, black pepper, white pepper, cumin, and smoked paprika. Divide the flour into 2 shallow dishes. Place a dish of buttermilk between the dishes of flour. Dredge the chicken in the flour, then dip in the buttermilk, and then dredge in the second dish of flour. Fry 2 or 3 pieces of chicken at a time for 6 to 7 minutes, until crispy and deep golden. Drain the chicken pieces. Transfer the cooked chicken to a rack and keep in the hot oven.

CONSTRUCT THE SANDWICHES: bun bottom, white onions, lettuce, pickles, fried chicken, hot sauce and/or hot honey, bun top.

Spicy Pickleback and Beer / MAKES ONE DRINK

1½ ounces rye whiskey

1 slice of fresh jalapeño

1 sprig of fresh dill

1½ ounces pickle juice

1 can lager beer

JOHN SAYS: What chefs really *drink*. Bottoms up!

POUR THE WHISKEY into a shot glass.

MUDDLE THE JALAPEÑO and dill at the bottom of a cocktail shaker. Add the pickle juice, shake well with ice, and double strain into a shot glass.

DRINK THE SHOT of whiskey and chase immediately with the pickle juice shot. Follow with the can of beer while you eat late-night greasy food.

Epilogue: The Next 50

January 17 is Michelle Obama's birthday. And on that day this year in 2019, *I* was the one who got a great gift! Mrs. Obama's staff reached out to me, asking if I would like to join her on tour for her memoir, *Becoming,* as her moderator in one or two cities. Wow was all I could think, as I quickly said yes. A little over a month later, we met up in Austin, bringing together one of my favorite places and one of my favorite people, all in front of a crowd of 17,000. It was electric, and one of the biggest highlights and honors of my life so far.

It reminded me that in America, anyone can become a Rachael Ray or a Michelle Obama. She's from a working class family from the South Side of Chicago. I'm a girl from Upstate New York with what I thought were no special talents. My grandpa came here as a child from Sicily, one of fourteen children, and managed to provide for ten children of his own. My mom, the first of those ten, successfully ran companies and kitchens for more than fifty years. Here, anything is possible. Every day we wake up is another opportunity to grow, to try something new, to become something more. I am grateful to be working and growing and learning every day of my life. I am enthusiastic and childlike in my excitement for the years to come.

It's been another busy year: a reboot of *30-Minute Meals* on Food Network for a new generation of hungry viewers. The daytime show hits its fourteenth season, and my magazine, my marriage, and my Isaboo will be fourteen this year, too. There are also many new beginnings. I'm celebrating year one of our online community/shopping site, Moxie Made, and my own line of sustainable handbags and accessories, Convalore. My furniture and home brands continue to grow, as well as our pet and human food businesses. Also, because of the support of these businesses, I have been able to contribute more money to help kids, my community, and animals than I ever dreamed I would earn in my lifetime.

I've never worked for the pursuit of money. I simply worked hard and I am very grateful for every job from dishwasher to daytime television host. I end each of my days knowing I left it all on the field, with the prayer my mom taught me when I was a little girl. It makes me feel closer to her and reminds me of who she wants me to be. Who I want to be.

> *Goodnight dear God, I love you dear God*
> *Please give me the knowledge and the courage*
> *To help others and to do good*
> *God bless, help, protect, and forgive*
> *Amen*

I hope to keep doing all of the above for another fifty.

Acknowledgments

I wanted to make a list of all the people who have developed our shows, magazine, books, and licensing brand to date, everyone who helped me along the way. But to thank every soul from my first fifty years, I'd need a registry as thick as this book.

Thank you to all my colleagues, from interns to executives. I apologize for my learning process and for all the times when I was impatient or just didn't listen. Some of you have been with me for decades—whoa! Together we've come a long way, and I hope it was not for me but for what we all believe in—that everyone deserves a sense of adventure, better food, and an easier way in life. We believe a rich life has less to do with money and more to do with love. I'm so grateful for all you do and all you are.

Thank you to everyone at CBS, Watch Entertainment, *Rachael Ray Every Day* and the Meredith Corporation, Food Network/Scripps/Discovery, and the Rachael Ray brand.

Thank you to the people who helped me get my start at Food Network, Bob Tuschman and Kathleen Finch. (Kathleen recently hired me again to cook up more *30 Minute Meals* for a new generation of cooks!) Mark Dissin produced the original series, every episode. My PIC and food producer Emily Reiger not only gave me my legs at FN, but has been with me every workday

since, including the 2,100+ episodes (so far) of the daytime show. That show would never have existed without Brooke Johnson, former president of Food Network, who took me to syndicated TV and kept me on cable. She became and remains a mentor and dear friend. Wade Sheeler was our fearless leader. Brian Lucky Lahaire and Marc and Nancy Daniels, our gang: We all remain friends to this day and our crazy adventures were priceless though sometimes painful. Thanks to Ray and Norma Rios, Michael Corsello, Joe and Agatella Musco, Donna Carnevale.

Special shout-out to my dear friends Mini and Pat—Cara and Patrick Jammet—who are my sous chefs and moral support "before and after" the parties; to Anne Burrell for her spirit, laughter, helping hands, and amazing desserts; to Mary Giuliani for her support in and out of kitchens and for making us cry for *good* reasons; to Victoria and Andrew Cusimano, for always dancing; and to Giancarla and Co., the food and beverage team at Monteverdi, for giving me the night off on Friday. To Michael Schlow and Kenny Orringer and all the chefs who welcomed me into their fold. To Lee Brian Schrager and Pat LaFrieda and everybody who ever made a burger for our Bash. To Andrew Kaplan and Charlie Dougiello for their tireless hard work supporting me and my brands.

It's always hard for people to throw me a birthday party, because I'm usually upstate working in late August. Zanna Roberts Rassi and Mazdack Rassi, my dear friends, you solved this by throwing me a surprise fiftieth-birthday party at your fabulous Milk Studios in New York City . . . in November! It was the biggest, nicest party thrown for me since my wedding, and while I usually hate surprises, I had such a good time that I forgave you! You guys are the kindest people; you literally always have smiles on your faces and I can't believe you got all those people to come out in the middle of the biggest snowstorm in a decade.

To the team at Ballantine Books, thank you for your efforts on behalf of *RR50*. Special thanks (and a little pity) to Pamela Cannon and Lauren Iannotti for being on the front lines of this project and trying to edit me. Hope you ladies kept wine and/or tequila on hand throughout. To Christopher Testani, Barrett Washburne, and the rest of the photo team for the beautiful food photography in this book. And thanks, as always, to Michelle Boxer for everything I know nothing about that she simply handled.

To my dogs, Boo and Isaboo, and to my family: Thank you for your love, support, and appetites. John, you get extra thanks for the cocktails.

Recipes by Category

Index

Page numbers of illustrations appear in italics.

Photo Credits

ABOUT THE AUTHOR

RACHAEL RAY is a multi–Emmy Award–winning syndicated television star, an iconic Food Network personality, bestselling cookbook author, founder and editorial director of her own lifestyle magazine, *Rachael Ray Every Day,* and founder of the Yum-o! organization and The Rachael Ray Foundation. She splits her time between New York City and the Adirondacks with her husband, John, her family, and her beloved pit bull, Isaboo.

rachaelrayshow.com

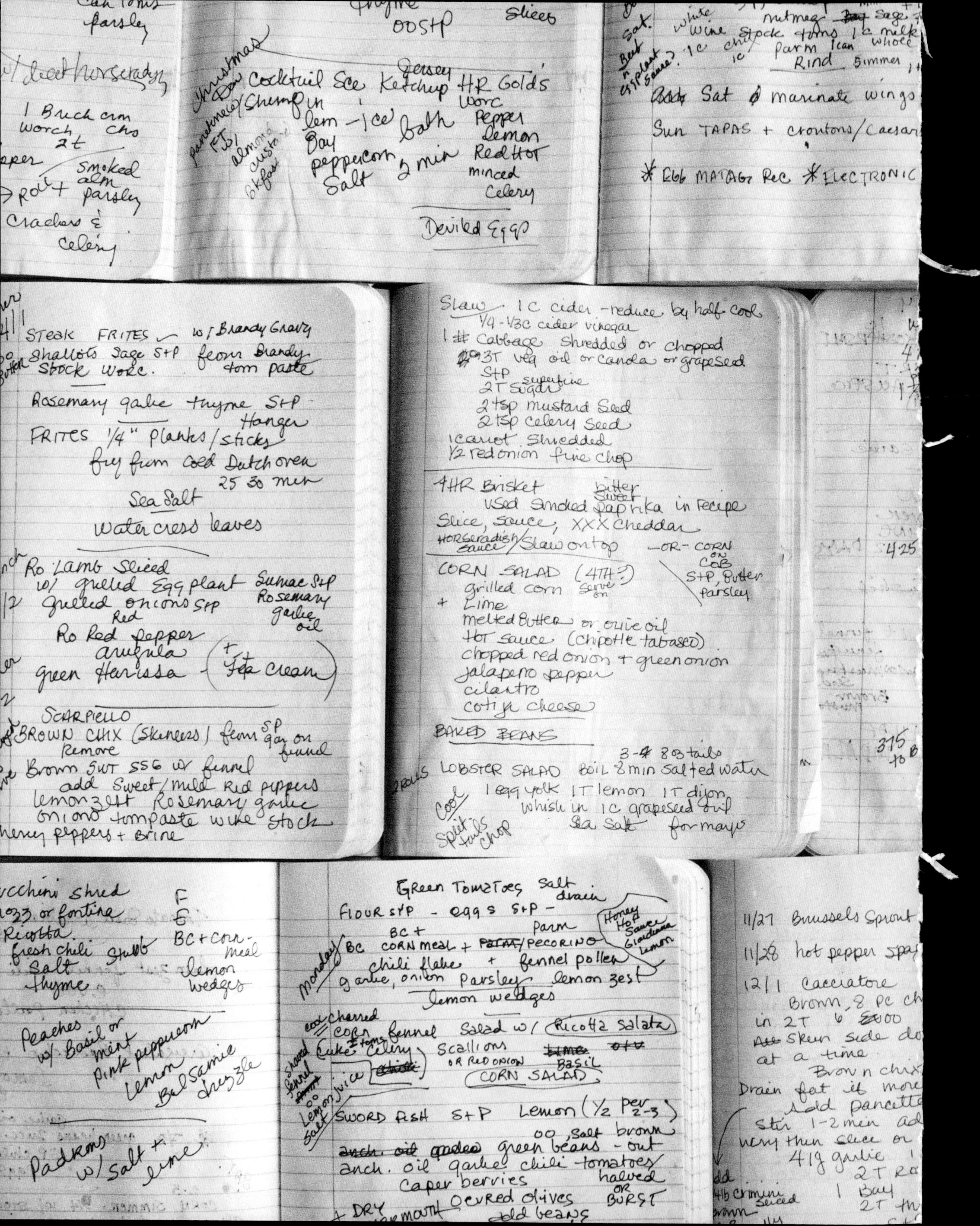

Top left page

/ beef horseradish

1 Buck cm
worch chs
2T
...per
→ Roll + smoked alm
parsley
Crackers &
Celery

Top middle-left

Christmas
panner... / Champ in
almond custard
8 fast

Top middle

Cocktail Sce Jersey HR Gold's
Ketchup
lem - ice Worc
Bay bath Pepper
peppercorn Lemon
Salt 2 min Red Hot
minced
Celery

Deviled Eggs

Top right

Sat. white nutmeg Sage
Beef Wine Stock toms 1c milk
n'plant .1c chick Parm 1can whole
crispsauce 1c Rind 5 immer

Add Sat ∅ marinate wings

Sun TAPAS + croutons/Caesar

* R66 MATAG Rec * ELECTRONIC

Middle left page

4/1

STEAK FRITES — w/ Brandy Gravy
Shallots Sage S+P deom Brandy
Butter Stock Worc. tom paste

Rosemary garlic thyme S+P
Hanger
FRITES 1/4" planks/sticks
fry from cold Dutch oven
25 30 min
Sea Salt
Water cress leaves

Ro Lamb Sliced
w/ grilled Eggplant Sumac S+P
grilled onions S+P Rosemary
Red garlic oil
Ro Red pepper
arugula (+
green Harissa (Feta cream)

SCARPIELLO
BROWN CHIX (Skinless) deom S+P gar on
Remove fennel
Brown SWT SSG w/ fennel
add Sweet/mild Red peppers
lemon zest Rosemary garlic
onions tompaste w/ke stock
honey peppers + Brine

Middle right page

Slaw - 1C cider - reduce by half- cool
1/4 -1/3C cider vinegar
1# Cabbage Shredded or chopped
3T veg oil or canola or grapeseed
S+P
2T sugar superfine
2 tsp mustard Seed
2 tsp celery Seed
1 carrot Shredded
1/2 red onion fine chop

4 HR Brisket bitter sweet
used Smoked paprika in recipe
Slice, Sauce; XXX Cheddar
Horseradish sauce/Slaw on top -OR- CORN
on COB
CORN SALAD (4TH!) S+P, Butter
grilled corn serve on Parsley
+ Lime
melted Butter or olive oil
Hot Sauce (chipotle tabasco)
chopped red onion + green onion
Jalapeno pepper
cilantro
cotija cheese

BAKED BEANS
3-4 8oz tails
2 Rolls LOBSTER SALAD Boil 2 min Salted water
Cool 1 egg yolk 1T lemon 1T dijon
whisk in 1C grapeseed oil
Split tails chop Sea Salt for mayo

Bottom left

...cchini shred F
...33 or fontina E
Ricotta BC + corn-
fresh chili grub meal
Salt lemon
Thyme wedges

Peaches
w/ Basil or mint
Pink peppercorn
Lemon
Balsamic drizzle

Padrons
w/ salt + lime

Bottom middle

Green Tomatoes Salt
drain
FLOUR S+P - eggs S+P -
BC + Parm Honey Hot Sauce Giardiniera Lemon
Monday BC CORN MEAL + POTATO/PECORINO
chili flakes + fennel pollen
garlic, onion Parsley lemon zest
lemon wedges

charred
corn Fennel Salad w/ (Ricotta Salata)
Sword Cuke toms Celery Scallions
fennel OR RED ONION Basil
lemon juice chili (CORN SALAD)
Lemon Salt

SWORD FISH S+P Lemon (1/2 per 2-3)
00, Salt brown
anch oil green beans - out
anch oil garlic chili tomatoes
caper berries halved or BURST
Oc red olives BURST
DRY vermouth add beans

Bottom right

11/27 Brussels Sprout
11/28 hot pepper spag
12/1 Cacciatore
Brown, 8 Pc ch
in 2T 6 Evoo
Skin side do
at a time
Brown chix
Drain fat if more
add pancetta
Stir 1-2 min ad
very thin slice or
41g garlic
2T Ro
4 lb crimini 1 Bay
sliced 2T th